A Brain-Focused Foundation for Economic Science

Richard B. McKenzie

A Brain-Focused Foundation for Economic Science

A Proposed Reconciliation between Neoclassical and Behavioral Economics

palgrave
macmillan

Richard B. McKenzie
Paul Merage School of Business
University of California, Irvine
Irvine, CA, USA

ISBN 978-3-030-08295-6 ISBN 978-3-319-76810-6 (eBook)
https://doi.org/10.1007/978-3-319-76810-6

Cover image: © Lasse Kristensen/Alamy Stock Photo
Cover design by Tjaša Krivec

Printed on acid-free paper

This Palgrave Macmillan imprint is published by the registered company Springer International Publishing AG part of Springer Nature
The registered company address is: Gewerbestrasse 11, 6330 Cham, Switzerland

For
Jack William Shelton

Preface

This small book takes its inspiration from British economist Lionel Robbins' small book, *An Essay on the Nature and Significance of Economic Science*, first published in 1932. In his book, Robbins posited that economics as a discipline was, at the time, being held in check by a lack of a unifying construction of the discipline broadly adopted by practicing academic economists. Robbins contended that economists seemed to be dealing with the same issues but were at odds over what was their core unifying concern. The problem, according to Robbins, was not a single definition, but a multiplicity of definitions, all of which he found wanting for assorted reasons and which I will consider in Chapter 2. He argued the discipline would be well served by an agreed-to definition, or just a methodological focus, that provided clarity of purpose for economists' disparate investigations. He concluded that *scarcity*, or the conflict between human wants and means, had to be at the core of the unifying definition. His construction of the discipline's methodological focus, was broadly adopted by textbook authors within two decades.

The discipline has marched on since Robbins walked the halls of the London School of Economics. As in Robbins era, the discipline is now fractured with competing visions of what economists do, and should be doing, or how they should be doing whatever they are doing—not always without crisscrossing barbs and at least some professional acrimony. I have written this book with the view that the profession has another "Robbins moment," meaning an opportunity to rethink, in light of how much the profession has evolved since Robbins' day, the ultimate foundation of the discipline. The short version of my central thesis is this: Robbins' construction of the discipline's organizing cornerstone, *scarcity*, and all that has been derived from it since Robbins' no longer generate general consent among economists. Moreover, economic "generalizations," which Robbins held out as the ultimate goal of all sciences, no longer attract general consent among academics who wear the disciplinary mantel of "economist," and the methodological divide among economists is growing.

Since Robbins' *Essay*, economists, and other social scientists, have learned a great deal about human decision-making and about the human brain, the lynchpin of human decision-making, which Robbins and his cohorts could not have imagined. I propose to do here for the modern era what Robbins did, to reimagine and reconstruct the foundation of economic science. I hold dear Robbins' concern for "scarcity," but with a radically different focus, enlightened by behavioral and cognitive psychology and neuroscience—which have given rise to counterparts, behavioral economics, and neuroeconomics—over the eight decades since Robbins found his unity in disparate investigations within the discipline.

I posit that the human brain is the ultimate scarce resource. The human brain must first optimize on itself before it (or humans) can optimize on the scarce resources available in the external world, the latter being Robbins' conceptual domain for scarcity. Economists in their investigations must do the same as their subjects, which is to optimize on their own scarce neuronal and energy resources to efficiently devise their generalizations of how an economy works, and can be predicted to work.

I posit that by starting with the scarcity of neurons (and other resources) in the human brain, which must cope with an immense inflow of sensory data and develop an equally immense number of internal and external decisions, there is the potential for a "unified field theory" that reconciles, albeit partially, many differences among divergent groups of contemporary economists, not the least of which are neoclassical (or mainstream) economists (who grew up intellectually on Robbins' construction of the discipline) and the newly established force of behavioral economists, with adherents taking their intellectual cues mainly from psychology and neuroscience. In short, I offer a brain-centric foundation for economic science.

As a practical matter, behavioral economists and neuroeconomists are right when they find faults (lots of them) with neoclassical economists' premise that people are not only *rational*, they are *perfectly rational* (or can be assumed to be perfectly rational for modeling purposes). I acknowledge that perfect rationality is an evolutionary nonstarter. Perfectly rational humans, if they happened to emerge, would not likely survive for long in a world of scarce resources they confront internally and externally. This is the case because they would have to spend so much time refining their decisions that they would have starved to death for never making timely decisions, or they would have been eaten by, say, sabertoothed tigers before deciding to flee (*if* the standard for their decisions were perfection in considering all aspects of fleeing). Surely in a world beset with scarcity of everything, economists and their subjects would not go so far as place a valuation on all conceivable combinations of goods (and units of the goods within all possible combinations) that could be consumed (which is implicitly, if not explicitly, subsumed in economists' indifference-curve analytics in which every point on the graph, even those far beyond the budget line, which are unobtainable by design, are given a relative evaluation). Such analysis is patently self-contradictory, as well as representing decision makers as "hyperrational," to use a coined phrase of behaviorists, by the standards of the underlying analytics. Indifference-curve analytics assumes mental resources and decision time is unbounded in a world in which everything else is assumed to be scarce.

Perfect rationality (or hyperrationality) in an economy is no more likely than perfect efficiency in engineering, and for much the same economic reason: as perfection is approached, the added gains of added perfection would likely diminish while the added costs would likely escalate, at least beyond some point. Also, why would a rational person take the time to place valuations on unlimited combinations of goods that are far from achievable? The question answers itself.

Moreover, in repositioning the scarcity and rationality foundations of the discipline from the perspective of a neoclassical economist, I accept a number of tenets of behaviorists. Perfect rationality would likely be inferior to some lower, imperfect level of rationality, which accounts for the economy of the human brain that has far more to do than it can accomplish. This is to say that perfect rationality can come close to being its obverse, "perfect irrationality." The clinching argument is that if people were perfectly rational, economists would not have to tell their students that, nor would they have to draw out all of premise's implications. Students would know them (naturally?). Perfect rationality, in effect, denudes economics of any didactic purpose. Would perfectly rational people (students) need economic instruction? If for some odd reason they did, why would economic instruction be as difficult as it is for many people on both sides of the lectern?

But alas, behavioral economists and neuroeconomists, in pointing to numerous ways people fall short of perfectly rational decisions—through so-called, at times, "biases" and "irrationalities" and, at other times, "anomalies"—they have saved neoclassical economics from such self-contradictions in what could be viewed as a wayward approach. With my brain-focused foundation for economics, I can explore five lines of argument that seem, on the surface, to be at odds with one another.

- First, the many (not all) identified biases, irrationalities, and anomalies in decision-making can be reconciled: they are to be expected when the human brain must first optimize on its own resources and even on its own level of rationality, given its evolutionary constraints and given its need for energy conservation to do all that it is called on to do. (And the human brain is a true physiological "gas guzzler," given that it soaks up a fifth of all energy consumed by the human body.) Many of the so-called biases, irrationalities, and anomalies are no different than the inevitable "wastage" in production processes, and they, like production waste, can contribute to greater efficiency in decision-making and use of external resources than would otherwise be possible. They are also, in critical ways, similar to calculated "mistakes" that are bound to emerge from investment strategies devised to elevate risk-taking and increase a portfolio's overall rate of return (even after accounting for the added risk costs).
- Second, if people were, in fact, perfectly rational, there would be little didactic value to economic instruction. There is nothing in economics that can improve (the efficiency of) decision-making and the use of external resources. With the acknowledged lapses in decision-making (e.g., as behaviorists have found, many people ignore opportunity costs, consider sunk costs, and discount future costs and benefits "defectively" and "inconsistently"), economics has a potentially efficiency-enhancing role, that of "improving" decision-making and, hence, the efficiency in the use of external resources.
- As will be argued, economics harbors the potential for slowing down decision-making, guiding students away from the pitfalls of "fast and furious" decision-making that novice students have likely

adopted, for evolutionary reasons, and toward avenues for more complete consideration of costs and benefits, both now and in the future. From my perspective, economics training, in its best form, is intent on showing students the value of key economic principles, which take the form of heuristics (ignore sunk costs and equate at the margin both) recommended for use in students' personal and commercial lives. These heuristics, even though flawed, can potentially improve the rationality of students' decisions and, thereby, potentially increase students' personal welfares and their firms' profitability. (From my perspective, it is far more instructive for "economic heuristics" to be substituted for "economic principles.")

- Third, in neoclassical economics, with its roots grounded in Robbins construction of the discipline's foundation, the rationality premise is imposed on the analytics. It is exogenous, and largely arbitrary (and if not arbitrary, made a necessity by the employment of mathematically precise analytics). The same could be said about behavioral economics in that behaviorists have sought to show how deficient human decision-making is, using perfect rationality as the standard, without a conceptual deductive framework for conceptualizing people's optimum rationality (at least from my reading of the behavioral literature). I seek here to develop the missing framework that allows economists to recognize that many (if not most) deficiencies in all forms of decision-making can be every bit as rational as farmers' decisions to allow vegetables to rot in their fields and car makers to plan for deficiencies in the performance of their cars.
- Fourth, in neoclassical economics, human rationality cannot be improved. The central concern is then directed to the efficiency in the allocation of external resources with no potential feedback effects on rationality. When rationality is optimized as the brain seeks to optimize on its own resources, rationality can, indeed, be improved by instructions, and an improvement in rationality can improve decisions on the allocation of external resources, which can have feedback effects on the brain's optimized rationality.
- Fifth, the limits of the human brain also place limits on how economics is done. The subject matter—human interactions in a variety of institutional settings, including markets, politics, and organizations—is extraordinarily complex, far too complex to be understood and appreciated in its totality. The core problem melds with Robbins' construction: Too much "data" and too few available

> neurons. This means that those interactions *must* be considered in reduced, simplified form, in one way or another. Neoclassical economics concedes to the limits of people's (and economists') brain power through simplified models along with a founding premise, perfect rationality, that is far from descriptive of how people make—and must make—their decisions. Behavioral economists do much the same thing in a radically different way, by taking subjects into controlled and constrained laboratories that are also far removed from descriptive reality of the complex social and economic interactions that are at play outside their laboratories. The goal of both approaches is designed to gain insight that would not otherwise be accessible. By making economics brain-focused, rationality is made endogenous, which gives new meaning to "economic efficiency" and "welfare gains" from decision-making, even when they are flawed.

In neoclassical economics, external efficiency is the core concern, as noted. The extent of market competitiveness (or market power) and government regulations, for examples, can only affect the efficiency of external resource allocations. From my perspective, such market forces can affect the level of rationality adopted by the brain, which can, through sensory feedback loops between the external world and the brain (which can result in adjustments in mental algorithms and heuristics), efficiency in the allocation of external resources can be enhanced beyond what is conventionally thought and taught in neoclassical economics. Indeed, from my perspective, specialization of resources and trades aren't simply innate propensities of humans, which reduce production costs, as Adam Smith and every economist since have argued, they are means of relieving demands on people's mental resources and processes, enhancing mental rationality, and thereby further improving economic efficiency. If competitive pressures and feedback loops are denied, as they often are in behaviorists' sterilized laboratory experiments, no one should be surprised if findings of irrationalities abound, at least more so than in the real world beyond the walls of laboratories.

* * * * *

With that said, I begin my inquiry into the "nature and significance of modern economic science," starting with a brief evolutionary history of economic methodology. My goal is daring, to develop economic generalizations by starting with an economic theory of how the human brain works. Because the interactions of the human brain could be as complex as the interactions of the normal domain of economics, the economy, I will simplify, mainly by assuming that the human brain (or "mind") seeks to optimize on the body's limited physiological resources (including energy intake and reserves, as well as the internal forms of chemical and electrical communication systems and "memory" available in the brain and elsewhere, say, muscles). That task requires the brain to optimize use of its own limited cognitive resources (e.g., neurons, glia cells, and electrical and chemical communication systems) available for decision-making. I emphasize the evolutionary origins of the brain, among the many forces that constrain what and how the brain's performance is constrained, as I also stress the extent to which the brain cannot possibly absorbed the enormous inflow of sensory data or make with intensive care all the decisions it is called upon to make. This means that the brain must find ever-evolving ways of economizing on—or seeking as best it can to optimize on the use of—its resources.

As noted, in neoclassical economics, rationality (most often, perfect rationality) is superimposed on economic models. From my brain-centric view of the discipline, rationality, whatever its level, is endogenous, which means it is an outcome of the brain's economizing processes. I posit that the brain seeks an *optimum rationality* (or rational rationality), given its admirable capacity to cope with a multitude of physiological constraints, grounded in evolutionary forces which shape the boundaries of how the brain must operate internally, as well as the ever-evolving external forces that shape the incoming sensory data with which the brain must cope.

In behavioral economics and psychology, uncovered biases, anomalies, and flaws in decision-making are often treated as evidence of the limits of predictive value of neoclassical economics, and even as evidence of that paradigm's intellectual bankruptcy, and irrelevancy. From my perspective developed, such "flaws" are expected, or predicted, and the consequence of a "meta-rationality" that transforms (at least, potentially) "flaws" into sources of greater efficiency in decision-making, which can imply greater efficiency in the employment of limited internal and external resources to satisfy human wants.

Readers should note that my coverage of various literatures—evolutionary biology, neuroscience, neoclassical economics, behavioral economics, and psychology—is not intended to be exhaustive, as if complete coverage were possible, given the breadth of the literatures and my intention to contain the length of this book. My goal is to cover only enough of the relevant literatures to convince readers that many economists in modern times use radically different methodological approaches and draw radically different "generalizations," which are often at odds with one another. I seek only to persuade readers that it is time to seek a new methodological foundation, one that harbors a chance of unifying economists' disparate investigations and conclusions. I seek to reconcile, partially, the competing methodological perspectives of neoclassical and behavioral economics, mainly by retaining the deductive methods of neoclassical economics organized around the constructs of scarcity, maximization/optimization, and equilibrium and providing rational explanations for many, if not most, of the inductive findings of behaviorists. I suggest my approach can be best crystalized as "brain-focused neoclassical microeconomics (or just economics)."

In writing this book, I have sought to extend themes in my earlier work on methodology, *Predictably Rational? In Search of Defenses for Rationality in Economics* (Springer 2010). I have drawn on that work liberally but always with revisions, updates, and upgrades in the analysis, and always with the goal of devising a new way of thinking not considered in the earlier book. Also, readers will notice that key themes and arguments in the book are often repeated. This is the case partially not only because of the conventional need to tie the arguments in the different chapters together but also because the chapters of the book will be made available for download separately.

I must thank strongly Dwight Lee for his many corrections and suggested improvements in his critical and insightful review of an early draft of the book. I also need to thank Elizabeth Graber and Allison Neuburger at Palgrave Macmillan for easing the problems of moving the book through the editorial and production processes. Finally, I am very pleased to dedicate this book to my grandson, Jack William Shelton, who will be one-year-old at the time of the publication.

Irvine, USA
January 2018

Richard B. McKenzie
Walter B. Gerken Professor (Emeritus)

Contents

CHAPTER 1

Economists' Founding Concerns in the History of Economic Thought

Contemporary economists have variously defined their discipline over the two-plus centuries since its intellectual emergence from the work of Adam Smith. However, there is widespread agreement among contemporary economists that the one word that captures the core organizing concern of neoclassical economics is *scarcity*, which economists almost always interpret to mean the inescapable conflict that occurs when people's virtually unlimited (and ever-expanding) human wants grounded on subjective, mind-based evaluations (the product of myriad, often unspecified, neurological and physiological and external forces) are pitted against the known but limited or finite resources in the external physical world that are available for satisfying human wants.

The Foundations of Economics, Scarcity, and Analytical Methods

The venerable Paul Samuelson first published his once dominant introductory economics textbook in 1948 without scarcity being the focus of his construction of the discipline, possibly because he was then more concerned with introducing students to the management of the overall level of a country's aggregate economic activity with the introduction of the then still relatively new Keynesian macroeconomics.[1] However, in later editions he fully adopted scarcity as the core organizing concept for the disciplines: "Economics is the study of how people and society

R. B. McKenzie, *A Brain-Focused Foundation for Economic Science*,
https://doi.org/10.1007/978-3-319-76810-6_1

end up choosing, with or without the use of money, to employ scarce productive resources that could have alternative uses, to produce various commodities and distribute them for consumption, now or in the future, among various persons and groups in society. It analyzes the costs and benefits of improving patterns of resource allocation."[2]

During the first half of the 1960s, Campbell McConnell's introductory textbook began to seriously erode Samuelson's market share in part because he adopted Samuelson's model of placing heavy and early emphasis on macroeconomics with microeconomics relegated to the last half of the textbook (taken up usually in the second semester of the then traditional year-long introductory course). Perhaps, McConnell's market share was also boosted somewhat by his greater emphasis on the scarcity paradigm as the chief organizing concept for both macroeconomics and microeconomics: "Recalling that wants are unlimited and resources are scarce, economics can be defined as *the social science concerned with the problem of using or administering scarce resources* (*the means of producing*) *so as to attain the greatest or maximum fulfillment of our unlimited wants (the goal of producing)*" (emphasis in the original).[3]

In an even later edition, Samuelson with his adopted co-author William Nordhaus defined economics (which in the 2010s had been in print for nearly seven decades) with greater brevity, as "the study of how societies use scarce resources to produce valuable commodities and distribute them among different people."[4] In his widely adopted introductory textbook, first published in 1998, that follows in the Samuelson/Nordhaus tradition (but with more emphasis on microeconomics), Gregory Mankiw writes that "the management of society's resources is important because they are scarce. *Scarcity* means that society has limited resources and therefore cannot produce all the goods and services people want." Accordingly, he defined economics in much the same way that Samuelson/Nordhaus (and what seems to be an ever-changing horde of other textbook writers) did, as "the study of how society manages its scarce resources."[5]

Again, the conventional construction of scarcity in economics is largely grounded in the boundedness of resources in the external real world in which people must survive (or, as the case might be) prosper and the unboundedness of people's capacity to imagine things they want and ways to obtain what they want.

In short, scarcity occurs at the intersection of the physical and subjective universes (as economists conceive and limit them). Scarcity also constrains, if not determines (in some tightly constructed mathematical models), people's decision-making and economists' analytics. Scarcity in the external world defines the subject matter of economics, as well as defines and largely guides what and how economists do what they do, as well as teach what they do.

In economists' conceived "state of nature," not all human wants, obviously, can be satisfied. Choices must be made. Modern economics as a discipline is most often seen as bounded, but only by those arenas in which people have meaningful choices and make decisions among viable options. That is, economics is not generally thought to extend to those realms of human behavior in which people do not have two or more meaningful alternative courses of action, as may be the case after people are lifted into the vortex of a tornado or when they are tightly shackled. Until the advent of sexual reassignment surgeries, economics played no (or a thought-to-be little) role in "gender" identity matters. People had no choice about their sexual orientation (at least, as once presumed by economists, and almost all other social scientists, in their modeling).

Scarcity implies (or so economists who adopt scarcity as their core concern, founding analytical presumption) that in making choices people will seek to maximize attainment of utility from the fulfillment of wants that, in turn, implies optimum use of resources. Why would people, within the constraints of their volition, do anything less, at least for modeling purposes? The presumption of maximizing behavior implies people have some rational capacity, which is to say that they have some ability to weigh off the relative value of various wants that can be fulfilled—and to fulfill with some consistency, within constraints, those wants that have the greatest value.

For Samuelson, McConnell, Mankiw, and a generation of economists who followed textbook writers' lead on "unlimited wants," scarcity did not extend to the generation of wants (for the most part). Wants are just "there," unaffected by anything, or are unaffected by resource constraints, and are, effectively, beyond economists' concerns (as Lionel Robbins insisted in the early 1930s was the case, a point I take up in the next chapter).

Modern economists have sometimes parted ways on just how rational people can be in real life from economists who followed the methodological framework laid down in clearest terms by Milton Friedman in the early 1950s. The overwhelming majority of contemporary economists have assumed some variant of *perfect rationality*, some as a matter of conviction that people's level of rationality is close enough to perfect rationality that little is lost in descriptiveness in assuming perfect rationality, while others have assumed perfect rationality as a means of easing their analytics, an approach that elevates the importance of testing empirically the accuracy of their theories' predictions.[6]

Neoclassical (or mainstream) economists have acknowledged their own and their subjects' mental limitations in one important theoretical regard. As Friedman contended, the founding premise of all theories dealing with complex phenomenon must, to one degree or another, be "unreal," or not strictly in accord with how people make decisions in the "real world." The real world is complex and messy, with "what is" at any point in time or within any period of time necessarily the consequence of myriad, ongoing, and continually interacting economic and noneconomic variables. The real world is made ever messier by a multitude of humans imposing varying and different evaluations and actions on life in all arenas, not just business.

Understandably, Friedman reasoned that theories could not be "complete," or fully descriptive, and, by chance, if a theorist tried to devise a truly complete theory, he or she could not understand or be able to work with it. A complete theory would overtax the limited mental capacities of economists, which is why theories are devised to reduce (or abstract from) complex reality to a manageable form. Understandably, Friedman concludes, as a matter of human mental limitations and scientific necessity, "the legitimacy of and justification for this abstraction [that people maximize or act fully rationally or markets are frictionless] must rest ultimately, as with any other abstraction, on the light shed and the power to predict what is yielded by the abstraction."[7]

Economists might as well simplify their analytics as much as possible to facilitate their analyses, and progressively simplify them so long as nothing, or little of consequence, is lost in the insightfulness and accuracy of predictions from the theory. The usefulness of economic analytics is determined by the congruence between theoretical deductions and empirical findings.

In neoclassical economics, the rationality premise is grounded on the type of decision-making consumers and producers are likely to adopt, or to be pressured to adopt generally (but not necessarily everywhere and always), in a world of pervasive scarcity. The premise, in other words, has a grounding in reality, not just in the creative imaginations of economists whose first and only purpose is to ease their analytics. Seen from this perspective, the rationality premise is a necessary starting point, which need not be proven but does require general consent for its reasonableness from a community of scholars, for a deductive science, a *means* to an *end*, the development of predictions that can be falsified. If they are not falsified in repeated tests, the following analytics can give rise to acceptable insights into, or generalizations about, human behavior in face of changing market forces, including government policies. Because the premise is accepted as being less than fully descriptive of how people think and behave, then empirical tests are crucial in neoclassical economics (but not in, say, Austrian economics). Otherwise, without testing, neoclassical predictions might just be totally misleading, a product of a lack of coherence between the unreality of the founding premise and complex reality.

By the same token, inductive empirical studies not guided by some general theory, founded on an agreed-upon premise, can also be misleading, because the studies are not testing predictions. The data series created within or abstracted from and selected for study of complex reality, which encompasses a multitude of variables (all of which can't be considered), might not be representative of complex reality (or even a portion thereof) and, thereby, no better than the product of ad hoc, uninspired and unguided thinking. These problems are especially worrisome within social science studies of human behavior because humans, presumably, can introduce major complexities of their own into reality because of human's capacities to respond to external forces with purpose and creativity (problems that don't afflict the natural sciences, which deal with substances and objects that have no internal evaluative and responsive processes). This is to say, both deductive and inductive scientific methods suffer similar potential conceptual problems.

George Stigler, Gary Becker, and others have argued that the deductive economic paradigm has allowed economists to develop an array of tools of analysis that, effectively, make economics a *method of analysis*, distinctive from the analytical methods of other disciplines. As Becker has written, "The combined assumptions of maximizing behavior, market equilibrium, and stable preferences, used relentlessly and unflinchingly, form the heart of the economic approach as I see it."[8] Moreover, Becker dares to assert the broad-based inclusiveness of the economic approach:

> Indeed I have come to the conclusion that the economic approach is a comprehensive one that is applicable to *all* human behavior, be it behavior

> involving money prices or imputed shadow prices, repeated or infrequent decisions, large or minor decisions, emotional or mechanical ends, rich or poor persons, adults or children, brilliant or stupid persons, patients or therapists, businessmen or politicians, teachers or students.[9]

Economics has not been so conceived generally by the profession over the more than two centuries of the discipline's history since the writings of Adam Smith (with Phillip Wicksteed being a notable exception in the early 1900s, as we will see). Economics has evolved from having no distinctive boundaries (in the late eighteenth century) in terms of topics subject to analysis, as might be expected when the subject was not recognized as a discipline in Smith's days, to being neatly defined by scarcity in the 1930s and for nearly a half-century afterward. In the late 1900s, the discipline came to be defined not so much by topic, or even by scarcity, as by evolved methods of analysis that were anchored in scarcity, albeit without full recognition of the scarcity's continuing central role in theory. Methods of dealing with scarcity, not scarcity per se, became the evolved core of the discipline.

The venerable Austrian contrarian Friedrich Hayek worried that economics students would be seduced by economists' economic lecture, textbooks, and public commentaries that, with study of the discipline, would adopt a "fatal conceit," that they would be able to manage "society's scarce resources" from, say, their perch in some government planning council. Hayek warned that such a task was impossible, and would ultimately fail. The basic problem is that the societal managers would lack the information on the scope and value placed on a diverse population's wants and resources, subjective considerations they could not possibly gather and would be overwhelmed if they ever tried to use and collect the colossal amount of information collected on people's (not overlords') diverse subjective preferences that would be needed to allocate resources diverse preferences at a state level.[10] In short, if economists intended their students to be able to solve the scarcity problem for states, they had founded the discipline on a false premise and an unattainable goal.

The Overriding Goal of the Book

The overriding goal of this book is to provide a history of the methodology of economics from the discipline's inception with the works of Adam Smith until today. This history can provide context for the now divergent, and still diverging, conceptions of how economics should be done. More importantly, I seek a methodological means of reconciling the analytics of the two major (and, to a nontrivial degree, warring) methodological camps, behavioral economic and neoclassical economics. I accomplish this end by focusing attention on the ultimate scarce resource in doing economics—the one that governs how economists must think about using and allocating all other scarce resources and do their science—on the *human brain*, which has evolved to be an economy unto itself, to resolve its own scarcity conflict with purposeful allocation decisions. I show how neoclassical economic analytics can be applied to how the brain works and can predict many (not all) of the findings of behavioral economics, and much more.

My goals are, indeed, ambitious, but I submit I have achieved it in a relatively small book, with a relatively simple shift in the focus and methodology of the discipline. As a teaser, my methodological perspective enables me to predict that a perfectly rational brain (which I argue is a plausible founding premise, and far more plausible than the assumption that people are perfectly rational) will not always make perfectly rational decisions, as neoclassical economists assume. It also predicts that specialization and trade are consequences of the human brain seeking to optimize its own limited, scarce resources. This suggests that restrictions on specialization and trade undercut human welfare by more than neoclassical economists suggests. Why? Stay tuned.

The Fracturing of Economics

More recently, over, say, the last two to five decades (or longer), the discipline has been fracturing into subdisciplines with different premises and analytical methodologies that go by the names of neoclassical economics, behavioral economics, neuroeconomics, institutional economics, experimental economics, public choice economics, institutional economics, and Austrian economics—with economists representing the different subdisciplines not always respecting, and often ignoring, the work of economists in other subdisciplines. Behaviorists from several disciplines (most prominently, economics, psychology, law, and neuroscience), who are the focus of attention here (because they have recently been in ascendency in their disciplinary prominence and now seem to represent the strongest threat to the primacy of neoclassical economics), have made substantial careers of finding "anomalies," or outright contradictions, of fundamental tenets (especially the perfect rationality premise) undergirding much neoclassical economics.

Behavioral economist—and recently anointed Nobel Laureate in Economics—Richard Thaler and legal scholar Cass Sunstein muse (with some disdain for neoclassical economists' work in general), "If you look at economics textbooks, you will learn that *homo economicus* can think like Albert Einstein, store as much memory as IBM's Big Blue, and exercise the will power of Mahatma Gandhi."[11] Thaler and Sunstein suggest *homo economicus* stands in stark contrast with real *homo sapiens*—whom they cite as "Humans"—who stand in sharp contrast with the "Econs" of neoclassical economic models—who readily forget birthdays, have trouble with math, and regret hangovers.[12] Thaler doubts the instructiveness of economics as a discipline because there is no way to test whether consumers "equate price ratios to marginal rates of substitution."[13]

Contrary to Friedman and Becker (and many other economists), who stressed economics was a *positive science* (of "what is") as distinct from "normative science" (of what "should be"), Thaler and his behavioral cohorts stress that economics is not so much a deductive positive science, as it is, at best, a prescriptive one (if science can be prescriptive without contradiction), with the prescriptions devised from microeconomic investigations not necessarily directed (or maybe only in a loose way directed) by a deductive theory that causes them to doubt the didactic value of much neoclassical economics: "Setting price so that marginal cost equals marginal revenue is the right answer to the problem of how to maximize profits. Whether firms *do* that is another matter. I try to teach my MBA students that they should avoid the winner's curse and equate opportunity costs to out-of-pocket costs, but I also teach them that most people don't" (emphasis in the original).[14]

Marketing researchers Thanos Skouras, George Avlonitis, and Kostis Indounas in their survey of the differences in approaches to research by people in marketing and economics parrot the Thaler/Sunstein criticism of neoclassical economics, as do a growing chorus of other behaviorists (citing Kahneman 1994; Kahneman and Tversky 2000; Thaler 2001).

> The weakest part [of "economists' theoretical edifice"] is surely the notion of utility-maximization by rational consumers. This is not only implausible as a general description of buyers' behavior but there are many instances in everyday experience of most people that seem to contradict it. Moreover, the work of psychologists and several psychological experiments

have shown beyond any doubt that rationality and utility-maximization can hardly be considered as universal and ever-present traits of consumer behavior.[15]

Economists' Methodologies

In this book, I will be first concerned with a brief review of the evolution of the definition of economics through the centuries of its development, starting with Smith and concluding with the integration of psychology and neuroscience into subdisciplines of economics. Along the way, I will take issue with the commonly accepted construction of the discipline based on scarcity in the form described by Robbins (which I cite as "external scarcity"). My major goal, however, will be to seek a restatement of the foundation of economics as a science in such a way that various, sometimes warring, economists in the subdisciplines that have emerged since (external) scarcity became the widely adopted founding paradigm can once again find a sense of unity in purpose and method.

In effect, much as did Robbins in the 1930s (1932), I seek a new methodological foundation that will achieve (hopefully) broad consent among economists in the different subdisciplines and that will unify the efforts of economists who adopt different methodological approaches that now seem in conflict. As we will see, by reconstituting the discipline's methodological foundation, economists in the various subdisciplines may be able to better understand and appreciate their commonalities and complementarities.

Adam Smith's admirers and critics through time seem to agree on one point: Smith's core concern revolved around people's individual pursuit of their self-interest, which is taken to mean individuals' pursuit of their private betterment, however individuals define in various ways their individual "betterment." Unlike many contemporary neoclassical economists, Smith never founded his economics on people "maximizing" or "optimizing" their welfare, with scarcity being the core concern. As do modern behavioral economists, Smith would likely have scoffed at any presumption that people's pursuit of their self-interest was organized with "perfect rationality," or anything close. His emphasis was on people's pursuit of *improvement* in their economic well-being, given their personal rational limitations and their imperfectly known interests, through production and trade, which suggests people necessarily must pursue their goals, whatever they are, imperfectly, or as best they could.[16]

Indeed, Smith might very well agree that the actual pursuit of perfection on any margin of real life is a nonstarter in a world of pervasive scarcity. With his emphasis on trade being directed by costs and prices, he clearly believed in the power of incentives on human welfare, which means he clearly believed that people can conceive of their own wants in some ordered (imperfect) preference function and could make purposive choices and decisions with some level of rationality, albeit at some distance from perfect rationality.

Smith reasoned that even under what some might construe as the worst of market conditions, when market participants pursue solely their own individual self-interests, however narrowly and imperfectly defined and pursued, the individuals' pursuits can, under *some* very constraining conditions, lead to the betterment of society (as if by Smith's much-heralded "invisible hand," which suggests that people generally might not understand well, or even at all, how their private pursuits generated societal betterment). Smith wrote,

> As every individual, therefore, endeavours as much as he can both to employ his capital in the support of domestic industry, and so to direct that industry that its produce may be of the greatest value; every individual necessarily labours to render the annual revenue of the society as great as he can. He generally, indeed, neither intends to promote the public interest, nor knows how much he is promoting it. By preferring the support of domestic to that of foreign industry, he intends only his own security; and by directing that industry in such a manner as its produce may be of the greatest value, he intends only his own gain, and he is in this, as in many other cases, led by an invisible hand to promote an end which was no part of his intention. Nor is it always the worse for the society that it was no part of it. By pursuing his own interest he frequently promotes that of the society more effectually than when he really intends to promote it. I have never known much good done by those who affected to trade for the public good. It is an affectation, indeed, not very common among merchants, and very few words need be employed in dissuading them from it.[17]

Both Smith's admirers (including the author) and critics have read into such isolated passages in *The Wealth of Nation* that Smith believed that people who were left free to pursue their self-interests, whatever they are, would, without fail, do good works for broader society because self-interest would generally, but not always, be checked and guided by competitive market forces. Self-interested people would, more or less, be blindly guided by market forces to produce more efficiently than otherwise with prices charged reasonably in line with production costs, but, again, only within bounds.

Note that Smith does not say that the invisible hand works its market magic with perfection, partially because people don't always know with clarity what their self-interests are as they work their way through market processes (which are better characterized as mazes than known operations that mechanically follow one another in sequence). For example, Smith writes that "profusion" and "magnanimity" may be the result of a "defect of the proper attention to the objects of self-interest" and "magnanimity" could be due to "too weak a sentiment of our own worth and dignity."[18]

Also, note that in his famous invisible-hand passage above, Smith merely asserts that individuals' pursuit of their self-interest "frequently promotes" larger society's interest "more effectually than when he really intends to promote it." He adds that pursuit of society's interest is "not very common among merchants," which is to say that Smith did not think that people's pursuit of narrow selfish ends per se is all-controlling. People, in other words, could be variously motivated, although pursuit of personal ends could be dominant. Even pursuit of societal interests was simply "not very common" among the commercial classes, but that suggests that Smith did not believe merchants' pursuit of societal interest is altogether absent either.

True enough, Smith did put selfishness at the core of his discussions of how trade can elevate the wealth of any nation. He famously stressed that people don't expect their meals from the "the butcher, the brewer, or the baker" out of "benevolence." Rather,

> We address ourselves, not to their humanity but to their self-love, and never talk to them of our own necessities but of their advantages. Nobody but a beggar chuses to depend chiefly upon the benevolence of his fellow-citizens. Even a beggar does not depend upon it entirely.[19]

Smith's critics (and many followers) have wrongly deduced, from my reading, that Smith believed that "self-love" was at the core of all human behavior, and his nascent construction of economics as a discipline. No doubt, he believed much human behavior is driven by self-love, which is especially true in market trades that involve merchants. After all, his prominent merchant-class examples—"the butcher, the brewer, or the baker"—are at some distance from people's close circles of friends and family. In market trades, buyers and sellers at some distance apart hardly know each other well in matters outside of their commercial lives and frequently contact each other only for completing their trades. In the vernacular of economics, they have little reason to allow for the motivational forces of love and benevolence to work their way into their "interdependent utility functions" (hardly Smith's choice of words), which are largely (if not exclusively) related to their trades.

Surely, Smith would allow, at least to some degree, for love and benevolence and other motivation forces to constrain and guide behaviors within circles of families and friends who share common goals and resources (and from my reading of Smith, I see no reason for him to rule out altogether such motivations in commercial life). In his *Logic of Collective Action*, Mancur Olson argued a point that Smith appears to have understood intuitively, if not explicitly, close to two centuries before Olson, the motivational power of common goals loses its force as groups grow in size and numbers because the actions of individuals become progressively less perceptible and meaningful as people's collective output expands.[20]

In *Wealth of Nations*, Smith could also very well have felt he could focus narrowly on the drive of self-interest because he had covered other nonself-love foundations for behaviors in his *Theory of Moral Sentiments*, published seventeen years before *The Wealth of Nations*. In *Moral Sentiments*, Smith gave homage to people who displayed "perfect virtue,"[21] writing with some eloquence and, seemingly, approval about perfectly virtuous people:

> The man of the most perfect virtue, the man whom we naturally love and revere the most, is he who joins, to the most perfect command of his own original and selfish feelings, the most exquisite sensibility both to the original and sympathetic feelings of others. The man who, to all the soft, the amiable, and the gentle virtues, joins all the great, the awful, and the respectable, must surely be the natural and proper object of our highest love and admiration.[22]

Moreover, he contended that people's more honorable motivations were sometimes cultivated, in part, by their self-interest:

> Regard to our own private happiness and interest, too, appear upon many occasions very laudable principles of action. The habits of oeconomy,

> industry, discretion, attention, and application of thought, are generally supposed to be cultivated from self-interested motives, and at the same time are apprehended to be very praise-worthy qualities, which deserve the esteem and approbation of every body. The mixture of a selfish motive, it is true, seems often to sully the beauty of those actions which ought to arise from a benevolent affection.[23]

Smith was an ardent advocate of a "system of natural liberty," under which governments would have three chief duties, that of providing national defense, systems of justice, and "certain public goods" (which actually gave governments substantial latitude in the duties they assumed).[24] But Smith's main interest in limited government was to constrain people's (especially rich and politically connected people's) pursuit of their own narrow interests through government, under the guise of pursuing some societal interests. Smith stressed the beneficial tie between free trade and economic growth, that free trade could expand markets and could, therefore, increase the potential for the realization of economies of specialization (as highlighted in pin production at the start of *Wealth*), which could translate into a growth in the wealth of nations. However, he also opposed trade restrictions because they were all too often imposed by governments to pad the pockets of special interests with government influence. That is, bounded government would contain what modern economists have tagged as "rent seeking" and, thus, along with the exploitation of *absolute* advantages in production, promote long-term growth in the wealth of nations. (Smith did not appreciate the advantages that could be drawn from exploitation of *comparative* advantages in production, which had to wait for "discovery" by David Ricardo in the early 1800s.)

Moreover, Smith's complete system of natural liberty was not intended to afford people opportunities to do whatever they wished within constrained government. The commercial class would be constrained by external market competition from domestic and foreign sources, as now widely recognized. They would be constrained and directed by an unheralded second "invisible hand," which emerges from people's willingness to defer to their individually devised "impartial spectators," which emerge from cultural and religious influences and which people carry with them throughout life.[25]

People's impartial spectators judged the rightness of behaviors partially based on their sense of "beneficence"[26] and perhaps fear of eternal damnation from the "author of nature," or God, for seeking to gain at the expense of others.[27] Smith even allowed for behavior to be guided by "pity," "compassion," "pride," and "vanity."[28] Smith clearly did not forsake his broad view of human nature when he turned to matters of commerce and fortune in *Wealth*:

> How selfish soever man may be supposed, there are evidently some principles in his nature, which interest him in the fortune of others, and render their happiness necessary to him, though he derives nothing from it except the pleasure of seeing it. Of this kind is pity or compassion, the emotion which we feel for the misery of others, when we either see it, or are made to conceive it in a very lively manner. That we often derive sorrow from the sorrow of others, is a matter of fact too obvious to require any instances to prove it; for this sentiment, like all the other original passions of human nature, is by no means confined to the virtuous and humane, though they perhaps may feel it with the most exquisite sensibility. The greatest ruffian, the most hardened violator of the laws of society, is not altogether without it.[29]

But then, Smith seems conflicted over the role of self-interest in guiding people's behavior. In *Moral Sentiments*, he also wrote, "We are not ready to suspect any person of being defective in selfishness."[30] A fair reading of his two classics, taken together, suggests that for Smith there were two interlocked and inseparable invisible hands at work in people's interactions inside and outside of markets, with the second invisible hand remaining largely unrecognized, that of people's impartial spectators that induce them to do the right things even in markets. Again, in *Moral Sentiments* he wrote as much:

> But though the virtues of prudence, justice, and beneficence, may, upon different occasions, be recommended to us almost equally by two different principles; those of self-command are, upon most occasions, principally and almost entirely recommended to us by one; by the sense of propriety, by regard to the sentiments of the supposed impartial spectator. Without the restraint which this principle imposes, every passion would, upon most occasions, rush headlong, if I may say so, to its own gratification. Anger would follow the suggestions of its own fury; fear those of its own violent agitations. Regard to no time or place would induce vanity to refrain from the loudest and most impertinent ostentation; or voluptuousness from the most open, indecent, and scandalous indulgence. Respect for what are, or for what ought to be, or for what upon a certain condition would be, the

> sentiments of other people, is the sole principle which, upon most occasions, overawes all those mutinous and turbulent passions into that tone and temper which the impartial spectator can enter into and sympathize with.[31]

Such a fair reading of his books suggests that Smith probably held the view that the invisible hand of the market would be lame without the invisible hand of people's impartial spectators.[32] Without the second invisible hand, markets might not emerge or when they emerge, might be more narrow in influence than could be achieved with only the first invisible hand. Without the prevalence of people's impartial spectators, the welfare gains from specialization of labor (and other resources) and trade would be delimited, which means the growth in the wealth of nations would come up short of nations' potential growth. That is, any folding of the second invisible hand would crimp the first, and the growth in the wealth of nations. Modern economists have documented the importance to economic prosperity and growth of widespread trust within market economies, with trust being inspired by and emerging from constraining moral principles invoked and enforced by people's impartial spectators, and fortified by an all-knowing, omnipresent, and all-powerful God.[33]

While Smith surely recognized the scarcity of resources (without ever using the word "scarcity"), he never posited a theory of people maximizing their welfare in the way (and with the precision) modern economists do. Rather, he seemed mainly concerned with how people, and their governments, could *improve* the general welfare, or the wealth of nations, through the freeing of markets. Freeing markets from trade restrictions, both domestic and foreign, had much the same economic effects of what might be called a "third invisible hand": Freer markets allowed for an expansion of markets that, in turn, increased people's opportunities to increase their production scale and efficiency through greater specialization—and increase total production and the wealth of nations.[34]

In summary, many of Smith's critics focus their ire on the prominence of "self-love," or just "self-interest," in Smith's support of open markets. Read more generously and accurately, with both of his treatises in mind, he seems to have intended to argue that even under unexpected and unfavorable conditions—when self-interest is largely driving market participants—then markets, through the "invisible hand," can generate broad-based social gains—*but* only so long as competition and rules of behavior constrained market participants and government powers to favor politically influential groups were held at bay.

Twixt Smith and Wicksteed

While Adam Smith clearly recognized that worker competition for jobs could hold down worker welfare, he still deduced reasons for economic optimism, or sources of at least some economic improvement in production and wealth over time.[35] The overarching source of wealth creation came from the ever-widening of markets that could be achieved partially by ever-eroding government-inspired trade barriers that had been erected for the benefit of special interest groups. Several luminaries in the budding discipline of economics, or "political economy," through much of the 1800s, adopted a more dismal view of the plight of humankind, most notably, Thomas Robert Malthus, David Ricardo, and Karl Marx.

Malthus

By way of contrast to Smith, Thomas Robert Malthus (1766–1834) was a raving pessimist. His population theory, which he laid out in *An Essay on the Principle of Population* (1798), held out minimal to no hope for economic improvement for ordinary people (which he characterized as "inferior," "unproductive," and "menial" workers) who were doomed to live at subsistence. If by a turn of passing events (say, a contraction in the labor supply from wars or diseases), worker wages were to rise above the subsistence level, the "passion of the sexes" would kick in and more children would survive to become workers, leading to a greater supply of labor and a return of worker wages to subsistence.[36] Aid for subsistence workers grounded in benevolence on the part of the well-off was all but futile:

> An amelioration of society to be produced merely by reason and conviction, wears much more the promise of permanence, than any change effected and maintained by force. The unlimited exercise of private judgement, is a doctrine inexpressibly grand and captivating, and has a vast superiority over those systems where every individual is in a manner the slave of the public. The substitution of benevolence as the master-spring, and moving principle of society, instead of self-love, is a consummation devoutly to be wished. In short, it is impossible to contemplate the whole of this fair structure, without emotions of delight and admiration, accompanied with ardent longing for the period of its accomplishment. But, alas! that moment can never arrive. The whole is little better than a dream, a beautiful phantom of the imagination. These "gorgeous palaces" of happiness and immortality, these "solemn temples" of truth and virtue will dissolve, "like the baseless fabric of a vision," when we awaken to real life, and contemplate the true and genuine situation of man on earth.[37]

Clearly, in Malthus' worldview, people's welfares were checked by resource constraints. After all, his population theory was grounded in the relatively more rapid rate of growth in population than in the food supply. However, the most important conflict was between, on the one hand, the limited availability of jobs for the masses of workers and a more or less fixed "wage fund" that had to be ever more finely divided in a growing population.

Malthus' construction of scarcity never caused him to posit rationality—much less, perfect rationality—on the part of ordinary people in working through their economic affairs. He scoffed at William Godwin's philosophical musing founded on people as "rational beings" being "beautiful and engaging," but such theorizing would be found "baseless" under careful scrutiny "when we awaken to real life, and contemplate the true and genuine situation of man on earth."[38] In addition to their sexual passions, ordinary people's choices were also tightly constrained by other forces:

> The cravings of hunger, the love of liquor, the desire of possessing a beautiful woman, will urge men to actions, of the fatal consequences of which, to the general interests of society, they are perfectly well convinced, even at the very time they commit them... [A]nd under all the circumstances of their situation with these bodily cravings, the decision of the compound being is different from the conviction of the rational being.[39]

In short, ordinary people were led by a Malthusian "invisible hand" of cravings toward economic self-destructive ends, not exactly what Smith envisioned for the broad swath of humanity for the long run. The only hope Malthus held out for economic improvement of the masses was a slim one, that of people delaying marriage. When subsisting, workers had precious little room to carefully weigh off options and choose consistently. They merely did what was required by their tight constraints, subsist.

Malthus' pessimistic assessment of the plight of workers was probably more in tune with the reality of the economics of the times (prior to the early to mid-1800s) than was Smith's more optimistic assessment. University of California, Davis economic historian Gregory Clark has observed that there was precious little economic progress in the world before 1800. Indeed, he found that in the millennium prior to 1800, annual economic growth average at best a scant .05% (if not closer to zero or negative), which meant that, prior to 1800, it took about 1400 years for the then measly average income of workers to double. Moreover, he found,

> Jane Austen may have written about refined conversations over tea served in china cups. But for the majority of the English as late as 1813 conditions were no better than their naked ancestors of the African savannah. So, even according to the broadest measures of material life, average welfare, if anything, declined from the Stone Age to 1800. The poor of 1800, those who lived by their unskilled labor alone, would have been better off if transferred to a hunter-gatherer band.[40]

Malthus' great failures were that he did not see the Industrial Revolution taking form as he wrote up his dismal assessment of the future of the vast majority of workers. From the historical record he had at hand, technological progress could easily be overpowered by people's sexual proclivities and derivative population growth. The reverse was the actual future history, with the added benefits of economic growth, at least beyond some point, curbing Malthusian population growth.

Ricardo

David Ricardo (1772–1823) in his *On the Principles of Political Economy and Taxation* (first published in 1817) adopted with admiration Malthus' population theory that led to the "iron law of wages," or the press of worker wages toward the subsistence level with a growth in the labor supply.[41] In Ricardian theory of income distribution, prices had little to do with people's subjective evaluation of goods or the interaction of supply and demand. Aside for a few goods ("rare statutes and pictures, scarce books and coins, wine of a peculiar quality"), even goods' scarcity had little to nothing to do with their prices.[42] Prices had everything to do with their labor content, which would ultimately be checked by diminishing returns in production.[43]

Workers' welfare might be improved for a time by an expansion in international trade, which, he recognized for the first time, could be founded on *comparative* cost advantages, not just *absolute* cost advantages (which was at the foundation of Smith's gains from freer trade).[44] Moreover, in Ricardo's construction of the impact of expanded trade, the grip of diminishing returns of production would be relieved by the greater use of land (lowering the labor/land ratio), which, in turn, would reduce the rents of landlords.

Nevertheless, with added income, the Malthusian "passion of the sexes" would kick in, driving up the labor supply, driving down worker wages, and, eventually, driving up the rents of landlords and capitalists. As with Malthus, rationality was far from central to Ricardian economics. External forces largely, if not completely, controlled the welfare of the masses.

Marx

Karl Marx (1818–1883) integrated Malthus' population theory and Ricardian central concern for the distribution of income—along with the labor theory of value that both Malthus and Ricardo viewed as central to establishing relative prices of goods—to form his Marxian theory of labor exploitation and theory of the ultimate demise of capitalism into (somewhat paradoxically) a workers' paradise, as laid out in his *Communist Manifesto* (1848) and *Das Capital* (1867). Marx's theory of the downfall of capitalism was grounded on something of new form of scarcity centered on deficient consumer demand (driven by the suppression of workers' wages by the masters of capital) not keeping up with the production capacity (driven by capitalists' attempt to find new ways to invest the surplus value of labor that the capitalists siphoned from worker contributions to the value of production). Marx called for an uprising of the proletariats because they "have nothing to lose but their chains" and have the opportunity to win the "whole world," which suggests Marx believed that incentives to create capital were of little consequence.[45] Capitalists, like workers, were cogs in an economic machine. Their behaviors through time were largely driven by a "historical materialistic dialectic."

Nevertheless, Marx posited a theory that capitalism would, in the process of usurping labor's rightful productive value, build up (through some largely exogenous dialectic forces) the world's productive base, so much that problems of scarcity would be so suppressed that workers could take over the economic system and take from the "haves" and give to the "have-nots," with no material consequences for output. Incentives did not matter in the historical demise of capitalism and would not matter in his worker paradise.

Marx never seemed to worry that capital, most prominent in the brick and mortar of factories all about, could be as ephemeral, elusive, and mobile as the steam that powered the Industrial Revolution and, supposedly, worker suppression. In formulating his theory of workers' overthrow of capital, Marx was taking a page from Adam Smith who had observed that then modern methods of factory production, which was built so much on the specialization of labor, had dehumanized and subjugated workers to the monotony of repetitive work, reducing them to close to babbling idiots. Smith elaborated on the downside of specialization on workers' character:

> In the progress of the division of labour, the employment of the far greater part of those who live by labour, that is, of the great body of the people, comes to be confined to a few very simple operations, frequently to one or two. But the understandings of the greater part of men are necessarily formed by their ordinary employments. The man whose whole life is spent in performing a few simple operations, of which the effects are perhaps always the same, or very nearly the same, has no occasion to exert his understanding or to exercise his invention in finding out expedients for removing difficulties which never occur. He naturally loses, therefore, the habit of such exertion, and generally becomes as stupid and ignorant as it is possible for a human creature to become. The torpor of his mind renders him not only incapable of relishing or bearing a part in any rational conversation, but of conceiving any generous, noble, or tender sentiment, and consequently of forming any just judgment concerning many even of the ordinary duties of private life. Of the great and extensive interests of his country he is altogether incapable of judging, and unless very particular pains have been taken to render him otherwise, he is equally incapable of defending his country in war. The uniformity of his stationary life naturally corrupts the courage of his mind, and makes him regard with abhorrence the irregular, uncertain, and adventurous life of a soldier. It corrupts even the activity of his body, and renders him incapable of exerting his strength with vigour and perseverance in any other employment than that to which he has been bred. His dexterity at his own particular trade seems, in this manner, to be acquired at the expence of his intellectual, social, and martial virtues. But in every improved and civilized society this is the state into which the labouring poor, that is, the great body of the people, must necessarily fall, unless government takes some pains to prevent it.[46]

Bastiat

During the first half of the 1800s, following the lead of Ricardo, economics was to one extent or another relegated to price theory, or how prices are determined and how they affect the distribution of income, as well as the distribution of resources, with the focus of various political economists on the dominance of self-interest in directing people's market transactions. French economic journalist and satirist Frederic Bastiat (1801–1850) felt that it was all very nice for political economists to recognize the noble motives of people, but he concluded that the thrust of political economy inquiry must be guided by the "cold domain of self-interest."[47] He then narrowly defined economics as seeking understanding of market transactions:

> What does it [political economy] deal with? With transactions carried on between people who do not know each other, who owe each other nothing beyond simple justice, who are defending and seeking to advance their own self-interest. It deals with claims that are restricted and limited by other claims, where self-sacrifice and unselfish dedication have no place. Take up the poet's lyre, then, to speak of these things. I would as soon see Lamartine consult a table of logarithms to sing his odes.[48]

Bentham, Mill, and the Marginalists

Jeremy Bentham (1748–1832) made utility maximization at the individual level the heart of economic inquiry in *An Introduction to the Principles of Morals and Legislation* by observing that

> Nature has placed mankind under the governance of two sovereign masters, *pain* and *pleasure*. It is for them alone to point out what we ought to do, as well as to determine what we shall do. On the one hand the standard of right and wrong, on the other the chain of causes and effects, are fastened to their throne. They govern us in all we do, in all we say, in all we think: every effort we can make to throw off our subjection, will serve but to demonstrate and confirm it. In words a man may pretend to abjure their empire: but in reality he will remain subject to it all the while. The *principle of utility* recognizes this subjection, and assumes it for the foundation of that system, the object of which is to rear the fabric of felicity by the hands of reason and of law. Systems which attempt to question it, deal

> in sounds instead of sense, in caprice instead of reason, in darkness instead of light. (emphasis in the original)[49]

John Stuart Mill (1806–1873), in his *Principles of Political Economy*, first published in 1848 and widely adopted for university classes until the late 19th century, shifted emphasis in price determination from the labor theory of value advocated by Smith, Ricardo, and Marx to a subjective theory of value and contended that market competition would push prices to the upper limit of goods' respective subjective values.[50] In so articulating the core concern of economics, Mill set the stage for the "marginal revolution" pushed separately in the last third of the 1800s by William Stanley Jevons (1835–1882), Leon Walras (1834–1910), and Carl Menger (1840–1921).[51] The marginalists argued that it was the marginal value of goods, or what Jevons called the "final degree of utility" and Phillip Wicksteed later called "marginal utility," that determined competitive prices.[52] Again, the core concern of economics remained price determination and variation, but their emphasis on marginal values was a precursor to economists discussing maximization in terms of equating marginal values of goods.

Marshall

In critical ways, mainly through his widely and long used textbook *Principles of Economics*, Alfred Marshall (1842–1924) pressed for formalization of economic inquiry, adding key concepts and graphical devices that continue to be used in contemporary economics courses, including supply-and demand curves, equilibrium, and short and long run time periods. He placed the first set of supply-and-demand curves in a footnote (reflecting his effort to downplay their importance to economic analytics), but he used them to make the point that prices were determined by forces that could be treated *as if* they captured the clearly separated two sides of the market, consumer subjective evaluations and production costs (when, in reality, market forces could not be so clearly demarcated, he argued).[53] In explaining how equilibrium prices are determined in market, he laid out an explanation some variant of which many contemporary economists still use in their classes:

> We might as reasonably dispute whether it is the upper or the under blade of a pair of scissors that cuts a piece of paper, as whether value is governed

> by utility or cost of production. It is true that when one blade is held still, and the cutting is effected by moving the other, we may say with careless brevity that the cutting is done by the second; but the statement is not strictly accurate, and is to be excused only so long as it claims to be merely a popular and not a strictly scientific account of what happens.[54]

However, he cautioned that devices employed in economic analysis should be understood for what they are, *devices* to make analyses manageable and to develop insight, and were not to be taken as founding truths in themselves regarding how markets really work in their full complexity:

> The forces [in economics] to be dealt with are however so numerous, that it is best to take a few at a time; and to work out a number of partial solutions as auxiliaries to our main study. Thus we begin by isolating the primary relations of supply, demand and price in regard to a particular commodity. We reduce to inaction all other forces by the phrase "other things being equal": we do not suppose that they are inert, but for the time we ignore their activity. This scientific device is a great deal older than science: it is the method by which, consciously or unconsciously, sensible men have dealt from time immemorial with every difficult problem of ordinary life.[55]

As Marshal simplified his assumptions about human motivations, market partitions in terms of goods and time periods, and his analytical constructions, he mused at the "mischief" that could be created by economists crystalizing their behavioral premises and then believing them to be fully descriptive of human motivations. He worried about past misuses of "economic man," who was assumed, in his market dealings and elsewhere and for purposes of pursuing "abstract science," to be devoid of "ethical influences and who pursues pecuniary gain warily and energetically, but mechanically and selfishly"[56]:

> But they [past economists] have not been successful, nor even thoroughly carried out. For they have never really treated the economic man as perfectly selfish: no one could be relied on better to endure toil and sacrifice with the unselfish desire to make provision for his family; and his normal motives have always been tacitly assumed to include the family affections. But if they include these, why should they not include all other altruistic motives the action of which is so far uniform in any class at any time and place, that it can be reduced to general rule?[57]

Marshall added, cautioning students about his mode of analysis in his own textbook:

> There has always been a temptation to classify economic goods in clearly defined groups, about which a number of short and sharp propositions could be made, to gratify at once the student's desire for logical precision, and the popular liking for dogmas that have the air of being profound and are yet easily handled. But great mischief seems to have been done by yielding to this temptation, and drawing broad artificial lines of division where Nature has made none. The more simple and absolute an economic doctrine is, the greater will be the confusion which it brings into attempts to apply economic doctrines to practice, if the dividing lines to which it refers cannot be found in real life. There is not in real life a clear line of division between things that are and are not Capital, or that are and are not Necessaries, or again between labour that is and is not Productive.[58]

Marshall simply saw economics as a method of analysis made necessary by the subject matter, complex human behavior in production, consumption, and exchange. He pressed for simplifying the subject matter into four time periods that held out the prospects for separable price equilibriums in each, at least in theory,[59] although he firmly held to the "Principle of Continuity" (caps in the original), implying "continuous gradation" in all things, goods and time and evaluations (which shows up in is smoothly downward-sloping demand curve).[60] He wrote, "For the element of Time, which is the centre of the chief difficulty of almost every economic problem, is itself absolutely continuous: Nature knows no absolute partition of time into long periods and short; but the two shade into one another by imperceptible gradations, and what is a short period for one problem, is a long period for another."[61]

Marshall was also willing to accept gradations in the motivations of people in different spheres of life, which means that people in "business-like" classes could, and likely were, more motivated by personal gain than elsewhere in life (within, families and circles of friends, for example):

> Thus stress [in economics] is laid on the fact that there is a continuous gradation from the actions of "city men," which are based on deliberate and far-reaching calculations, and are executed with vigour and ability, to those of ordinary people who have neither the power nor the will to conduct their affairs in a business-like way. The normal willingness to save,

> the normal willingness to undergo a certain exertion for a certain pecuniary reward, or the normal alertness to seek the best markets in which to buy and sell, or to search out the most advantageous occupation for oneself or for one's children—all these and similar phrases must be relative to the members of a particular class at a given place and time: but, when that is once understood, the theory of normal value is applicable to the actions of the unbusiness-like classes in the same way, though not with the same precision of detail, as to those of the merchant or banker.[62]

Moreover, people so segmented differed in their "personal affections," "conceptions of duty," and "reverence of high ideals." He was willing to accept that "it is true that the best energies of the ablest inventors and organizers of improved methods and appliances are stimulated by a noble emulation more than by any love of wealth for its own sake."[63] True, magnanimous cooperation among everyone might yield greater social welfare than competitive market, but such is a romantic view of the world as it can be observed, but he warned, "Such is the Golden Age to which poets and dreamers may look forward. But in the responsible conduct of affairs, it is worse than folly to ignore the imperfections which still cling to human nature."[64]

Marshall was willing to follow the logic of his analytics founded on an intentionally narrow portion of the spectrum of human motivations—self-interest—because he placed analytical boundaries on the scope of human interaction under considerations.[65] He saw economics mainly as a study, in limited (not fully scientific way), "of men as they live and move and think in the ordinary business of life" and was chiefly concerned "with those motives which affect, most powerfully and most steadily, man's conduct in the business part of his life," where people—namely business people—were "deliberate in their courses of actions and were mainly motivated by monetary rewards."[66]

In short, Marshall saw economics as a simplified method of analysis of a complex and interactive segment—albeit an important segment—of human society. He was willing to assume that within the business world "city men" could be expected to base their business moves "on deliberate and far-reaching calculations" that "are executed with vigour and ability" relative to those "ordinary people who have neither the power nor the will to conduct their affairs in a business-like way."[67] Given the importance of the Principle of Continuity in Marshall's analytical framework, it is altogether reasonable to deduce that economic analysis, as he constructed it, would lose its predictive power as economists moved from tackling strictly commercial topics to topics involving "unbusiness like classes" and personal relationships. This is because the "force of motives" (maximization of personal or firm gain) would dissipate.[68]

I suggest that by insisting that economics was most relevant to people in commerce, Marshall was implicitly recognizing people were not, and could not be, innately perfectly rational, and were far from it. They shuffled through combinations of several drives in different spheres of life, especially in the long run. People in business, while doing business, would likely adopt to a greater degree the thinking like *homo economicus* than ordinary people outside of business classes, mainly because business people self-selected business as a life course and were surrounded by competitive pressures to do so. Given variety of cost/benefit calculations in business, business people also had ample opportunities to refine their thinking over time and to discover the economic way of thinking and to become trained economists. And people who were inclined to think like economists more or less "naturally" may have been predisposed to go into business. Those who were not so inclined and refused to refine their thinking could be pushed out of the market by those who did through competitive forces.

Because of the tenor of his methodological musings, I have to believe Marshal was not inclined to assume that in their commercial lives, business people were exclusively self-interested. After all, trust among other virtues infuses business relationships, as noted. I suspect, given his emphasis on continuity in thinking, he was unwilling to define the extent of the self-interest drive in different people or to assume everyone had the same self-interest drive.

Given his emphasis on noncommercial motivations and his insistence on limiting economics to "the ordinary business of life," I suspect he would agree that the extent of a person's self-interested drive in commercial life was set by marginal considerations, which is to say that he probably thought of the extent of the self-interest motivation in business endeavors would be checked by its declining marginal value of extending the drive relative to other motivations, with the achievement of an equilibrium of sorts for the several motivations he identified. People's equilibriums on motivations could vary as much as equilibriums in different markets.

Wicksteed

Philip Wicksteed (1844–1927), a contemporary of Marshall's, had his main influence on the economics discipline through his textbook, *Common Sense of Political Economy* (1910). He shared much of Marshall's predilections toward trying to model market interactions. However, while Marshall saw supply and demand as completely separate market forces, Wicksteed saw supply and demand as mirror images of each other, with the supply curve being producers' (or holders') of goods reservation demand curves.[69]

More importantly, while Marshall viewed economics as mainly concerned with commercial relations, in which people were mainly calculating, Wicksteed was Becker's forerunner. Wicksteed saw economics as far more expansive mainly because people in their noncommercial lives had to deal with their "personal economies," in which they could not have everything they wanted (implying scarcity of means for satisfying wants) and in which they were involved in "the administration of the *affairs and resources* of a household in such a manner as to avoid waste *and* secure efficiency." This meant that the discipline could be construed as "the study of the principles on which the *resources* of a community should be so regulated *and* administered as to secure the communal ends without waste" (emphasis in the original).[70]

Marshall argued that people in commercial spheres could be thought of as seeking their own narrow ends for strictly personal gain, within commercial spheres. In effect, Wicksteed argued that people in their commercial lives could be, and should be, thought of as pursuing a variety of ends, ranging from strictly selfish to strictly selfless ends. The ends didn't matter. Market forces would be activated and augmented by whatever ends people pursued for market analyses.[71] Wicksteed argues that the core concern of the economics discipline was not the underlying motives for "personal economy," but the nature of the resulting relationships, mainly in market settings:

> Accordingly, I shall try to shew that it is time frankly and decisively to abandon all attempts to rule out this or that "motive" from the consideration of the Economist, or indeed to attempt to establish any distinction whatever between the ultimate motives by which a *man* is actuated in business and those by which he is actuated in his domestic or public life. *Economic relations* constitute a complex machine by which we seek

> to accomplish our purposes, whatever they may be. They do not in any direct or conclusive sense either dictate our *purposes* or supply our *motives*. We shall therefore have to consider what constitutes an *economic* relation rather than what constitutes an *economic* motive. And this does away at a stroke with the hypothetically simplified psychology of the *Economic Man* which figured so largely in the older books of Political Economy, and which recent writers take so much trouble to evade or qualify. We are not to begin by imagining *man* to be actuated by only a few simple motives, but we are to take him as we find him, and are to examine the nature of those relations into which he enters, under the stress of all his complicated impulses and desires—whether selfish or unselfish, material or spiritual,—in order to accomplish indirectly through the action of others what he cannot accomplish directly through his own.[72]

A key attribute of "successful" economic relations for Wicksteed consisted of "purposeful selection between alternative applications of resources; and the ultimate value or significance of such success depends on the nature of the objects at which the administrator aims."[73] Having conceived of the discipline as he did, Wicksteed anticipated Becker's expansive view of economics as a methodology that is widely applicable. Wicksteed wrote,

> We have thus arrived at the conclusion that all the heterogeneous impulses and objects of desire or aversion which appeal to any individual, whether material or spiritual, personal or communal, present or future, actual or ideal, may all be regarded as comparable with each other; for we are, as a matter of fact, constantly comparing them, weighing them against each other, and deciding which is the heaviest. And the question, "How much of this must I forgo to obtain so much of that?" is always relevant. If we are considering, for example, whether to live in the country or in the town, such different things as friendship and fresh air or fresh eggs may come into competition and comparison with each other. Shall I "bury myself in the country," where I shall see little of my dearest friends, but may hope for fresh eggs for breakfast, and fresh air all the day? Or shall I stay where I am, and continue to enjoy the society of my friends? I start at once thinking "how much of the society of my friends must I expect to sacrifice? Will any of them come and see me? Shall I occasionally be able to go and see some of them?" The satisfactions and benefits I anticipate from a country life will compensate me for the loss of some of their society, but not for the loss of all of it. The price may be too high. In such a case as this the terms on which the alternatives are offered are matter of more or less vague

surmise and conjecture, but the apparent dissimilarity of the several satisfactions themselves does not prevent the comparison, nor does it prevent the quantitative element from affecting my decision. Using the term price then in its widest extension, we may say that all the objects of repulsion or attraction which divide my energies and resources amongst them are linked to each other by a system of ideal prices or terms of equivalence. We may conceive of a general "scale of preferences" or "relative scale of estimates" on which all objects of desire or pursuit (positive or negative) find their place, and which registers the terms on which they would be accepted as equivalents or preferred one to the other.[74]

Concluding Comments

Clearly, some notion of scarcity has long undergirded economics (or as the discipline was initially known, political economy), or at least the perspectives of the discipline's luminaries covered in this chapter—Smith, Ricardo, Malthus, Marx, Marshall, and Wicksteed. Scarcity was subsumed by all, or otherwise it is hard to understand their attention to the implied goal of *improvement* in people's and countries' incomes and wealth through, for example, taking down trade barriers, broadening markets, and gaining efficiencies through greater labor specialization. However, by subsuming scarcity, many economists of the eighteenth, nineteenth, and early twentieth centuries felt no compunction to erect anything approaching consumer and producer choice theory grounded on some form of strictly mathematical-type optimization. They did not get bogged down in detailed discussions of "maximizing behavior, market equilibrium, and stable preferences," to use Becker's list of core concerns of the discipline. Rather, they were able to restrict their focus, for the most part, on the institutional framework and policies for growth in countries' aggregate wealth over time, which included freeing all trade as much as practical and restraining governments' as much as practical (generally for the purpose of containing rent seeking, which they considered counter-productive of the general welfare).

Smith founded the discipline of economics on the presumption that people's economic decisions were guided by a multiplicity of motives. His concern was, as was apparent from the title of his classic, primarily, the "the nature and causes of the wealth of nations." Ricardo, Malthus, and Marx diverted attention to matters of the struggle over the income distribution, with worker's welfare always constrained by the capitalist class and the "iron law of wages." Marshall reasserted Smith's expansive view of human motivations at the same time he returned economics to matters of theory building, but largely, if not exclusively, within commercial life and with the value of predictions from models limited by the underlying presumption of people's pursuit of personal gain, narrowly conceived. Marshall made economics a tightly confined method of analysis as he worried, at the same time, that the method could be misapplied and misused.

Wicksteed retained Smith's and Marshall's expansive view of human motivations and accepted that economics was a method of analysis, but he reconceived of economics as a disciplined bordered by the nature of the *relationships* people develop to achieve their different ends. At the same time, he argued that there was no reason to assume that economic relationships were devised solely by narrow self-interests.

Wicksteed was willing to accept economic methods and relationships developing far afield from Marshall's. He seems to have set the methodological stage for a host of following economists to apply economic methods to an unchecked array of topics, but only after Robbins cast economics as the study of the implications of scarcity. Robbins' repositioning of the discipline's core concern gave rise to a formal purified choice theory under which, ironically, people's capacities to precisely and accurately refine their preferences (implied by the premise of "perfect rationality") were not subject to the constraints of scarcity that gave rise to the need for choices. Interestingly, as economics evolved toward perfect rationality as the core premise, people retained the right to choose among goods, but not the right to choose among possible levels of precision in their decision-making.

In closing this chapter, what needs to be noted is that in so much of the writings of early economists, the notion of scarcity was construed simply as people not being able to obtain all that they want, because of the limitations of their incomes, due to suppression of wages checked by forces like trade barriers and population growth. The critical scarcity was in the physical world external to people. Little direct attention was given to the scarcity of people's mental capacities to make economic calculations and to seek what they want at whatever efficiency level was possible. If there was any boundedness to people's calculating ability it had to do with the intrusions of noneconomic, nonself-interested motives, such as concerns of ethics and humanism. Economists continued on this intellectual trajectory through Robbins' repositioning of the discipline in the 1930s, with internal, mental scarcity set further and further into the background until the 1950s (or, maybe, better, the 1970s), when psychology-grounded scholars began to question and then demonstrate empirically that real people's decision-making fell far short of the demands of "perfect rationality" that had, by the 1970s, become the workhorse premise in economists' modeling of behavior in commercial and noncommercial spheres of life.

We continue our review of the history of economic methodology in the following two chapters, mainly to show how behavioral economists have broken dramatically with economic thinkers of the past, as explained in Chapter 4. Then, in Chapters 4 and 5, I lay out how behavioral economists and psychologists have uncovered flaws in neoclassical economics, most notably with its founding premise of perfect rationality. In Chapter 6, the final chapter, I show how making scarcity within the limited capacities of the human brain holds considerable promise for reconciling the work of behavioral economists with the work of neoclassical economists. My goal is to show how applying economic analytics to scarcity within the brain can predict behaviorists' findings.

Notes

1. Samuelson (1948).
2. Samuelson (1976, p. 3).
3. McConnell (1960, p. 23).
4. Samuelson and Nordhaus (2009).
5. Mankiw (2011, p. 4).
6. Friedman (1953, Chapter 9).
7. Friedman (1962, p. 13).
8. Becker (1976, p. 5).
9. Becker (1976, p. 8).
10. Hayek observed in his classic "Use of Knowledge in Society,"

    > The economic problem is thus not merely a problem of how to allocate 'given' resources—if 'given' is taken to mean given to a single mind which deliberately solves the problem set by these 'data.' It is rather a problem of how to secure the best use of resources to any of the members of society, for ends whose relative importance only these individuals know. Or, to put it differently, it is a problem of the utilization of knowledge not given to anyone in its totality. (1945, pp. 519–520)

He added two decades later in his *Studies in Philosophy, Politics and Economics*

> One of the chief results so far achieved by theoretical work in these fields seems to me to be the demonstration that here individual events regularly depend on so much concrete circumstances that we shall never in fact be in a position to ascertain them all; and that in consequence not only the ideal of prediction and control must largely remain beyond our reach, but also the hope remain illusory that we can discover by observation regular connections between the individual events. (1967, p. 34)

11. Thaler and Sunstein (2008, pp. 6–7).
12. Thaler and Sunstein (2008, pp. 6–7).
13. Thaler (1991, p. xiii). In passing, it needs to be noted that Becker's demonstration of how the downward-sloping demand curves could be obtained from people acting randomly was a matter of intense debate between Becker and Austrian economist Israel Kirzner in the early 1960s, with Kirzner stressing that an assumption of random behavior on the part of economic actors was missing a major part of the process underlying rational behavior, which is that people are expected to revise in systematic ways their plans when confronted with new information as they interact with others who are continually revising their plans to new information. See Becker (1962, 1963) and Kirzner (1962, 1963).
14. Thaler (1992, p. 197).
15. Skouras et al. (2005, p. 362).
16. For example, Smith writes that "profusion" and "magnanimity" may be the result of a "defect of the proper attention to the objects of self-interest" and "magnanimity" could be due to "too weak a sentiment of our own worth and dignity" (1759, ¶ VII.II.16).
17. Smith (1776, ¶ IV.2.9).
18. Smith (1759, ¶ VII.II.16).
19. Smith (1776, ¶ I.2.2).
20. Olson (1965).
21. Smith wrote on perfectly virtuous people:

> The man of the most perfect virtue, the man whom we naturally love and revere the most, is he who joins, to the most perfect command of his own original and selfish feelings, the most exquisite sensibility both to the original and sympathetic feelings of others. The man who, to all the soft, the amiable, and the gentle virtues, joins all the great, the awful, and the

> respectable, must surely be the natural and proper object of our highest love and admiration. (1759, ¶ III.I.77)

22. Smith (1759, ¶ III.I.77).
23. Smith (1759, ¶ VII.II.87).
24. Smith wrote on the emergence of the "system of natural liberty," which in no way is a system without personal restraints on individuals, in *Wealth of Nations*,

> All systems either of preference or of restraint, therefore, being thus completely taken away, the obvious and simple system of natural liberty establishes itself of its own accord. Every man, as long as he does not violate the laws of justice, is left perfectly free to pursue his own interest his own way, and to bring both his industry and capital into competition with those of any other man, or order of men. The sovereign is completely discharged from a duty, in the attempting to perform which he must always be exposed to innumerable delusions, and for the proper performance of which no human wisdom or knowledge could ever be sufficient; the duty of superintending the industry of private people, and of directing it towards the employments most suitable to the interest of the society. According to the system of natural liberty, the sovereign has only three duties to attend to; three duties of great importance, indeed, but plain and intelligible to common understandings: first, the duty of protecting the society from violence and invasion of other independent societies; secondly, the duty of protecting, as far as possible, every member of the society from the injustice or oppression of every other member of it, or the duty of establishing an exact administration of justice; and, thirdly, the duty of erecting and maintaining certain public works and certain public institutions which it can never be for the interest of any individual, or small number of individuals, to erect and maintain; because the profit could never repay the expence to any individual or small number of individuals, though it may frequently do much more than repay it to a great society. (1776, ¶ IV.9.51)

25. Smith (1776, ¶ III.I.46).
26. Smith (1776, ¶ VI.III.55).
27. Smith (1759, ¶ III.I.106).
28. On nonself-interest motives, Smith observed:

> How selfish soever man may be supposed, there are evidently some principles in his nature, which interest him in the fortune of others, and render their happiness necessary to him, though he derives nothing from it except the pleasure of seeing it. Of this kind is pity or compassion, the emotion which we feel for the misery of others, when we either see it, or are made to conceive it in a very lively manner. That we often derive sorrow from the sorrow of others, is a matter of fact too obvious to require any instances to prove it; for this sentiment, like all the other original passions of human nature, is by no means confined to the virtuous and humane, though they perhaps may feel it with the most exquisite sensibility. The greatest ruffian, the most hardened violator of the laws of society, is not altogether without it. (1776, ¶ I.I.1)

See also Smith (1759, ¶ I.I.14).

29. Smith (1776, ¶ I.I.1).
30. Smith (1759, ¶ VII.II.87).
31. Smith (1759, ¶ VI.III.55).
32. Smith mused in *The Theory of Moral Sentiments*:

> In the same manner, to the selfish and original passions of human nature, the loss or gain of a very small interest of our own appears to be of vastly more importance, excites a much more passionate joy or sorrow, a much more ardent desire or aversion, than the greatest concern of another with whom we have no particular connexion. His interests, as long as they are surveyed from this station, can never be put into the balance with our own, can never restrain us from doing whatever may tend to promote our own, how ruinous soever to him. Before we can make any proper comparison of those opposite interests, we must change our position. We must view them, neither from our own place nor yet from his, neither with our own eyes nor yet with his, but from the place and with the eyes of a third person, who has no particular connexion with either, and who judges with impartiality between us. Here, too, habit and experience have taught us to do this so easily and so readily, that we are scarce sensible that we do it; and it requires, in this case too, some degree of reflection, and even of philosophy, to convince us, how little interest we should take in the greatest concerns of our neighbour, how little we should be affected by whatever relates to him, if the sense of

> propriety and justice did not correct the otherwise natural inequality of our sentiments. (1759, ¶ III.I.45)

Smith then added in *The Wealth of Nations*:

> Nature has lighted up in the human heart, that is thus capable of counteracting the strongest impulses of self-love. It is a stronger power, a more forcible motive, which exerts itself upon such occasions. It is reason, principle, conscience, the inhabitant of the breast, the man within, the great judge and arbiter of our conduct. It is he who, whenever we are about to act so as to affect the happiness of others, calls to us, with a voice capable of astonishing the most presumptuous of our passions, that we are but one of the multitude, in no respect better than any other in it; and that when we prefer ourselves so shamefully and so blindly to others, we become the proper objects of resentment, abhorrence, and execration. It is from him only that we learn the real littleness of ourselves, and of whatever relates to ourselves, and the natural misrepresentations of self-love can be corrected only by the eye of this impartial spectator. It is he who shows us the propriety of generosity and the deformity of injustice; the propriety of resigning the greatest interests of our own, for the yet greater interests of others, and the deformity of doing the smallest injury to another, in order to obtain the greatest benefit to ourselves. It is not the love of our neighbour, it is not the love of mankind, which upon many occasions prompts us to the practice of those divine virtues. It is a stronger love, a more powerful affection, which generally takes place upon such occasions; the love of what is honourable and noble, of the grandeur, and dignity, and superiority of our own characters. (1776, ¶ III.I.46)

33. See, for example, Zak and Knack (2001). Put in biblio http://onlinelibrary.wiley.com/doi/10.1111/1468-0297.00609/abstract.
34. In making the tie between specialization and wealth growth, Smith observed:

> As it is the power of exchanging that gives occasion to the division of labour, so the extent of this division must always be limited by the extent of that power, or, in other words, by the extent of the market. When the market is very small, no person can have any encouragement to dedicate himself entirely to one employment, for want of the power to exchange all

> that surplus part of the produce of his own labour, which is over and above his own consumption, for such parts of the produce of other men's labour as he has occasion for. (1776, ¶ I.3.1)

35. Smith also wrote that an overabundance of available workers and a highly responsive labor supply can make for subsistence living with little to no welfare improvement for workers over time, thus anticipating Malthus:

> Though the wealth of a country should be very great, yet if it has been long stationary, we must not expect to find the wages of labour very high in it. The funds destined for the payment of wages, the revenue and stock of its inhabitants, may be of the greatest extent; but if they have continued for several centuries of the same, or very nearly of the same extent, the number of labourers employed every year could easily supply, and even more than supply, the number wanted the following year. There could seldom be any scarcity of hands, nor could the masters be obliged to bid against one another in order to get them. The hands, on the contrary, would, in this case, naturally multiply beyond their employment. There would be a constant scarcity of employment, and the labourers would be obliged to bid against one another in order to get it. If in such a country the wages of labour had ever been more than sufficient to maintain the labourer, and to enable him to bring up a family, the competition of the labourers and the interest of the masters would soon reduce them to this lowest rate which is consistent with common humanity. China has been long one of the richest, that is, one of the most fertile, best cultivated, most industrious, and most populous countries in the world. It seems, however, to have been long stationary. (1776, ¶ I.6.5)

36. Malthus wrote,

> The passion between the sexes has appeared in every age to be so nearly the same that it may always be considered, in algebraic language, as a given quantity. The great law of necessity which prevents population from increasing in any country beyond the food which it can either produce or acquire, is a law, so open to our view, so obvious and evident to our understandings, and so completely confirmed by the experience of every age, that we cannot for a moment doubt it. The different modes which nature takes to prevent or repress a

> redundant population, do not appear, indeed, to us so certain and regular; but though we cannot always predict the mode, we may with certainty predict the fact. If the proportion of births to deaths for a few years, indicate an increase of numbers much beyond the proportional increased or acquired produce of the country, we may be perfectly certain, that unless an emigration takes place, the deaths will shortly exceed the births; and that the increase that had taken place for a few years cannot be the real average increase of the population of the country. Were there no other depopulating causes, every country would, without doubt, be subject to periodical pestilences or famine. (1798, ¶ VII.11)

37. Malthus (1798, ¶ X.2).
38. Malthus (1798, ¶ X.2).
39. Malthus (1798, ¶ XIII.3).
40. Clark (2007, p. 2).
41. Ricardo wrote admiringly of Malthus' population theory:

> Although the nature of rent has in the former pages of this work been treated on at some length, yet I consider myself bound to notice some opinions on the subject, which appear to me erroneous, and which are the more important, as they are found in the writings of one, to whom, of all men of the present day, some branches of economical science are the most indebted. Of Mr. Malthus's Essay on Population, I am happy in the opportunity here afforded me of expressing my admiration. The assaults of the opponents of this great work have only served to prove its strength; and I am persuaded that its just reputation will spread with the cultivation of that science of which it is so eminent an ornament. Mr. Malthus, too, has satisfactorily explained the principles of rent, and shewed that it rises or falls in proportion to the relative advantages, either of fertility or situation, of the different lands in cultivation, and has thereby thrown much light on many difficult points connected with the subject of rent, which were before either unknown, or very imperfectly understood; yet he appears to me to have fallen into some errors, which his authority makes it the more necessary, whilst his characteristic candour renders it less unpleasing to notice. One of these errors lies in supposing rent to be a clear gain and a new creation of riches. (1821, 32.1)

42. Ricardo (1821, ¶¶ 1.5 and 1.6).
43. Ricardo explained his labor theory of value this way: "In speaking then of commodities, of their exchangeable value, and of the laws which regulate their relative prices, we mean always such commodities only as can be increased in quantity by the exertion of human industry, and on the production of which competition operates without restraint" (1821, ¶ 1.7).
44. Ricardo explained how trade could occur from comparative cost advantage this way:

> To produce the wine in Portugal, might require only the labour of 80 men for one year, and to produce the cloth in the same country, might require the labour of 90 men for the same time. It would therefore be advantageous for her to export wine in exchange for cloth. This exchange might even take place, notwithstanding that the commodity imported by Portugal could be produced there with less labour than in England. Though she could make the cloth with the labour of 90 men, she would import it from a country where it required the labour of 100 men to produce it, because it would be advantageous to her rather to employ her capital in the production of wine, for which she would obtain more cloth from England, than she could produce by diverting a portion of her capital from the cultivation of vines to the manufacture of cloth. (1821, ¶ 7.16)

45. Marx (1848, p. 81).
46. Smith (1776, ¶ V.1.1.178).
47. Bastiat (1850, ¶ 2.19). Bastiat elaborated,

> This fact is unfairly forgotten when we reproach political economy with lacking the charm and grace of moral philosophy. How could it be otherwise? Let us challenge the right of political economy to exist as a science, but let us not force it to pretend to be what it is not. If human transactions whose object is wealth are vast enough and complicated enough to constitute a special science, let us grant it its own special appeal, and not reduce it to talking of self-interest in the language of sentiment. I am personally convinced that recently we have done it no service by demanding from it a tone of enthusiastic sentimentality that from its lips can sound only like hollow declamation. (1850, ¶ 2.19)

48. Bastiat (1850, ¶ 2.19).
49. Bentham (1781, ¶ I.1).

50. Mill (1848, ¶ III.1.9).
51. Jevons published his *The Theory of Political Economy* in 1871. Walras published his *Elements of Pure Economics* in 1874, and Menger published his *Principles of Economics* in 1871.
52. Wicksteed (1888).
53. Marshall (1890, ¶ V.III.27).
54. Marshall (1890, ¶ V.III.27).
55. Marshall (1890, ¶ p. 20).
56. Marshall (1890, ¶ p. 3).
57. Marshall (1890, ¶ p. 30).
58. Marshall (1890, ¶ p. 8).
59. Marshall (1890, ¶ V.V.38; and ¶ V.XV.7).
60. Marshall (1890, ¶ pp. 3–4).
61. Marshall (1890, ¶ p. 5).
62. Marshall (1890, ¶ p. 4).
63. Marshall (1890, ¶ I.II.1).
64. Marshall (1890, ¶ I.I.21).
65. Marshall reflected on economics as a partial view of human life in this way:

    > Everyone who is worth anything carries his higher nature with him into business; and, there as elsewhere, he is influenced by his personal affections, by his conceptions of duty and his reverence for high ideals. And it is true that the best energies of the ablest inventors and organizers of improved methods and appliances are stimulated by a noble emulation more than by any love of wealth for its own sake. But, for all that, the steadiest motive to ordinary business work is the desire for the pay which is the material reward of work. The pay may be on its way to be spent selfishly or unselfishly, for noble or base ends; and here the variety of human nature comes into play. (1890, ¶ I.II.1)

66. Marshall (1890, ¶¶ I.II.1 and p. 4). On the importance of monetary measurements to assessing economists predictions, Marshall wrote,

    > But the motive is supplied by a definite amount of money: and it is this definite and exact money measurement of the steadiest motives in business life, which has enabled economics far to outrun every other branch of the study of man. Just as the chemist's fine balance has made chemistry more exact than most other physical sciences; so this economist's balance, rough and imperfect as it is, has made economics more exact than any other branch of social science. But of course,

> economics cannot be compared with the exact physical sciences: for it deals with the ever changing and subtle forces of human nature. (1890, ¶ I.II.1)

67. Marshal (1890, ¶ 4). Marshall wrote in full,

> Thus stress [in economics] is laid on the fact that there is a continuous gradation from the actions of "city men," which are based on deliberate and far-reaching calculations, and are executed with vigour and ability, to those of ordinary people who have neither the power nor the will to conduct their affairs in a business-like way. The normal willingness to save, the normal willingness to undergo a certain exertion for a certain pecuniary reward, or the normal alertness to seek the best markets in which to buy and sell, or to search out the most advantageous occupation for oneself or for one's children—all these and similar phrases must be relative to the members of a particular class at a given place and time: but, when that is once understood, the theory of normal value is applicable to the actions of the unbusiness-like classes in the same way, though not with the same precision of detail, as to those of the merchant or banker. (1890, ¶ 4)

68. Marshall (1890, ¶¶ 3, I.III.4, III.III.18, V.V.90).
69. Wicksteed wrote on the similarity of supply and demand:

> I say it boldly and baldly: there is no such thing [as a meaningful distinction between supply and demand]. When we are speaking of marketable commodities, what is usually called the supply curve is, in reality, the demand curve of those who possess the commodity, for it shows there exact place which every successive unit of the commodity occupies in their relative scale of estimation. The so-called supply curve is, therefore, simply a part of the total demand curve ... The separating of this portion of the demand curve and reversing in the diagram is a process which has its meaning and its legitimate function ... but it is wholly irrelevant to the determination of price. (1914, p. 13)

70. Wicksteed (1910, p. 14).
71. Wicksteed stressed early in his book,

> Economic *relations* constitute a complex machine by which we seek to accomplish our purposes, whatever they may be. They do not in any direct or conclusive sense either dictate

> our *purposes* or supply our *motives*. We shall therefore have to consider what constitutes an economic relation rather than what constitutes an economic motive. And this does away at a stroke with the hypothetically simplified psychology of the Economic Man which figured so largely in the older books of Political Economy, and which recent writers take so much trouble to evade or qualify. We are not to begin by imagining man to be actuated by only a few simple motives, but we are to take him as we find him, and are to examine the nature of those relations into which he enters, under the stress of all his complicated impulses and desires—whether *selfish* or un*selfish*, material or spiritual,—in order to accomplish indirectly through the action of others what he cannot accomplish directly through his own. (1910, p. 4)

Wicksteed explained his position on motivations that moved markets by citing the example of Paul the tentmaker:

> And yet the ground on which this stubborn prejudice rests is obvious enough, and the example of the apostolic tentmaker has already suggested it. We have seen that although Paul was certainly not thinking of himself or of his own advantage when he was making tents in Corinth, yet neither was he necessarily or even probably thinking, in any disinterested or enthusiastic manner, of the advantage of those for whom he was working and whose wants he was immediately supplying. In his attitude towards himself and "others" at large, a man may be either *selfish* or un*selfish* without affecting the economic nature of any given relation, such as that of Paul to his customers; but as soon as he is moved by a direct and disinterested desire to further the purposes or consult the interests of those particular "others" for whom he is working at the moment, then in proportion as this desire becomes an ultimate object to him (so that he is directly fulfilling one of his own purposes in supplying these wants) the transaction on his side ceases to be purely economic. No doubt Paul took conscientious pains with his tent-making. So far as this was with a view to business it was done in obedience to an economic force. So far as it was an expression of his own personality or of his independent sympathy with his employers it was not. If you and I are conducting a transaction which on my side is purely economic, I am furthering your purposes, partly or wholly perhaps for my own sake, perhaps entirely for the sake

of others, but certainly not for your sake. What makes it an economic transaction is that I am not considering you except as a link in the chain, or considering your desires except as the means by which I may gratify those of someone else—not necessarily myself. The economic relation does not exclude from my mind everyone but me, it potentially includes everyone but you. You it does indeed exclude, and therefore it emphasizes, though it does not narrow or tighten, the limitations of the altruism of the man who enters into it; for it calls our attention to the fact that, however wide his sympathies may be, they do not urge him to any particular effort or sacrifice for the sake of the person with whom he is dealing at the moment. An economic relation may be entered upon equally well from egoistic or altruistic motives; but as long as it remains purely economic, it must remind us that no man's altruism is undiscriminating to the extent of lavishing itself upon all persons or all purposes at all times. Short of this, clearly the most altruistic person may enter into a relation with another man, the purpose of which is to further the good of those who are other than himself, and also other than the person with whom he is dealing. In that case his action is altruistic because it is inspired by a desire for the good of someone other than himself, and the relation is economic because it is entered into for the sake of someone other than his correspondent. (1910, p. 173)

72. Wicksteed (1910, p. 4).
73. Wicksteed (1910, p. 14).
74. Wicksteed (1910, ¶ I.1.28).

References

Bastiat, Frederic. 1850. *Economic Harmonies*, ed. George B. de Huszar, 1996, Irvington-on-Hudson, NY: The Foundation for Economic Education, Inc., trans. W. Hayden Boyers, accessed December 22, 2007 from http://www.econlib.org/library/Bastiat/basHar2.html.

Becker, Gary S. 1962. Irrational behavior and economic theory. *Journal of Political Economy* 70 (1, February): 1–13.

Becker, Gary S. 1963. A reply to Israel Kirzner. *Journal of Political Economy* 71 (February): 82–83.

Becker, Gary S. 1976. *The Economic Approach to Human Behavior*. Chicago: University of Chicago Press.

Bentham, Jeremy. 1781. *An Introduction to the Principles of Morals and Legislation*. Oxford: Clarendon Press, 1907, accessed December 26, 2007 from https://www.econlib.org/library/Bentham/bnthPML1.html.

Clark, Gregory. 2007. *A Farewell to Alms: A Brief History of the World*. Princeton, NJ: Princeton University Press.

Friedman, Milton. 1953. *The Methodology of Positive Economics*. Chicago: University of Chicago Press.

Friedman, Milton. 2007. *Price Theory: A Provisional Text*. New Brunswick, NJ: Transaction Publishers (first published in 1962).

Hayek, F.A. 1945. The use of knowledge in society. *American Economic Review* 35 (4, September): 519–530.

Hayek, F.A. 1967. *Studies in Philosophy, Politics and Economics*. Chicago: University of Chicago Press.

Kahneman, Daniel. 1994. New challenges to the rationality assumption. *Journal of Institutional and Theoretical Economics* 150 (1): 18–36.

Kahneman, Daniel., and Amos Tversky. 2000. Prospect theory: An analysis of decision under risk, as reprinted in *Choices, Values, and Frames*, ed. Daniel Kahneman and Amos Tversky, 17–43. Cambridge, UK: Cambridge University Press.

Kirzner, Israel M. 1962. Rational action and economic theory. *Journal of Political Economy* 70 (4, August): 380–385.

Kirzner, Israel M. 1963. Rejoinder. *Journal of Political Economy* 71 (August): 82–83.

Malthus, Thomas Rober. 1798. *An Essay on the Principle of Population*. Indianapolis, IN: Liberty Fund, available online from http://oll.libertyfund.org/titles/malthus-an-essay-on-the-principle-of-population-1798-1st-ed.

Mankiw, N. Gregory. 2011. *Principles of Economics*, 6th ed. New York: Cengage Learning.

Marshall, Alfred. 1890. *Principles of Economics*. London: Macmillan and Co., Ltd, 1920, available online from https://www.econlib.org/library/Marshall/marP1.html.

Marx, Karl. 1848. *The Communist Manifesto*. Chicago: Henry Regnery Co., reissued in 1954.

McConnell, Campbell R. 1960. *Elementary Economics: Principles, Problems and Policies*. New York: McGraw-Hill.

Mill, John Stuart. 1848. *Principles of Political Economy*, ed. William James Ashley, 1909: London: Longmans, Green and Co. Available online from https://www.econlib.org/library/Mill/mlP1.html.

Olson, Mancur. 1965. *The Logic of Collective Action: Public Goods and the Theory of Groups*. Cambridge, MA: Harvard University Press.

Ricardo, David. 1821. *On the Principles of Political Economy and Taxation*. London: John Murray, 1821, accessed December 20, 2007 from https://www.econlib.org/library/Ricardo/ricP1.html.

Robbins, 1935. *An Essay on the Nature and Significance of Economic Science.* Auburn, AL: Ludwig von Misses Institute (first published in 1932 and revised and reissued in 2007).
Samuelson, Paul A. 1948. *Economics.* New York: McGraw-Hill.
Samuelson, Paul A., and Peter Temin. 1976. *Economics*, 10th ed. New York: McGraw-Hill.
Samuelson, Paul A., and William Nordhaus. 2009. *Economics*, 19th ed. New York: McGraw-Hill.
Skouras, Thanos, George J. Avlonitis, and Kostis A. Indounas. 2005. Economics and marketing on pricing: How and why do they differ. *Journal of Product and Brand Management* 14 (6): 362–374.
Smith, Adam. 1759, vol. I of the Glasgow Edition of the Works and Correspondence of Adam Smith. *The Theory of Moral Sentiments*, ed. D.D. Raphael and A.L. Macfie. Indianapolis: Liberty Fund, 1982.
Smith, Adam. 1776 (reprinted 1904). *An Inquiry Into the Nature and Causes of the Wealth of Nations.* London: Methuen & Co. (available online from the Liberty Fund) http://oll.libertyfund.org/titles/smith-aninquiry-into-the-nature-and-causes-of-the-wealth-of-nations-cannan-ed-vol-1.
Thaler, Richard H. 1991. *Quasi Rational Economics.* New York: Russell Sage Foundation.
Thaler, Richard H. 1992. *The Winner's Curse: Paradoxes and Anomalies of Economic Life.* New York: Free Press.
Thaler, Richard H. 2001. Anomalies. *Journal of Economic Perspective* 15 (1): 219–232.
Thaler, Richard., and Cass R. Sunstein. 2008. *Nudge: Improving Decisions About Health, Wealth, and Happiness.* New Haven, CT: Yale University Press.
Wicksteed, Philip H. 1888. *Alphabet of Economic Science.* New York: Kelley & Millman, reprinted in 1955.
Wicksteed, Phillip H. 1910. *The Commonsense of Political Economy, Including a Study of the Human Basis of Economic Law.* London: Macmillan, 1910. Available online from https://oll.libertyfund.org/title/1415.
Wicksteed, Philip H. 1914. The scope and method of political economy in the light of the "marginal" theory of value and of distribution. *Economic Journal* 24 (93, March): 1–23, presidential address to Section F of the British Association, 1913.
Zak, Paul, and Stephen Knack. 2001. Trust and growth. *Economic Journal* 111 (470, March): 295–321.

CHAPTER 2

Lionel Robbins and Scarcity

British economist Lionel Robbins (1898–1984) first published his small, but influential book *An Essay on the Nature and Significance of Economic Science* in 1932, only to revise it over the next three years for republication to account for hostile criticisms from his fellow academic economists. In the end, Robbins was able to have his definition of the discipline, organized around his construction of scarcity, adopted widely in the profession. Indeed, ever since the publication of his book, an untold count of students in their first economics course have had to parrot Robbins on his construction of scarcity on their first tests.

Disunity in Economic Inquiries

Robbins started his book with the observation that the economics discipline was beset with the problem of having various and divergent definitions with no unifying theme. He offers several prominent definitions he drew from "standard works" available in the early 1930s, which failed to show a unifying theme in what all economists do, or so he contended[1]:

- Alfred Marshall: "Economics is the study of mankind in the ordinary business of life; it examines that part of individual and social action which is most closely connected with the attainment and with the use of the material requisites of well-being."[2]
- Herbert Davenport: "Economics is the science that treats phenomena from the standpoint of price."[3]

R. B. McKenzie, *A Brain-Focused Foundation for Economic Science*,
https://doi.org/10.1007/978-3-319-76810-6_2

- Edwin Cannan: "The aim of Political Economy is the explanation of the general causes on which material well-being of human beings depends."[4]
- William Beveridge: Economics is "the study of the general methods by which men co-operate to meet their material needs."[5]
- Arthur Pigou: Economics is the study of economic welfare, but mainly (if not only) "that part of welfare which can be brought directly or indirectly into relation with the measuring rod of money."[6]

Robbins concludes, "We all talk about the same things [generalizations], but we have not yet agreed what it is we are talking about."[7] According to Robbins, any science must evolve with the definition of a discipline following the development of its content: "Indeed, it follows from the very nature of science that until it has reached a certain stage of development, definition of its scope is necessarily impossible," Robbins muses. He cites, approvingly, John Stuart Mill's observation made a century earlier: "Like the wall of a city it has usually been erected, not to be a receptacle for such edifices as might afterwards spring up, but to circumscribe an aggregate already in existence."[8]

Robbins posits that it was not possible until "quite recent times" that the "identity of the problems underlying these different enquiries ... [could] be detected"[9]: "At an earlier stage, any attempt to discover the ultimate nature of the science was necessarily doomed to disaster. It would have been a waste of time to have attempted it."[10] Robbins justifies his own search for a unifying definition for the discipline because a sufficient range of economic "generalizations" had then been devised that were in need of "unification" through the identification of a common theme. Moreover, finding the "unity" would encourage progress in economic science and reduce misguiding conceptual distractions:

> Unless one has grasped what this unity is, one is apt to go off on false scents. There can be little doubt that one of the greatest dangers which beset the modern economist is preoccupation with the irrelevant – the multiplication of activities having little or no connection with the solution of problems strictly germane to his subject... moreover, if these solutions are to be fruitfully applied, if we are to understand correctly the bearing of Economic Science on practice, it is essential that we should know exactly the implications and limitations of the generalizations it establishes.[11]

Robbins acknowledges that the concept of "material" was common in widely used definitions of economics (see Marshall's, Cannan's, and Beveridge's definitions above), but he insisted that economic generalizations went beyond solely material concerns. However, if such matters were "of the order of marginal cases" that invariably fall outside the confines of any definition for a discipline, there is a more important consideration, the definition's "capacity to describe exactly the ultimate subject-matter of the main generalizations of the science."[12] Robins pointed to labor economics that is greatly concerned with wage determination, and wages in themselves often fit poorly with any people's material concerns. He added that "the wages of the members of an orchestra, for instance, are paid for work which has not the remotest bearing on material welfare"[13] and that workers might buy bread with his earnings, which fits within the material construction of the discipline, but the worker might also buy a seat in a theater. The "immaterial" uses of wages are so great as to make any material-based definition of economics "arbitrarily delimited."[14]

Moreover, a great variety of workers—for example, dancers and opera singers—also produce goods and services that lack material content, and citing Irving Fisher, Robbins contended that "the income from a material object must in the last resort be conceived as an 'immaterial' use." Indeed, in the words of Fisher, the income from valets and opera singers "perishes in the moment of its production,"[15] a line of reasoning that caused Robbins to conclude, "Whatever Economics is concerned with, it is *not* concerned with the causes of material welfare as such" (emphasis in the original).[16] Besides, with any meaningful distinction between "economic" and "non-economic"—which is tantamount to "material" and "non-material"—sources of welfare, "there is still an economic problem of deciding between the 'economic' and 'non-economic'" uses of the fixed amount of time in a day.[17]

Scarcity, the Unifying Theme in Economic Inquiries

Feeling confident that he had demolished any reliance on the "material" sources of "economics," Robbins moves on to take up the presumption that exchange is the delimiting issue of the discipline. He insists that there are four conditions that, ultimately, give "economic" meaning to life, even for people isolated from one another, which can be embraced by economists:

- Even "isolated man" (Robinson Crusoe is Robbins' favorite metaphor) wants both real income and leisure.
- "Isolated man" does not have the wherewithal to fully satisfy his desires for both real income and leisure.
- He can seek more real income and leisure in varying proportions.
- Various isolated people can be expected to seek different combinations of real income and leisure.

These four conditions also apply generally to people in all social settings, but they do not apply to all behaviors. A "multiplicity of ends" is of no interest to economists if all the ends can be satisfied. Similarly, limited means, by themselves, is not a matter of concern when the means can only be used in the satisfying one given end: "The Manna which fell from heaven may have been scarce, but if it is impossible to exchange it for something else or to postpone its use, it was not the object of any activity with an economic aspect."[18] He concludes that

> The economist studies the disposal of scarce means. He is interested in in the way different degrees of scarcity of different goods give rise to different ratios of valuation between them, and he is interested in the way in which changes in conditions of scarcity, whether coming from changes in ends or changes in means – from the demand side or the supply side – affect these ratios.[19]

By finding fault with alternative definitions of the discipline, Robbins presumes he then puts himself in a position to offer a more representative and inclusive definition of the discipline, "the science which studies human behavior as a relationship between ends and scarce means which have alternative uses."[20] Accordingly, the purview of economists extends to "any kind of human behaviour" so long as the activity involves choices, or the sacrifice of some ends when others are achieved[21]: "There are no limitations on the subject-matter of Economic Science save this," Robbins boldly asserts.[22]

At the same time, Robbins doubles back on where he comes down on the limits of economics—a couple of times, in fact. At one point, after asserting "no limitations," he argues that "economic generalizations" are not so applicable to those of "isolated man," or the Robinson Crusoes of the world, because they would be "uninteresting." The task of the isolated man is merely to apply his "productive powers to this or that."

Moreover, Robbins then followed Ludwig von Mises' advice by noting how economic generalization would not apply (at least, not fully) to central planners in communist countries because the dictates of the "executive" would not be guided by "prices and costs" and would, hence, be completely "arbitrary," which is to say that "economic analysis has [the] most utility in the exchange economy." Nevertheless, Robbins insisted that economic analysis still applies to isolated man because, after all, every isolated person's decisions are limited by the prevalence of scarcity.[23] Even the decisions of the "executive" in communist/centrally planned economy is constrained by scarcity. They both must choose how best to employ their "productive power."[24] Again, consistency in argument is not always a hallmark of his essay.

Robbins goes on to explore the relevance of ends and means taken separately. In themselves, "ends" are of little consequence for economists, and it matters little what they are: "The ends may be noble or they may be base. They may be 'material' or 'immaterial'—if ends can be so described." For ends to be relevant for economic analysis, "the attainment of one set of ends involves the sacrifice of others."[25] Even for monks, economics applies because they have to work out the distribution of their time "between prayer and good works," with good works, in turn, having "its economic aspect equally with the distribution of time between orgies and slumber."[26] Anticipating the "economic imperialism" (or the spread of economic analysis beyond business and into subjects covered in other social sciences that emerged in force in the 1960s, led by economists, such as Gary Becker and James Buchanan), even prostitution and other "indulgences" can be subject to economic analysis because the service must also confront the consequences of scarcity—and choices and tradeoffs.[27]

In Robbins' view, the *ends* themselves, taken separately from means, don't matter in economics, which distinguishes economics from ethics, a discipline consumed with *what ends* matter. To Robbins, what is important to the discipline is the ends/means conflict that requires choices and tradeoffs. Then what matters even more are the deductions economists can draw in theory from the ends/means conflict.[28] With similar arguments, Robbins delimits economic analysis further:

- Economic analysis is not concerned with engineering-based "motion studies." The discipline is independent of technologies and is only concerned with how technologies affect the ends/means conflicts, that is, the extent to which they are constrained by scarcity and, in turn, affect people's choices. And one of the "main dangers" that comes from natural sciences is the inability of natural scientists to distinguish between what is "economic" and what is "technical"[29]: "[T]he problem of technique arises when there is one end and a multiplicity of means, the problem of economy when both the ends and the means are multiple."[30] Economics, therefore, is the study of the implications of particular "relationships," between, on the one hand, the "ends as the possible objective of conduct" and, on the other, "the technical and social environments on the other."[31]

- Economic theory describes the "forms" of the relationships. Economic history describes the "substance" of the isolated relationships through time," or, rather, "the changing network of economic relationships" from time period to time period.[32]
- Robbins delimits economics in a way that seems to contrast with Marx's materialistic dialectic evolution of economy: "[T]here is nothing in economic analysis which entitles us to assert that all history is to be explained in 'economic' terms, if economic is to be used as equivalent to the technically material."[33]
- For Robbins, given the prevalence of scarcity and the changes in ends and means, "changes in relative evaluations are data," and evaluations are necessarily relative—that is, relative to the available resources to satisfy the pressing ends, which makes wealth an "essentially relative concept." Similarly, "productive power" is relative to the capacity of means to satisfy ends, with "productive power" changing with demand.[34]
- For many economist, scarcity occurs because of the conflicts that emerge when *limited* means confronts *unlimited* wants. All Robbins insists is necessary for scarcity to be prevalent is for the "*given* ends" to exceed the "*given* means," or that not all ends can be satisfied (emphasis in the original).[35] He doesn't hang his concept of scarcity on the notion that ends, or wants, need to come close to being unlimited, as any number of modern economists seem to do (at least as represented by undergraduate textbooks).
- For Robbins, a key ingredient to *economic* scarcity was the introduction of human evaluation. Quantities of goods and resources considered apart from their evaluation by people may be meaningful to disciplines such as accounting and engineering, but have

no meaning for economists' analytical interests. Even then, marginal evaluations of goods will not be positive without the quantity demanded exceeding the quantity that is available, or can be made available.[36] This suggests that for Robbins, *opportunity cost* is not merely *what* is given up in choices. Rather, it is the *value* of what is foregone in choices. Choices must be made based on some common denominator, which necessarily involves subjective evaluations of options subject to choice (a point that suggests he recognized that options far removed from being viable options would not be given separate evaluations, contrary to what is often presumed in modern choice theory).

- For Robbins, absolute scarcity was of no (or maybe of little) consequence to economists. Absolute scarcity had no more meaning than absolute distance or absolute speed, meaning without their consideration being a matter of relationships with other distances and speeds. What was important, and meaningful, in economic analysis was relative scarcity, or how scarce something was relative to the scarcity of other things, which showed up in "relative valuation" and relative prices. Prices taken separately "mean nothing": "Value is a relation, not a measurement."[37] Economic choices are always and everywhere made based on the *relative* evaluations of options.
- Prices in the future can affect prices today, but prices, in and of themselves, have no meaning when compared with prices of the past. Prices of the past have meaning in relationship to the prices of other things then, and the same must be said of prices today. Without knowledge of *relative* prices, nothing can be understood by the comparisons of prices of given goods today with prices in the past.[38] "Bygones are forever bygones," Robbins points out repeatedly, which means that prices of the past can't affect prices today (a position that behavioral economists and neuroeconomists will now, no doubt, dispute with evidence and, maybe, some glee).[39]

Rebukes of Historical and Psychological Analytics

Having defined economics as a matter of drawing out the implications of scarcity, Robbins insists that his "aim" is "not to discover how Economics should be pursued" but to assess the "significance" that can be given to the "results" (by which he appears to mean "economic generalizations," or principles and laws) that had been, to his writings, devised, for example, the emergence of "food queues" whenever "the fixing of prices" has been imposed in relatively free markets.[40] While Robbins references historical events, he argues that they are not a basis for economic generalization. Why? Because history cannot be counted on to repeat itself, contrary to a widely held belief: "[H]istorical induction, unaided by analytical judgment, is the worst possible basis of prophecy."[41] The flow of events through time are simply the consequence of myriad interacting and, thus, ever-changing forces.[42]

Moreover, in a rebuke to psychology (perhaps applicable, at least somewhat, to modern behavioral economics, grounded in psychological methods), Robbins also argues that economics cannot rest on "controlled experiments." Government policies may have been imposed at times in what approximates a controlled experiment, but "it would be very superficial to suppose that the results of these 'experiments' can be held to justify a proposition of such wide applicability," which suggests that controlled experiments would likely be a "very fragile body of economic generalizations."[43] Conditions in the real world are exceedingly complex and simply not likely to replicate very often the narrow (and, to one degree or another) artificial conditions of controlled experiments, especially since choices must be made "not between certainties, but rather between a range of estimated probabilities" (a point that behavioral psychologists, starting with Daniel Kahneman and Richard Thaler, would hardly dispute today but is a line of argument that will have to wait for exploration in Chapters 4 and 5).[44]

On what then can economic generalizations be founded? Very simply, "a series of postulates," with the chief postulates being "assumptions involving in some way simply and indisputable facts of experience" (with "experience" allowing for history to work its way into economic theory, contrary to Robbins protestations that historical prices have no role in good theory). One such "indisputable fact of experience" is that consumers can and do order their preferences (with economists shying from explaining why consumers affix different values to different goods[45]) and that producers can use alternative combinations of available factors of production.[46] Such founding presumptions do not have to be established by controlled experiments. Rather, "they are so much the stuff of our everyday experience that they have only to be stated to be recognized as obvious."[47] Indeed, Robbins cautions that the founding postulates might seem so obvious that critics might fault economists for assuming very little, or nothing, in their basic postulates, which means they risk not being able to deduce much of consequence from their basic postulates. Clearly, Robbins saw economics as an abstract deductive science with all derived postulates constrained mainly by what constitutes indisputable founding postulates and by the rules for logical consistency.[48]

Robbins was (apparently) conflicted over the value of psychologists operating as social scientists. At one point, he suggested that psychologists were pulled astray by "fads," or by what is "fashionable," in topics and methods of inquiry. Similarly, economists are pulled away from their central occupation of "recognizing the implications of choice in a world of scarcity …"[49] Still, economists, as economists, relied on people's "valuations" as "data," but had little to say about what people valued, a core concern of psychologists. For economists, people's values are a part of the "fundamental data" that—along with "technical possibilities of production" and "the ultimate factors of production"—that lead to generalizations.[50] Economists need values for drawing out their generalizations. They also need assumptions about details of some behavior of a "psychological nature" that are "approximations of reality." At times, economics can be founded on the assumption that people act in the role of "Economic Men" who are driven exclusively by self-gain (whether from selfish or selfless motives) or by money, and who are capable of choosing courses of action with some level of "rationality." However, Robbins makes clear that economists utilize such founding sterilized assumptions, which are hardly accurate descriptors of the driving forces of people's decisions and behavior, as "expository devices" that are "first approximations," all adopted "very cautiously." These expository devices "enable us [economists] to study, in isolation, tendencies which, in a world of reality, operate only in conjunction with many others and then … to turn back to apply the knowledge thus gained to the explanations of more complicated situations."[51]

Similarly, perfect rationality, which presumes people's choices are completely consistent, was, according to Robbins, "irrational" "just because the time and attention which such exact comparisons require are … better spent in other ways," which suggests the prospects of an "opportunity cost of 'internal arbitrage.'"[52] Nevertheless, economic actors may be assumed to be "rational," or even "completely [perfectly] rational," but, again, Robbins insists that economists must keep in mind that such characterization of human decision-making and actions are introduced to facilitate the development of insights that might otherwise be missed with more realistic but complex founding premises about human decisions and actions.

The rationality premise can be justified on two grounds. First, it can enable economists to draw out the implications of choices under conditions of scarcity that might otherwise be missed. Second, human decisions and behaviors must be rational at least in the sense that they are "purposive": "[I]f behavior is not conceived of purposive, the conception of the means-end relationships which economics studies has no meaning," which implies that without a presumption and reality of some level of purposive behavior, there is no "economic phenomenon."[53]

While economists might sterilize their founding premises, making them less than fully descriptive of the "indisputable facts of experiences" that are at the core of the founding premises of the discipline, "the concern of the economist is the interpretation of reality." However, in developing their interpretations of reality, economists confront an economic problem, that of using their limited resources in developing their theories and deductions.[54] This abstract quest for derived generalizations cannot fully mimic the methods of the hard sciences in two regards:

- First, economists' subjects harbor valuations for what they seek and do. Hard scientists' subjects—e.g., rocks—harbor no capability of valuations (or so we think!).
- Second, economists have an advantage in their inquiries over hard scientists: there is less reason to doubt the "real bearing" of economists' generalizations: "In Economics, ... the ultimate constituents of our fundamental generalization are known to us by immediate acquaintance." That is to say, economists can test their deductions/generalizations (at least in a preliminary way) by daily personal experiences and introspection, which natural scientists can't do: "In the natural science they [generalizations] are known only inferentially."[55]

Nonetheless, economists must constantly be testing the accuracy and breadth of the applicability of their generalizations and can use the tests for adjusting the underlying premises, uncovering "changing facts," and making predictions possible. However, Robbins argues, theory–some form of abstract thought based on "indisputable facts of experience"—must ultimately guide analysis and the development of deductions that are subject to testing with real-world experience, or else the analyses are "purposeless."[56] Even then, any devised predictions must of necessity be applicable to a narrow segment of the course of events, because of the methods used in analysis and because of the great complexity of the course of interrelated and interacting courses of events, which means that predicting "the complete course of an uncontrolled history" is beyond the reach of any science.[57]

To reiterate, the limits of economic analysis is first set by the "relative scales [of] valuation" that are assumed as "data," but that are ever-changing in unknown (and often unknowable) ways as time passes—made all the more complicated by some people having "financial incentives" to actively change the data (valuations).[58] In effect, economists must rediscover their "laws of gravitation from moment to moment"; some natural scientists (physicists) don't have to do that because of the total absence of values at "the core of their theories."[59]

He concludes that economics is likely to lose its force in matters of politics because the interests of political operatives, especially in "larger groups," are hard to pin down, or are "hard to foretell a process of change, with its manifest elements of contingency, persuasion, and blind force," which suggests that in "the last analysis the study of Economics, while it shows us a region of economic laws, of necessities to which human action is subject, [it also] shows us, too a region in which no such necessities operate." Consequently, politics is a sphere into which "we make no enquiry"—at least when Robbins was writing.[60]

Of course, while Robbins may have been a good methodologist, he was not very prescient about the future efforts of economists to generate economic generalizations, using the scarcity framework he articulated. Within two decades of the publication of his classic (in the 1950s and 1960s), Robbins protestations to the contrary, public choice economists began aggressively pushing the boundaries of economics beyond the disciplinary limits Robbins assumed and began studying politics, both in the development of political institutions (rules for voting, for example) and policies that would likely emerge under given political institutional constraints (for example, constitutions), all under the presumption that people did not shed their rational (or purposive) inclinations and pursuit of self-interest when they moved from commercial spheres to "political markets."[61]

Given Robbins' emphasis on how economics' founding premises and methods are inextricably bound to what economists do and know, he would not likely be surprised that, today, the discipline is in a state of some stress, given the substantial evolution, and divergence, in what economists do and have learned since the early 1930s. He would probably relent on his opposition to the integration of psychology methods to economics, as behavioral economists have shown can be done. Robbins would probably also welcome any effort to find another common denominator that might bring about the unity of purpose that he sought. As said early in this book, my goal is to do for my era what Robbins did for his.

The Significance of Economics

At the end of his book, Robbins asks, in so many words, what can be the significance, or redeeming value, of economic analysis for individuals and larger society? Surely, as he argued, it can't be simply the application of the "Law of Diminishing Marginal Utility" (caps in the original) to questions of redistributive income policies, as many economists in Robbins' day, and long before, thought could, and should, be done. While the law may (eventually) apply to individual's serial consumption of units of a good, it is grounded in subjective evaluations that cannot be assessed other than by the individuals consuming the good. There is no reason given by economic theory to expect the marginal value of an additional unit of a good to a poor person will necessarily be greater than it is to a rich person, no matter their absolute and relative levels of consumption. People, and economists, may make interpersonal utility comparisons for any number of reasons, but they have no scientific foundation, or economic foundation, from Robbins' perspective, for doing so.

Similarly, Robbins reasons that economics focuses on equilibrium analysis, but there is no "penumbra of approbation" for equilibrium theory; "equilibrium is just equilibrium." Even freedom, or free markets, is not necessarily an "ultimate good" deemed desirable for itself. There's nothing in economics that suggests that ends, whatever they are, are "good" or "bad," and economics per se is "neutral" between ends (not even on the end goals of wage controls).[62]

In answer to his question on the significance of economics, Robbins opines that economic analysis can help people with this type of question, "If you want to do this, you must do that." The discipline can also help people identify their ends and then help them see the implications of alternative courses of action and, hence, make rational judgments.[63] Robbins deduces, as in the case of tariff analysis, that economics "enables us to see what *sets* of ends are compatible with each other and what are not, and upon what conditions such compatibility is dependent.

And, indeed, it is just here that the possession of some such technique becomes quite indispensable if policy is to be rational" (emphasis in the original).[64] (In making these points Robbins lays out a basic presumption underlying Milton Friedman's methodological position on "positive economics," as we will see in the next chapter.)

Later, Robbins closes his *Essay* with a statement on the rationality premise that seems at odds with his focus on positive analysis: "[Economics] relies upon no assumption that individuals will always act rationally. But it does depend for its *raison d'etre* upon the assumption that it is desirable that they should do so," later adding, "The revolt against reason is essentially a revolt against life."[65]

In short, Robbins saw economics as having a didactic purpose, to instruct people and policymakers not so much on how people can be expected to behave, but on how they can make their decisions with greater rationality, which makes economic analysis, for Robbins, didactic. Still, Robbins draws up short of arguing that economic analysis instructs people on how they ***should*** behave (points that Friedman would find unobjectionable).

Concluding Comments

For Robbins, the core of economics was scarcity, or rather drawing out the implications of people having to make choices, individually and collectively. The discipline did not require an assumption of rational behavior, and certainly not perfectly rational behavior. Perfect rationality could be irrational behavior because of the time and energy, or costs, required to make perfectly rational decisions, which could easily be greater than the gains from greater precision in decision-making, at least beyond some point. However, the discipline did require "purposive" behavior, or else there was no ends/means dilemma for people to resolve. Robbins accepted the use of an assumption of perfectly rational behavior but only as a "convenient" means of thinking through the implications of scarcity—or rather as a means of coping with the scarcity conflicts embedded in thinking itself.

Thus, Robbins touched on the scarcity of people's mental capacities in determining the scope and methods of economic analytics. However, the *scarcity* at the core if the discipline that Robbins had in mind was largely the conflict that existed in the external world between the means and the internal world of subjective evaluations, both taken as exogenous data imposed on the analytics, not generated within the analytics. Purposive behavior is made necessary in the main when the means/ends dilemma is made the unifying theme of all economic analysis. Material and nonmaterial choices—indeed, all economic methods and generalizations—are made necessary by limited capacities for productive efforts and resources in the external world. The scarcity of people's (neuronal) resources was not central to the efforts of economists to draw out generalizations, in Robbins' view. Such internal constraints were set aside or, more aptly, assumed away for analytical convenience.

Robbins eschewed the issue of the centrality of the human brain is his scarcity paradigm. No doubt, Robbins recognized, seemingly in passing, people's mental limitations, but he doesn't seem to have considered—not directly and with care, at least—the brain's limitations in delimiting what economic actors do, or how economists conduct their investigations, or how economics can and should be taught. People might try to "optimize" in some rough and ready way, but he never explored how the human brain might be asked to do the same, which could affect how people—economic actors and economists—could be bounded mentally in what they could accomplish.

In constructing economics the way he did and being as persuasive as he was with other economists (and textbook writers) in getting them to adopt his scarcity construction of the core of the discipline, Robbins liberated economists to think in terms of maximizing and optimizing decision-making, and then make the leap to perfect rationality, and with an additional leap to perfect maximization and optimization. "Focus": Robbins accepted that data—resources and wants—are revealed through people's market interactions and are given to economic analytics.

The perfect rationality premise facilitated economists' exploitation of mathematics that further severed economists' analytics from "indisputable facts of experience," which Robbins believed had to anchor economic analytics. Not surprisingly, psychologists and behavioral economists (and behavioral and cognitive scientists in general) have jumped on contemporary economists for what they see are gross gaps between the promises of economic predictions and behaviors of real-world people who must deal with the internal scarcity of their mental capacities—before they can hope to come to grips with the external scarcity and the multitude of derivative choices people face.

Notes

1. Robbins (1935 (first published in 1932), pp. 1–2, note 1).
2. As quoted in Robbins (1935, p. 1, note 1.1).
3. As quoted in Robbins (1935, pp. 1–2, note 1.1).
4. As quoted in Robbins (1935, p. 2, note 1).
5. As quoted in Robbins (1935, p. 2, note 1.1).
6. As quoted in Robbins (1935, p. 2).
7. Robbins (1935, p. 1).
8. Mill (1848, p. 120).
9. Robbins (1935, pp. 2–3).
10. Robbins (1935, p. 3).
11. Robbins (1935, p. 3).
12. Robbins (1935, pp. 4–5).
13. Robbins (1935, p. 6).
14. Robbins (1935, p. 6).
15. Robbins (1935, p. 9).
16. Robbins (1935, p. 9).
17. Robbins (1935, p. 11).
18. Robbins (1935, p. 13).
19. Robbins (1935, p. 16).
20. Robbins (1935, p. 16).
21. Robbins (1935, p. 17).
22. Robbins (1935, p. 17).
23. Robbins (1935, pp. 18–20).
24. Robbins (1935, p. 20).
25. Robbins (1935, p. 25).
26. Robbins (1935, p. 26).
27. Robbins (1935, p. 28).
28. Robbins (1935, pp. 30, 32).
29. Robbins (1935, pp. 33, 34).
30. Robbins (1935, p. 35).
31. Robbins (1935, p. 38).
32. Robbins (1935, pp. 37–38).
33. Robbins (1935, p. 45).
34. Robbins (1935, pp. 45, 47).
35. Robbins (1935, p. 46).
36. Robbins (1935, Chapter 3).
37. Robbins (1935, p. 56).
38. Robbins (1935, p. 59).
39. Robbins (1935, pp. 62–63).
40. Robbins (1935, pp. 72, 73).

41. Robbins (1935, p. 74).
42. Robbins (1935, p. 74).
43. Robbins (1935, pp. 74–75).
44. Robbins (1935, p. 78).
45. Robbins (1935, p. 86).
46. Robbins (1935, p. 79).
47. Robbins (1935, p. 79).
48. Robbins (1935, p. 79).
49. Robbins (1935, p. 84).
50. Robbins (1935, p. 101).
51. Robbins (1935, pp. 94, 97).
52. Robbins (1935, p. 92).
53. Robbins (1935, p. 93).
54. Robbins writes, "The perception and selection of the basis of economic analysis is as much economics as the analysis itself" (1935, p. 106).
55. Robbins (1935, p. 105).
56. Robbins wrote, "[Realistic studies] may test the range of applicability of the answer when it is forthcoming. They may suggest assumptions for further theoretical elaboration. But is theory and theory alone which is capable of supplying the solution. Any attempt to reverse the relationship must lead inevitably to the nirvana of purposeless observation and record," which means he eschewed application of inductive science beyond the development of basic premises, which, necessarily, can't be deduced (1935, p. 120).
57. Robbins (1935, pp. 124–125).
58. Robbins (1935, pp. 127, 129).
59. Robbins (1935, p. 132).
60. Robbins (1935, p. 135).
61. See Buchanan and Tulloch (1962) and Buchanan (1975).
62. Robbins (1935, p. 143).
63. Robbins wrote, "It [economics] can make clear to us the implications of the different ends we may choose. It makes it possible for us to will with knowledge of what it is we are willing. It makes it possible for us to select a system of ends which are mutually consistent with each other" (1935, p. 152).
64. Robbins (1935, p. 154).
65. Robbins (1935, p. 157).

References

Buchanan, James M., and Gordon Tulloch. 1962. *The Calculus of Consent: Logical Foundations of Constitutional Democracy*. Ann Arbor, MI: University of Michigan Press.

Buchanan, James M. 1975. *The Limits of Liberty: Between Anarchy and Leviathan*. Chicago: University of Chicago Press.

Mill, John Stuart. 1848. *Principles of Political Economy*, ed. William James Ashley, 1909: London: Longmans, Green and Co. Available from https://www.econlib.org/library/Mill/mlP1.html.

Robbins, Lionel. 1935. *An Essay on the Nature and Significance of Economic Science*. Auburn, AL: Ludwig von Misses Institute (first published in 1932 and revised and reissued in 2007).

CHAPTER 3

From Robbins to Friedman and Beyond

The last chapter focused on why and how Lionel Robbins in the early 1930s delimited economic inquiry. In this chapter, I return to Robbins' scarcity foundation for the discipline with an emphasis on methodological and analytical issues he (largely) set aside, or he viewed as outside of his scarcity boundary for the discipline. I am mainly concerned in this chapter with how Robbins and other economists, before and after Robbins (from Alfred Marshall to Milton Friedman and beyond), have treated scarcity in the external world, and failed to consider the implications of scarcity problem that besets the human brain before it considers the scarcity problems in the external world. My brief methodological history will give context to my shifting the focus of the discipline from scarcity in the external world to the scarcity within the human brain later in the book. As we will see in Chapters 5 and 6, this seemingly slight shift in the scarcity foundation of the discipline will powerfully affect economists' derived "generalizations," the treasured goal of Robbins, Friedman, and the other economists covered.

Robbins and Scarcity, Once Again

Scarcity in Lionel Robbins' (and Robbins' followers') construction of economics as a discipline is not dissimilar to Alfred Marshall's construction of supply and demand models at least in one regard; both constructions can be viewed, metaphorically, as involving two "blades" of a pair of scissors operating against one another. For Robbins, one of the scissor

R. B. McKenzie, *A Brain-Focused Foundation for Economic Science*,
https://doi.org/10.1007/978-3-319-76810-6_3

blades is the limited means in the external world facing off against the other blade, so many subjectively conceived ends that not all ends can be satisfied. The two blades are interactive and interdependent, one without the other is largely meaningless.

Scarcity doesn't exist—and economics has no scientific function—without both blades working against one another, again, in Robbins' view (employing Marshall's metaphor). The valuations people place on their ends ultimately give economic meaning to means, and limited means and the surplus of ends (without any requirement that ends be unlimited), in both Marshall's and Robbins' constructions, give rise to relative valuations and, on the margin, to relative prices. The two blades come together and find a form of resolution in markets through exchanges and prices, which resolve countless (but not all) conflicts.

Fixed Rational and Purposive Behavior

Under Robbins' construction of the discipline, economics is defined not so much by its methodology as by its core interest, the development of generalizations that emerge from the unifying theme of ever-present scarcity. Any premise of rational or "purposive" (Robbins' preferred adjective) decision-making is assumed and imposed on the analysis. That is, rational or purposive decision-making and behavior is an unchanging feature of the human condition (and brain) and does not change in response to changes in the institutional setting, or anything else, in the external world in which the two blades of scarcity squeeze together (which is a reasonable inference from Robbins' discussion of rational and purposive decision making because he never considers different levels of rational or purposive decision-making and behavior). And in contemporary times, there is no mechanism in neoclassical microeconomic theory that would integrate *changes* in rational or purposive behavior into matters of, say, price determination. The level of rationality in decision-making (whether perfect or less than perfect) is subsumed, perhaps as a matter of making economic analysis manageable (because Robbins does seem to recognize that, along with economists from Smith to Marshall, the precision with which decisions are made is transparently variable, to one degree or another, in people's decision-to-decision daily lives). In the case of perfect rationality, precision in decision-making can't vary; it's always perfect, at least for analytical purposes.

Subjective evaluations, on the other hand, can change in Robbins' worldview with changes in the availability of means, at least on the margin. (Robbins recognized the prospects of diminishing marginal utility at the individual level, although, as noted, he considered interpersonal utility comparisons beyond the boundaries of economics.[1]) Nevertheless, he considered people's valuations of ends as data *given* to the analysis, with their determination largely, if not exclusively, the providence of other social sciences, most notably psychology. He suggests that subjective evaluations *must* and *should be* beyond the providence of economics.

Clearly, Robbins saw economics as a powerful set of analytical methods for understanding human behavior. At the same time, he saw the methods necessarily providing a partial view, given he excludes evaluation formation, as well as the subject matter of the hard sciences in which evaluations are totally absent. Presumably, he would agree that economists, in order to fully understand human behavior, would have to jump from one intellectual plain (and analytical method) to another, because of the absence of bridges among the plains.

Conventional contemporary microeconomics, which has been largely built on Robbins' scarcity view of the discipline, is grounded in a number of widely accepted postulates that contain the scope of the discipline's analytics:

- At least for analytical purposes, people are considered to be no less rational and purposive under subsistent scarcity conditions as they are under much less pressing conditions.
- As openly assumed by neoclassical economists, while market equilibrium prices are tied to people's evaluations through supply and demand forces, the prices people are willing to pay for goods—for that matter, their demand schedules—do not affect people's evaluations of the goods, in total and on the margin, except under special circumstances that have been posited since the 1930s (e.g., network goods). This means that prices that represent "good deals" do not affect people's evaluations of goods subject to trades. The values of goods are not affected by the difference between the prices people actually pay and the prices they expected to pay. That is, prices and evaluations are assumed to be independent (even though economists, Marshall and Robbins, seem to agree that any founding premise must be founded on "indisputable facts of experience").

- Costs and prices can change with the forces of scarcity, but rational and purposive decision-making and behavior do not change with the degree of scarcity of goods and prices, at least in economic theory at the center of Robbins' construction of the discipline.
- When trade is undertaken to exploit comparative cost advantages, the resulting welfare improvement does not affect the rationality or purposiveness of production and consumption decisions. Moreover, people's rationality is unaffected by how trade allows for greater specialization of, say, labor. No consideration is given to how specialization of labor permits specialization of neuronal resources within the brain, which can affect the efficiency and rationality of decision-making within the brain.
- The competitiveness of market structures (from perfect competition to pure monopoly) does not affect the precision with which resources are used in production and costs are minimized. Costs are everywhere minimized (as represented by conventional cost curves or functions); profits are maximized within the operative competitive restraints. Perfect competitors, who are very likely principals in their respective small firms and who stand at all times on the cusp of being eliminated from the market for any market miscalculation, will minimize costs and maximize profits (to the extent that they can) with the same dedication as the agents within a monopoly firm (even when imagined, for analytical purposes, to be a cartel of former perfect competitors) protected by entry barriers. The monopolist's only assumed meaningful function is limited to making its good scarcer than otherwise in order to collect monopoly rents. A monopolist's protected market position, in other words, leaves the rationality and purposiveness of decision-making unaffected under the Robbins' paradigm.
- When economic activity is shifted from the private sphere to the government sphere, the rationality or purposiveness of decision-making is also assumed to remain unaffected by the institutional shift from perfect competition or pure monopoly to government bureaucracies, and vice versa. The efficiency of decisions and behaviors, of course, change, but only because the external constraints on decisions and behaviors change, not because the shift in constraints affects exactly how people are inclined to make decisions and conduct their behaviors.

- Scarcity is a "problem" that must be solved (or just abated) for welfare to be enhanced. Economists rarely mention, must less explore, how the persistence of the "problem" itself, and its (partial or limited) abatement, can add to people's welfares. The presumption is that the advent of abundance (if it could ever be achieved, which is ruled out by people's capacity to create new wants) cannot lower people's welfares because they no longer have challenges in life, which can have value in themselves. People's rationality is assumed to be the same regardless of the extent of "the problem," or the extent of life challenges.

All said, in Robbins' worldview, shared widely by economists for nearly a century, efficiency in production and consumption is achieved under an (implicit) assumption of constant rationality. If rationality were allowed to change, then the concept of *efficiency* would take on a different meaning.

Under Robbins' construction of economics, the human brain is literally a "black box" that is taken as a given and that does its work "behind the scenes" (not Robbins' characterization), so to speak, outside the scope of economic analysis. Little to nothing is said under the Robbins' scarcity paradigm about the limitations of the brain and how those limitations can affect human decision-making and behavior, or, for that matter, how those limitations can place boundaries on the subject matter of economics or how economists conduct their analyses (other than economists' mental limitations that require them to devise theories that are sufficiently simple to be manageable). The brain works its magic apart from the binding constraint of scarcity that is assumed to be true of all resources capable of delivering value—aside for the human brain. Again, the human brain is simply a given, not subject to variation within individuals or across them. But then, it must be remembered that Robbins, and his disciplinary forbearers and followers for decades to come, had at best a primitive understanding of the workings of the human brain. While people's understanding of the human brain remains primitive today (given how much is not understood), neuroscience has, in recent decades, unmasked some (or is it "much"?) of the prior mystery of how the brain works.

Under Robbins' construction, economists' forte is, first, recognizing the pervasive ends/means conflicts and, second, drawing out economic generalizations that emerge from thinking of people making unavoidable choices and tradeoffs, all purposively. Scarcity implies choices that imply costs for all choices, which means that people must engage in some form of purposive and optimizing behavior, whether precisely or roughly executed.

In Robbins' construction of the discipline, mental limitations on understanding the external world are not totally absent, just substantially downplayed as central to what economists do and how they do what they do. After all, Robbins noted how rationality at some level is, in the real world of decision-making, necessary to presume people have ends and choose among them: "And thus in the last analysis Economics does depend, if not for its existence, at least for its significance, on an ultimate valuation—the affirmation that rationality and ability to choose with knowledge is desirable."[2] At the same time, he never uses "perfect rationality" because there had to be cost/benefit limits to process of refining decisions. In effect, for Robbins any proposed perfect rationality as a foundation for economic decision-making had to be an evolutionary nonstarter. Similarly, he warned against jettisoning rationality in economics altogether, in favor of theories based only on ever-present influences of external forces or "irrationalities":

> If irrationality, if the surrender to the blind force of external stimuli and uneo-ordinated impulse at every moment is a good to be preferred above all others, then it is true the raison d'etre of Economics disappears. And it is the tragedy of our generation, red with fratricidal strife and betrayed almost beyond belief by those who should have been its intellectual leaders, that there have arisen those who would uphold this ultimate negation, this yearning for the deep unawareness of the unborn state, this escape from the tragic necessities of choice which has become conscious. With all such there can be no argument. In love with death, their love will overtake them. For them there can be no "way out" save the way which leads out of life. But for all those who still affirm more positive values, that branch of knowledge which, above all others, is the symbol and safeguard of rationality in social arrangements, must, in the anxious days which are to come, by very reason of this menace to that for which it stands, possess a peculiar and a heightened significance.[3]

Moreover, Robbins recognized that the economic models economists use are hardly fully descriptive of the world that they analyze, and they cannot be fully descriptive, given the complexity of the intertwined and interacting physical and social worlds. However, Robbins adds nothing else in the way of economic generalizations, or theoretical implications, to the implied insight that the human brain, which must be used to analyze scarcity, is itself in short supply and has functional limits and imperfections, just like all other means in the external world of pervasive scarcity.

In Robbins' world, the only human brains of any consequence to economic methods and generalizations are those possessed by economists' subjects (consumers, investors, and producers) who have to cope with complex human interactions under conditions of pervasive external scarcity. Subjects' brains might be recognized as a scarce resource that need to be used with care and with concern for costs, but subjects' brains are not considered on par with other factors of production—say, labor, capital, and technology—in economists' analytics. The limits or peculiarities of people's brain powers did not dictate economists' methods and generalizations derived, other than the admission that analytics must be made manageable with simplified models. Again, human brain power is treated as a side issue, if at all. Similarly, the brains of economists-qua analysts are not instrumental to their methods and generalizations, other than, I repeat, they force a reduction of complex reality into simplified economic models.

The Human Brain as a Scarce Resource

By excluding the scarcity of human brain power from economic analysis, Robbins (and his followers, including almost all conventional microeconomic theorists today) gave economists license to shift with conceptual ease from a realistic, or descriptive, assumption that people's decision-making and behavior were grounded in some form of rough and ready rational or purposive decision-making to an assumption of universal perfectively rational or purposive decision-making. After all, any assumption, no matter how refined, of less-than-rational or purposive decision-making necessarily had to be less than descriptive of actual decision-making among real-world people, especially given the (likely) substantial variation in the precision of decision-making across individuals. That is, any less-than-perfect decision-making premise could be (almost) as flawed as an assumption of perfect rationality and would certainly make the analysis more complex, perhaps unnecessarily so, with the models likely far less amenable to mathematical treatment. There is no basis in neoclassical economic theory for deciding on what level of less-than-perfect rationality premise, among a multitude of such premises, would be used. Unless all less-than-perfect-rationality premises are employed serially (making for an endless testing process), the decision on the founding premise must be arbitrary at best, as is, admittedly, the premise of perfect rationality. Hence, any assumption of less-than- perfect rationality would likely make economic theorizing convoluted and would not likely advance the derivation of economic generalizations that could be subject to real-world testing. Besides, the essential goal of theory in neoclassical economics is not to provide self-evident standalone *truths*, which is not possible. Rather, the essential goal of theory is far more modest (and realistic), to provide *insights*—via the generation of hypotheses—about people's behavior that might not otherwise be uncovered but that can be empirically tested at various levels of precision (from casual observations to sophisticated statistical analyses).

Friedman's Canonization of Robbins' Methodology

In the early 1950s, Milton Friedman canonized for generations of economists Robbins' view of the governing role of founding premises and theories in microeconomics in his *The Methodology of Economics.*[4] Following in the methodological footsteps of John Neville Keynes, whom he quotes with approval at the start of his essay, Friedman posits only two broad categories of economic analyses, *positive economics* and *normative economics.* As is commonly accepted (and parroted) today, the former is restricted to discussions of "what is," and totally "independent of any particular ethical position or normative judgment," at least in principle: "It's [positive economics'] task is to provide a system of generalizations that can be used to make correct predictions about the consequences of any change in circumstances. It's performance is to be judged by the precision, scope, and conformity with experience of the prediction it yields." Accordingly, positive economic analysis can be an "objective' science" in the sense that the physical sciences, especially physics, are viewed as objective.[5]

Of course, as Friedman concedes (as Austrian economists, including Ludwig von Mises insisted all economists must[6]), economics has major impediments in achieving objectivity that do not encumber the physical sciences: First, positive economics deals with the interactions of human beings with whom economists can feel intimate and communal connections. Second, economists themselves are a part of the "subject matter" of economic analysis, with their investigations potentially biased and distorted by their assessments of preferred findings from economic analysis (which means that positive economics can be infused with normative considerations, even when unintended).[7]

Another major difference between economics and physical sciences not acknowledged in Friedman's essay (but surely recognized by him and, for that matter, Robbins) is that a major force in people's economic interactions is their valuations of goods and services and alternative outcomes from changes in circumstances, which can be ephemeral and elusive as compared to the type of concrete and unalterable data points available to the physical sciences. The rocks of geology (presumably) are unconcerned with subjective valuations of their circumstances, or where they are headed or are moved, just as planets have no capacity to assess where they are heading and toward what end and to seek corrective courses of actions to optimize their subjective evaluation of their trips through space–time.

Similarly, chemicals in experiments react in their circumstances according to known physical laws, not to the chemicals' assessments of their circumstances and alternative circumstances they might imagine. Moreover, rocks, planets, and chemicals can't talk back to physical scientists (and influence how they are treated in experiments) and are not typically assumed to be affected by scientists' probes or their findings. There are no potential feedback loops between what the objects do and the scientists' findings, which can change the objects' "behaviors."

On the other hand, people can talk back to economists, or, at least, they can if allowed to do so. And findings of scientific, positive economic analysis can affect people's interactions and the policy constraints they face. Friedman insisted that a major objective of positive economics is to guide people's policy preferences and decisions within the sphere of normative economics: "[D]ifferences about economic policy among disinterested citizens derive predominantly from different predictions about economic consequences of taking action—differences that in principle can be eliminated by the progress of positive economics …."[8] (That is clearly a testable hypothesis that warrants testing, which I've not seen.)

Robbins emphasized the conflict between the limited resources and, essentially, unlimited wants and the generalization that could be drawn from the conflict itself, but left economic methods largely elusive (not that he didn't have a methodology in mind). Friedman subsumed

Robbins-type scarcity and focused on the method economists use to conduct their analyses, more or less exclusively positive in nature (with lots of room for error in predictions because of the complexity of the subject matter and because of the often-time subjective nature of their measurement of their data points).

In Friedman's view of the discipline, the economic method starts with theory, which is an "intermixture of two elements." The first is a "language," or a set of tautologies, that facilitates systematic, organized reasoning. As such, economics provides a "filing system" that facilitates the organization of "empirical material," enhancing understanding. As a filing system, economics can be judged by whether (or the extent to which) the identified categories in the filing system are sufficiently "precisely defined" to reduce, if not eliminate, ambiguity and sufficiently broad that they can be "exhaustive" in coverage of causative considerations. For Friedman, supply-and-demand models of markets work well as methodological "filing systems." The two functions are precisely defined, and virtually all market-moving considerations can be "filed" under "supply" or "demand" (as an acknowledged but often unstated proposition that the supply curve can be construed as a "reservation demand curve," and vice versa).[9]

The second "element," and prime purpose, of (micro) economic theory is, as with Robbins, to generate a "body of substantive hypotheses" that can only be judged by the theory's "predictive power for a class of phenomena which it is intended to explain," a role that requires "factual evidence" to settle the issue of whether the theory is "right" or "wrong," or, better yet, to determine whether the hypotheses are tentatively "accepted" or "rejected" as valid.[10]

Following Karl Popper's dictates for the pursuit of "science," theory is made necessary by the sheer complexity of the world external to the analyst. Complex reality cannot be understood in its full entirety because of limitations of the mind to handle the vast array of interconnected potential causative factors.[11] The best that analysts can hope to do is reduce the complexity to the proportion that are manageable by the human mind of the economist, which calls for "abstract models" that bring together in organized form "essential elements" of the world under study. Such models are hardly "abstract" in the sense that they are vague or have imprecise boundaries. On the contrary, they can be laid out precisely (even in detailed mathematical form) and are abstract only in the sense they are reduced forms of complex reality, again, encompassing only "essential elements" of complex reality.

Empirical tests of the hypotheses generated are made necessary because of the "highly simplified" nature of the models used, which means the models necessarily lack completeness. Also, the model used to generate hypotheses is, to an extent, arbitrary, given that there are, at least in social sciences, several alternative assumptions undergirding the theory to be presented: "The choice among such alternative assumptions is made on the grounds of the resulting economy, clarity, and precision in presenting the hypothesis," in Friedman's words.[12]

Accordingly, the assumptions underlying theory cannot be tested by their descriptiveness (or conformity to complex reality). To make analyses manageable, assumptions about human motivation can be, and must be, greatly simplified, if not sterilized into unrecognizable forms—perfect rationality, for example—because of the dictates of economy in theorizing, or the need to ease (make less costly) analyses, or just to clarify and make more precise the hypotheses subject to testing. Besides, more descriptive, assumption can often do little more than muddle the analyses: "Complete realism [in founding premises] is clearly unattainable, and the question whether a theory is realistic 'enough' can be settled only by seeing whether it yields predictions that are *good enough* for the purpose at hand or that are *better* than predictions from alternative theories" (emphasis added).[13]

But make no mistake about it, for Friedman, in economics, as in the physical sciences, the "construction of hypotheses is a creative act of inspiration, intuition, invention; its essence is the vision of something new in familiar material."[14] At the same time, theorizing about economic behavior in the external world (mainly in markets) was itself an economic problem, beset with cost/benefit comparisons with optimization of net gain always a goal. Friedman wrote about how it "does not always pay to use a more general theory because the extra accuracy it yields may not justify the extra cost of using it, so the question under what circumstances the simpler theory works 'well enough' remains important."[15] He suggests that an assumption that billiard players can make their shots *as if* they can make the complex mathematical calculations required to hit and sink balls can work reasonably well in making predictions about the course of play. Similarly, an assumption that firms rationally calculate their most profitable pricing and production decisions in "full knowledge of the data needed to succeed in this attempt *as if* … they knew the relevant cost and demand functions" can, within a "wide range of circumstances," yield theoretical contributions that make economic sense (emphasis in the original).[16] The fact that economic analysis, as imperfect and "unreal" as it is, has been accepted and used for such a long time and "the failure of any coherent, self-consistent alternative to be developed and be widely accepted is strong indirect testimony to its worth"[17] (a staked-out position that, as we will see in Chapters 4 and 5, the behaviorists now fervently challenge on all methodological margins with practically every study they publish).

Friedman's overriding point is that the founding premises of theories necessarily lack "realism" and are intended to provide an "economical mode of describing or presenting a theory." The founding premises are intended both to facilitate the drawing out of testable implications of the theory and to proscribe the circumstances under which the theory is expected to be valid.[18] Besides, Friedman reasoned that economic analysis did not cover all human behavior, but only that part of behavior that involved people's interactions, mainly their market-based interactions, in which there were checks on people acting in less than cost-minimizing and profit-maximizing ways:

> Confidence in the maximization-of-returns hypothesis is justified by evidence of a very different character. This evidence is in part similar to that adduced on behalf of the billiard-player hypothesis [that he shoots *as if* he can perform complicated calculations] – unless the behavior of businessmen in some way or other approximated behavior consistent with the maximization of returns, it seems unlikely that they would remain in business for long.[19]

By extension, people who act consistently irrational can either be driven to act more rationally than they would normally be inclined to do or they would lose market position to those market participants who acted more in line with the rationality assumption undergirding economic theory. For Friedman, his stretched assumptions regarding cost-minimizing behavior and optimizing behavior worked tolerably well within the sphere of his primary concern, markets: "The process of 'natural selection' thus helps to validate the hypothesis – or, rather, given natural selection, acceptance of the hypothesis can be based largely on the judgment that it summarizes appropriately the conditions for survival."[20] Thus, for Friedman rational decision-making is both a founding premise and a consequence of a *process* of people's interactions, surely within markets and maybe elsewhere. (This is to say that rational behavior is both a premise of economic modeling and, and not so widely appreciated, a prediction of market processes. Perhaps more accurately, Friedman suggests, in my reading of his "Essay," markets make people more rational, as a group, than they might otherwise be.)

As much as economists-qua-scientists would like their theories to be totally objective, such can't be, because of the embedded arbitrariness of the founding assumptions and the rules devised for the pursuit of science. Moreover, Friedman stresses, "there inevitably will remain room for judgment in applying the rules," and judgment requires experience in doing science within the "'right' scientific atmosphere," in which "amateurs" can be separated from "professionals" and, ultimately, real "scientists" from "crackpots."[21]

In Friedman's view, neoclassical microeconomics in the tradition handed down from Alfred Marshal has been "extremely fruitful," in spite of limiting consideration—ever-present subjective evaluations—in the conduct of economic science, which is a nonissue in the physical sciences, most notably physics.[22] Microeconomics has been "fruitful" because, as he notes in his acceptance of the Nobel Prize in Economics (with reference to the initial acceptance and eventual rejection of the Phillips curve), "[T]he body of positive knowledge grows by the failure of a tentative hypothesis to predict phenomena the hypothesis professes to explain; by patching up of that hypothesis until someone suggests a new hypothesis that more elegantly or simply embodies the troublesome phenomena, and so on ad infinitum."[23] Here, in my reading of Friedman, he leaves himself open, at least somewhat, to revisions in the way economic science is done—maybe some of those revisions proposed by behaviorists and maybe even the more radical revisions I propose later in this book.

Becker and Stigler

Friedman's University of Chicago colleagues Gary Becker and George Stigler adopted Friedman's analytical methodology (in large measure but not totally), especially the part allowing for sterilized unrealistic behavioral assumptions, but dropped altogether Friedman's implied boundaries on where the methodology could be applied. Becker, especially, made a career of applying the "economic approach" beyond the strict boundaries of markets and invading the traditional domains of other social sciences (1976). He pioneered work in discrimination (1971), human capital (1994), home production (1993), tastes, and the "economics of life" (1997), without apparent concern that Friedman's assumed market force of "natural selection" might not hold, at least not with the same force. Becker implicitly assumed (at least in his modeling and maybe in much of life) that people could be counted on to behave rationally without, necessarily, the constraining and directing force of market (-type) competition. Similarly, Stigler recognized how the economics of information affected people's market searches, making less-than-perfect decisions optimal and rational.[24] Becker and Stigler had no need for the feedback loops of competition on rationality because rationality can't be enhanced beyond perfection, which is embedded in their founding premise.

Stigler and Becker took Friedman to heart in crystalizing (and making unreal) the assumption underlying theory by asserting without qualification the fixity of preferences across people and time, at least for their analytical purposes:

> [T]astes neither change capriciously nor differ importantly between people. On this interpretation one does not argue over tastes for the same reason that one does not argue over the Rocky Mountains – both are there, will be there next year, too, and are the same to all men. ... On the traditional view [of tastes], an explanation of economic phenomena that reaches a difference in tastes between people or times is the terminus of the argument: the problem is abandoned *at this point* to whoever studies and explains tastes (Psychologists? Anthropologists? Phrenologists? Sociologists?). On our preferred interpretation, one never reaches this impasse: the economist continues to search for differences in prices or incomes to explain any differences or changes in behavior.[25]

Their goal was to move economic analysis away from the disputes that can easily arise over the explanatory role of taste differences, which are difficult, if not impossible, to handle scientifically. Tastes are necessarily founded in subjective evaluations, which makes them difficult (if not impossible) to quantify. Becker and Stigler intended to direct economists' analytical attention to variables subject to change and to measurement, the external constraints people face (primarily incomes and prices). They sought to add to people's understanding of behavior, in response to changes in constraints, not to their taste changes.

Clearly, for Stigler and Becker, rational behavior has a nonrational foundation, perhaps grounded in intuition or in what they see as the self-evident objective reality of the equivalence of subjective preferences and goods (and bads). Becker, especially, is renowned for recognizing that many purchased goods are inputs into household production functions.[26] But then, Stigler, Becker, and Friedman can't help but give goods an objective reality (which Austrian economists are reluctant to do). There is really no point in trying to do *science* (with economic science having any claim of being even remotely like the physical sciences), as a predictive endeavor, if subjective preferences don't have objective (measurable) counterparts in the external physical world in the form of identified "goods," "prices," and "incomes" that can be observed and measured with tolerable accuracy. (Of course, Austrians have objected to claims that economics is, or can be, a true *science*, equivalent to the physical sciences. Friedrich Hayek dubbed any attempt to draw an equivalence as "scientism."[27])

Again, Friedman, Stigler, and Becker do not openly acknowledge a need for considering how internal, evolutionary, and neurobiological, constraints affect just exactly *how* rational people can be, although we gather they would not object to extending economic models to allow for maximization under such evolutionary and neurobiological constraints, given how many different and new directions they took economic analysis. Becker introduced "home produced goods" to his "household production function," and Stigler assumed "information" on prices is a "good." They built their esteemed careers on the assumption, with flexibility, of rational behavior variously constrained by sometimes specifically tailored utility functions in which the "goods" are identified for the research topic at hand (e.g., information is good with attendant production costs in one of Stigler's seminal articles [1962]). For Becker, as with Friedman and Stigler, economics was defined much more by its method than by the external scarcity that Robbins emphasized. As Becker asserted, "The combined assumptions of maximizing behavior, market equilibrium, and stable preferences, used relentlessly and unflinchingly, form the heart of the economic approach."[28]

Opening for Criticisms

Modern neoclassical economists, of course, left themselves open for methodological assault on several fronts, which could, eventually, undercut (as the assaults have) the neoclassical economics preeminence among methods of doing economics. We consider several avenues of economic practitioners' assaults on the discipline's core methodology.

Predictions and Empirical Tests

Foremost, Friedman and other neoclassical economists staked the discipline's credibility of its methods' ability to make predictions, the accuracy and value of which must (like any science) be assessed by empirical evidence. Friedman probably had in mind predictions and policies to the effect: "A higher minimum wage will lead to a reduction in employment among the covered worker groups." However, there are a host of other predictions that emerge out of an assumption of perfectly rational people: Such people can be expected, for example (among many similar deductions), to

- equate (at least, in some approximate fashion) at the margin, both in their production and consumption decision-making,
- ignore sunk costs and consider opportunity costs,
- discount with reasonable accuracy and consistency the costs and benefits for time and risks, and
- take (at least with some consistency) the courses of action with the highest expected net values.

Granted, Friedman (and his followers) insisted that founding premises could not be judged by their "realism" (or maybe even by their coherence with deductions), but at the same time Friedman—and, for that matter, Robbins—was unwilling to say that selection of founding premises was unconstrained, or could be totally divorced from real-world human behavior, or could be made up out of thin air with no expected correspondence between behavior and predictions (deductions) listed above.

Friedman did seem to be comfortable with Marshall's and Robbins' position that the discipline's basic premise had to be connected to "indisputable facts of experience." A theory's predictions' also had to be "good enough" (or better than those of alternative theories to obtain the approval of a community of economists operating as "scientists," not "crackpots."

If such predictions don't hold up to agreed-upon empirical tests with some frequency, then Friedman's methodological position would, so it would seem, lead to a reassessment of the validity of theory, on the order of, well, maybe people are not nearly as rational as neoclassical economists claim, making the jump to perfect rationality for model purposes an untenable stretch. Such a reassessment might understandably cause practitioners of the discipline to seek some adjustment in the founding premise and methodology. If a large number of such predictions don't hold up to careful empirical (scientific) examination, maybe the rationality premise should be scrapped—or judged inferior to some other approach by recognized authorities within the discipline, to whom Friedman indicated he was willing to defer, and must defer, as final arbitrators, or what constitutes good economic science.

Possible Problems with Empirical Tests

As noted, Friedman writes as if empirical assessments of hypotheses generated with positive (scientific) methods could resolve with some finality and frequency normative policy disputes, or at least could be expected to reduce the frequency of disputes over normative ends (and maybe mitigate conflicts, if not hostilities, in policy debates). Friedman points specifically to the policy debate that arises when a hike in the minimum wage is proposed. He suggests that opponents and proponents are most likely in disagreement, not so much over the goal of helping low-wage workers, but over the unemployment and poverty effects (among a range of possible labor-market effects) of any minimum-wage hike. He seemed to accept the ***dominant*** empirical finding in the early 1950s and before that minimum-wage hikes undercut employment and seemed to believe that such empirical findings could (potentially, at least) settle the policy debate by undercutting support for hikes.

When he was writing in the early 1950s, Friedman did not seem to anticipate the growth in available data banks and the more rapid decline in the cost of computing power during the following half-century and more, which gave rise to a burgeoning econometric industry focused on assessing the employment and unemployment effects (or lack thereof) of minimum-wage hikes from a variety of competing academic and political perspectives. With the growing ability of economists and policy advocates to choose among data banks to test their theories, with differing measures of employment and unemployment for differing labor-market segments and to choose (with greater ease lower cost) among combinations of dependent variables, as well as independent variables, for their various (and sometimes numerous) regression equations (perhaps sometimes covertly concocted with policy agendas in mind), support for minimum-wage hikes has ebbed and waned over the past seven-plus decades. Through the late 1960s, proponents of hikes pressed for hikes, which made their way through Congress, with the real value of the federal nominal minimum-wage peaking in February 1968 at $1.60, equal to $12.15 in 2017 dollars, at the end of 2017 (the initial minimum wage of 25 cents passed in 1938 was equal to $4.34 in 2017 dollars).

However, the growing buildup of studies after 1968 predominantly showing negative employment effects of hikes eroded, as Friedman expected, political support for minimum-wage hikes through the 1990s, causing the substantial erosion of its purchasing power. Even editors of the *New York Times* (who first vehemently opposed the first federal minimum-wage law and gradually shifted to full support in the 1970s) reversed their position by the mid-1980s and editorialized in 1987 in favor of a "right" minimum wage of "$0.00," all on the grounds of saving jobs for menial workers, a position founded squarely on economists' then dominant findings of negative jobs effects of minimum-wage laws.[29]

In early 2018, the nominal federal minimum wage had not been hiked from $7.25 since 2009, leaving the real value of the minimum wage a third below real-dollar peak in 1968 (although states and municipal governments have raised their minimum-wage rates to as much as $15 an hour by late 2017).

Beginning in the early to mid-1990s, economists began to find market segments in which the employment effects of minimum-wage hikes were minimal, if not zero (and possibly positive).[30] Policymakers began to realize that even a substantial majority of past econometric studies of minimum-wage hikes revealed limited employment effects (with job losses most often less than 3% of covered workers), even for the presumed most vulnerable worker group, teenagers.[31] As a consequence, debates over proposed minimum-wage hikes have remained as divisive as ever, and maybe more so, with the policy debate devolving to the state and municipal level and with hope waning that the magnitude of the unemployment effects of wage hikes could be resolved by empirical findings.

This is to say that proponents and opponents can now choose among studies to support their normative—political—positions to an extent not available when Friedman and Robbins were laying out what they saw as core issues in economics. Policymakers can even point to studies that posit that the minor employment effects can be chalked up to employers forced by market competition to offset the cost effects of minimum-wage hikes with reductions in fringe benefits and increases in work demands.[32]

As of early 2018, proponents of minimum-wage hikes appeared to be gaining ground in policy debates at the state and municipal levels, with an array of hikes instituted in 2015 or scheduled for 2016 and beyond, with no end in sight for the spread of state minimum-wage hikes. California had scheduled annual hikes in its state minimum through 2020.[33]

The Economics of Doing Science

Given that the minimum-wage-policy debate remains unsettled, and as contentious as ever, might not Friedman (and Robbins) have missed something critical to how economics can be done, and maybe, should be done—and how doing economics can be expected to evolve (and will evolve) over time? Might the continuing minimum-wage debate reveal how undertaking positive economics leaves much room for normative judgments, if nothing else, over the quality of the databases and statistical methods used, as well as the extent to which normative considerations can drive the actual science done? After all, different scientific investigations can result in an array of assessments of what exactly are the effects of minimum-wage increases (not to mention healthcare benefits and mandates, farm subsidies, pollution taxes, and income-tax rates).

Put another way, as surely Friedman recognized, "what is" depends on any number of considerations, not the least of which is the ever-evolving technology and databases available for undertaking science. This means that reliance on conceptual models, which guide hypotheses testing, can be expected to be affected by the ease, or cost, of doing empirical research that, in turn, can be expected to affect the complexity and realism of economic models used to guide hypotheses testing. Indeed, no one should be surprised if the cost of accessing progressively larger databanks and doing sophisticated empirical assessments falls enough for economists to be less and less concern with model building of the type Robbins and Friedman thought was necessary for doing science, possibly at some point setting aside model development altogether and conducting science through computer-determined algorithms generated from "big data" bases, as seems to be a decided trend in economics and related fields (say, finance and marketing) in contemporary times.

Indeed, neoclassical microeconomic theory could predict that the way science is done will change with the prices of the various "inputs" of doing any type of "science," not the least of which for deductive and inductive science are concentrated thought on model building, available databases, and technology available for empirical tests (or just finding algorithms that provide the "best fit" for the available databases). If the costs of data analysis have, over the decades, fallen relative to the cost of model building, which seems highly plausible, then the pursuit of science should be expected to shift from deductive reasoning toward inductive reasoning. With low-cost statistical manipulations, there is less need, so it may be reasoned, for worrying about reducing the count of "relevant" variables to manageable proportions (as once constrained by the cost function of findings and statistically manipulating an ever-greater count of variables).

Under either methodology, inductive or deductive analyses, the prominence and sophistication of data analyses should have risen over the last half century (an empirical issue in itself), but one that seems to have been the case from the most casual perusal of economic journals and policy forums over the past century, with acceleration of statistical testing over the past half-century. During Robbins' career, published philosophical discussions in economic journals were not uncommon. Such publications appear far less frequently today. Indeed, they are rare, and sophisticated empirical tests of hypotheses (carefully derived from highly technical mathematical models) are often thought-to-be mandatory for publications today, as contemporary economics graduate students are taught, and as their programs of study have progressively emphasized mathematical model building and econometric courses, which can further forced sterilization of underlying assumptions and obscure the real-world relevance of the economic analyses to practitioners and to policymakers.[34]

With growing emphasis on mathematical models for economic analytics, "perfect rationality" has evolved in its meaning and has become more open to criticisms. Without the mathematics, "perfect rationality" can be construed as having something of an economic foundation, in that it could loosely be equated with a form of optimal rationality under constraints. When math is introduced, any lingering presumption of a rational rationality is readily jettisoned, just to keep the math manageable. "Perfect rationality" implies mathematical precision in decision-making, with all tangency conditions fully met in equilibrium, which is totally open to attack by critics who can see, by that standard, omnipresent flaws in human decision-making that can be easily validated empirically, even though empirical tests are hardly needed (other than to diehard economists who insist that their mathematical models are adequately, if not fully, descriptive of people's decision-making).

As economics become ever more mathematically precise in modeling human decision-making during the last half of the twentieth, psychologists, cognitive psychologists, evolutionary psychologists began demonstrating limitations and flaws in human decision-making that does not, and cannot, hope to match the precision economists' vision of mathematically precise rationality, as Richard Thaler and Cass Sunstein, and many others, have demonstrated with ease.[35] They ask their readers to consider drawings of two tables, adapted from the work of psychologist Roger Shepard.[36] One appears much longer and thinner than the other, which is how most subjects in laboratory trials "see" the tables, but both tables are exactly the same length and width. Psychologist Daniel Kahneman makes the Thaler/Sunstein point on people's visual limitations with two lines of equal lengths. However, the lines are displayed with two sets of "fins" on their ends. One set of fins for one line is pointing out and the other point in which makes one line look longer than the other.[37]

Similar visual illusions could readily be shown to exist among many subjects,[38] but this one illusion (among a host of illusions) makes the point psychologists of all stripes and behavioral economists frequently make: People subject to visual and other cognitive limitations cannot be as rational as economists suggest in their models. As we will see in Chapter 4, behavioural economists have expanded on an array of limitations and flaws in human decisions, so much so that some behaviourists reject the rationality premise altogether and argue for a theory grounded in pervasive and predictable irrationalities.[39]

The Emergence of Laboratory Economics

Even though Robbins and Friedman appreciated the need to simplify economic models to their essential features, both spurned laboratory experiments because they necessarily oversimplified complex realities of human interactions with built-in feedback loops that allow for corrections of misguided decisions, from which market outcomes emerge. However, Robbins and Friedman wrote at a time in which economists strongly doubted the credibility of what people would say they would do in imagined circumstances; they felt strongly that what people do, or are observed to do, in real-world settings was far more reliable and revealing of preferences and behaviors.

Robbins and Friedman also had little to no experience with laboratory experiments, and they plied their trade when the technology for conducting tolerably realistic laboratory experiments was highly constrained and primitive, partially because computer technology was embryonic. Might not developments in the technology for conducting laboratory experiments since the 1930s and 1950s, with growing reliance on computer recordkeeping on the interactions of laboratory subjects and computer simulations, have made laboratory experiments more credible and accepted within Friedman's community of scholars who, as noted, could separate real "scientists" from "crackpots"?[40]

The awarding of Nobel prize in economics in 2002 to economist Vernon Smith for initiating the development of experimental economics and to behavioral psychologist Daniel Kahneman for his inaugural work in behavioral economics (with Amos Tversky) that directly challenged economists' rationality premise. Then, in 2017, the Nobel committee saw fit to award the prize to another behavioral economists Thaler for his substantial advancement of the behavioral work of Kahneman and Tversky and many other of their students and converts. These scholars' selection testified to the shift of economic methodology, now ongoing for at least five and maybe seven decades, away from the methodology of Robbins and Friedman and their followers, constrained by deductive theory, to behaviorists' work, constrained by researchers' ingenuity in setting up laboratory experiments, often weakly constrained (if not totally unconstrained) by guiding hypotheses deduced from a general theory of the kind that Robbins, Friedman, Becker, and Stigler had in mind.

With neoclassical economics gradually discredited over the decades in a growing number of scholarly minds with a multitude of laboratory experiments, no one should be surprised if the standard for acceptable inductive science erodes, with experiments being reduced to simple, if not simplistic, survey questions of this sort: "Consider two options A and B [with specified values], which do you prefer?" The subjects' answers might be given credibility from a community of behaviorists, if they violate some predicted neoclassical tenet.

Economics as a Way of Thinking

The economics discipline has moved on in another important way, as noted with far greater emphasis on mathematics, which has made the core concern less about scarcity per se and more about mathematical technique. Granted, practically all (if not all) modern economics textbooks pay homage to Robbins' identification of economics with scarcity, with any number of textbooks dubbing scarcity as *the* economic problem (but often without reference to Robbins as the source of the scarcity paradigm).

However, the defining core concern of the discipline has moved in one major, largely unheralded way after Robbins wrote his *Essay*. Through the work of Friedman, Becker, and their key colleagues at the University of Chicago, the core unifying concern of economics has shifted from being focused on derived implications of scarcity to the *method* economists use to derive and test their generalizations, subsuming scarcity. As noted, Becker has crystalized the economic method as relentlessly following the logic of three key assumptions in economic models: maximizing behavior, market equilibrium, and stable preferences, with a key test of the theory remaining Friedman's, the method's predictive value, not the realism of the underlying premises and analytics.[41]

With the *method* of analysis central to economics, the array of topics open for investigation became unbounded. Economists were no longer tied to a confined area for investigation, for example, "business," as Marshall had confined the discipline, possibly because he, as did Friedman, believed business arenas were heavily populated by self-selected people who were inclined to think in strictly self-interested, cost-minimizing, and profit-maximizing terms. Moreover, business behaviors were heavily guided by competitive pressures that selected out those business people who (and their firms that) were relatively less inclined to think "rationally" (with self-interest, cost-minimizing, and profit-maximizing goals in mind).

Marshall, and to a lesser extent Friedman, would not be surprised that economists' expanded array of topics for investigation to social arenas (for example, families and friends, politics, gangs, marriage and divorce, dying, crime, religion, education, academic governance, and so forth, within which economic-grounded competitive pressures could guide, through feedback loops, decision-making) would reveal weaknesses in the discipline's predictive powers, as well as to reveal a growing gulf between economists' (perfect) rationality premise and people's real-world rationality (or lack thereof).

By maintaining that economics was a method of doing social science, Becker and those who followed him opened the discipline to a new challenge. If economics is a *method* that has no recognized bounded in application, there is no reason why the method should not be applied to all implications of the disciplines' own core methodology (below the level of, say, price will curb purchases). Rationality, especially the perfect variety, implies stark behavioral predictions, from which other predictions (the law of demand) are derived. As noted; rational people can be expected to equate at the margin, consider opportunity costs, ignore sunk costs, choose consistently, discount the values of choice options for risk and time. Behavioral economics has arisen in part to assess the validity of these predictions and, hence, the relative merit and reliability of economics as a method of doing science.

Concluding Comments

The domain of economic analysis expanded dramatically during the twentieth century. Alfred Marshall focused economic analysis on people as they work their ways through problems relating to business, fairly narrowly limiting its scope to market exchanges in which money plays a major role. Robbins found all such set boundaries for economic analysis limiting (for example, "business" or "material welfare"), because much economic science was pursued outside of business dealings and much production involved nonmaterial goods and services. He tagged scarcity as the pervasive and unifying concern of economists. He argued that economics was delimited by the "relationship between ends and means which have alternative uses," which means that Crusoe, stranded on his island by himself, faced economic challenges.[42]

Friedman accepted Robbins' reformulation of the discipline organized around scarcity, but he suggested, maybe only in passing, that the economic method was more likely to apply fruitfully to market settings. Competitive pressures were an important force that helped to legitimatize the founding rationality, or maximizing, premise of the discipline, which implied cost-minimizing decision-making. Markets helped to select out market participants who failed systematically, to one degree or another, to make rational, cost-minimizing, and profit-maximizing decisions, causing market outcome to be more rational and efficient than people might naturally be predisposed to be. Adam Smith's "invisible hand" continued to rule in Friedman's methodology, but with greater emphasis on the selective pressures on the rationality of market participants than Smith may have had in mind.

We have to think Friedman would reason (accepting Marshall's "continuity principle") that the less competitive markets (or other social environments) were and the less weeding pressures there were in those environments, the less appropriate economic methods would be. Beyond some point is moving away from competitive market pressures, the economic methods could become more or less impotent in terms of generating insights, or so we (or Friedman's community of authoritative scholars) might surmise, at least in retrospect.

Friedman never registered full frontal attack on economists expanding economic inquirer beyond markets (and commercial spheres). However, from his passing suggestions, I suspect that Friedman was not always fully comfortable with his University of Chicago colleagues (and many other economists) applying economic methods in environments devoid of competitive and weeding pressures to push out decision makers who felt little pressure to respond to market forces and economize. At the same time, Friedman began, in limited ways, to shift economic analyses away from boundaries defined by subject matter or content (business, in the case of Marshall, and scarcity, in the case of Robbins) to boundaries defined by analytical methods, or "approach." For example, Friedman remains well known today for applying simple economic analytics to the efficiency of the military draft (relative to an all-volunteer army), the relative efficiency of different forms of welfare grants, and to educational choice.

For Becker, Stigler, and following economists, key organizing elements of economic analyses were, again, "the combined assumptions of maximizing behavior, market equilibrium, and stable preferences, used relentlessly and unflinchingly."[43] At the same time, any discomfort Friedman may have felt toward economic imperialism could have been modulated by his recognition of the many insights his close, in-house colleagues, and others were generating outside of market settings.

As economic analyses evolved during the last half of the twentieth century, the method of economics became ever more detached from the analytical constraints that are imposed by the brain with which both analysts and subjects confront. Scarcity in the external world remained centrally important to the economic approach, but the scarcity of mental resources was never fully integrated into neoclassical economic analyses as an analytical constraints or variable. (After all, a working premise of "perfect rationality" sets aside any and all scarcity constraints within the human brain.)

Psychologists, neuroscientists, and economists favoring behaviorists' methods took notice of the many predictions that fell out of economic models were at odds with their casual and research observations and laboratory experiments, but had been sidestepped by neoclassical economists. In the process, behavioral economists cast doubt on the value of achieving the kind of *improved* understanding with economic methods that Friedman held as a treasured goal of "science." The behaviorists across several disciplines began to see the generation of criticisms of economic methods as the equivalent of "shooting fish in a barrel" and set out to supplant the neoclassical microeconomic modeling of Friedman, Becker, Stigler, and many other economists with a theoretical paradigm that the behaviorists believed, and still do, meets with Friedman's criteria for any disciplines that aspire to be *science*, insights, and predictions empirically tested.[44] By the last half of the twentieth century, behaviorists had honed their laboratory and statistical skills in their search for "what is," but this time not through deductive testing of hypotheses, but simply by observing what real people do, and don't do in settings that they find congenial and productive of insights, but that Robbins and Friedman would likely find more than a little problematic, because of the absence of an undergirding general theory capable of producing deduced hypotheses subject to testing.

Notes

1. Robbins (1935, Chapter 6).
2. Robbins (1935, p. 141).
3. Robbins (1935, p. 141).
4. As included in Friedman (1953, pp. 3–46).
5. In his *The Ultimate Foundation of Economics* (1962) and several of his other works, Ludwig von Mises insisted that while the objects, animate and inanimate devoid of any capacity to form preferences, of hard science could be expected to behave in "regular patterns," human beings could form values and make preference judgements and pursue their difficult-to-predict ends. Accordingly, they could change the course of events,

making predictions of human events difficult, if not impossible, to predict. According to Mises, Friedman, and other neoclassical economists, in pressing for the adoption of a variant of logical positivism, were succumbing to their "shocking ignorance of everything concerning the science of human action," which required a manner of thinking not applicable to the hard sciences, with physics believed to be the "paragon of science." Friedman, however, insisted that economics should follow the physics paradigm.

6. Mises (1962, pp. v and 11).
7. Friedman (1953, p. 4).
8. Friedman (1953, p. 5).
9. Friedman (1953, p. 7).
10. Friedman (1953, p. 8).
11. Friedman makes the problems of working with complex descriptive theories clear in this passage:

> A completely realistic theory of the wheat market would have to include not only conditions directly underlying supply and demand for wheat but also the kinds of coins or credit instruments used to make transactions; the personal characteristics of the wheat traders, such as the color of each trader's hair and eyes, his antecedents and education, the number of members of his family, their characteristics, the weather prevailing during the growing season; the personal characteristics of the farmers growing the wheat and of the consumers who will ultimately use it; and so on indefinitely. Any attempt to move very far in achieving this kind of "realism" is certain to render a theory utterly useless. (1953, p. 32)

12. Friedman (1953, p. 40).
13. Friedman (1953, p. 41).
14. Friedman (1953, p. 43).
15. Friedman (1953, p. 16).
16. Friedman (1953, p. 21).
17. Friedman (1953, p. 23).
18. Friedman (1953, p. 23).
19. Friedman (1953, p. 20).
20. Friedman (1953, p. 20).
21. Friedman (1953, p. 25).
22. By way of contrast, macroeconomics had not yet, in the early 1950s, fulfilled the promise of being organized around something approximating "the" theory, again, according to Friedman ([1953, pp. 41–42]).
23. Friedman (1976, p. 267).

24. Stigler (1962, pp. 213–225).
25. Stigler and Becker (1977, p. 76).
26. Becker (1993).
27. See Hayek (1943, 1944).
28. Becker (1976, p. 5).
29. Editors, *New York Times*, July 17, 1987. For a history of the ever-changing position of the *New York Times* editors on the minimum wage, see McKenzie (1994).
30. Card and Krueger (1995).
31. For review of the literature on the labor-market effects of minimum-wage hikes, see Brown et al. (1982), Peterson and Stewart (1969, pp. 151–155), Kosters and Welch (1972), Ragan (1977), and Neumark and Wascher (2008).
32. For a review of the literature of this perspective on the labor-market effects (or non-effects) of minimum-wage hikes, see McKenzie (2014).
33. For a listing of the various state and municipal minimum-wage hikes in 2015 and 2016 and beyond, go here. http://www.xperthr.com/quick-reference/minimum-wage-rates-by-state-and-municipality/7038/.
34. Schabas (2014).
35. Thaler and Sunstein (2008, pp. 17 and 18).
36. Shepard (1981, 1990). Shepard's tabletop illusion is illustrated here. http://www.michaelbach.de/ot/sze_shepardTables/.
37. Kahneman (2011, p. 27).
38. See Michael Bach's collection (n.d.) of 130 optical illusions and visual phenomena here. http://www.michaelbach.de/ot/index.html.
39. See Ariely (2008).
40. Friedman (1953, p. 25).
41. Becker (1976, p. 5).
42. Robbins (1935, p. 16).
43. Becker (1976, p. 5).
44. Friedman (1953, p. 41).

References

Ariely, Dan. 2008. *Predictably Irrational: The Hidden Forces That Shape Our Decisions.* York: HarperCollins.

Becker, Gary S. 1971. *The Economics of Discrimination.* Chicago: University of Chicago Press (originally published in 1957).

Becker, Gary S. 1976. *The Economic Approach to Human Behavior.* Chicago: University of Chicago Press.

Becker, Gary S. 1993. *A Treatise on the Family* (expanded edition). Cambridge, MA: Harvard University Press.

Becker, Gary S. 1994. *Human Capital: A Theoretical and Empirical Approach*. Chicago: University of Chicago Press.
Becker, Gary S. 1997. *The Economics of Life*. Chicago: University of Chicago Press.
Brown, Charles, Curtis Gilroy, and Andrew Kohen. 1982. The effect of the minimum wage on employment and unemployment. *Journal of Economic Literature* 20: 487–528.
Card, David, and Alan B. Krueger. 1995. *Myth and Measurement: The New Economics of the Minimum Wage*. Princeton, NJ: Princeton University Press.
Editors. 1987. The right minimum wage: "$0.00." *New York Times*, January 14.
Friedman, Milton. 1953. *The Methodology of Positive Economics*. Chicago: University of Chicago Press.
Friedman, Milton. 1976. Inflation and unemployment. *Nobel Memorial Lecture*, December 13.
Hayek, F.A. 1943. Scientism and the study of society: Part II. *Economica* 10 (37): 34–63 (reprinted in Hayek, 2010).
Hayek, F.A. 1944. Scientism and the study of society: Part III. *Economica* 11 (41): 27–39 (reprinted in Hayek, 2010).
Kahneman, Daniel. 2011. *Thinking, Fast and Slow*. New York: Farrar, Straus and Giroux.
Kosters, Marvin, and Finis Welch. 1972. The effects of minimum wages on the distribution of changes in aggregate employment. *American Economic Review* 62: 323–31.
McKenzie, Richard B. 1994. *Times Change: The Minimum Wage and the New York Times*. San Francisco: Pacific Research Institute.
McKenzie, Richard B. 2014. Why are there so few job losses from minimum-wage hikes? Dallas: National Center for Policy Analysis, Study 354, April 9.
Mises, Ludwig von. 1962. *The Ultimate Foundation of Economics*. New York: Martino Fine Books (republished in 2012).
Neumark, David, and William L. Wascher. 2008. *Minimum Wages*. Cambridge, MA: MIT Press.
Peterson, John M., and Charles T. Stewart. 1969. *Employment Effects of Minimum Wage Rates*. Washington, DC: American Enterprise Institute for Public Policy Research.
Ragan, James F. 1977. Minimum wages and the youth labor market. *Review of Economics and Statistics* 59: 129–36.
Robbins, Lionel. 1935. *An Essay on the Nature and Significance of Economic Science*. Auburn, AL: Ludwig von Misses Institute (first published in 1932 and revised and reissued in 2007).
Schabas, Margaret. 2014. *A World Ruled by Number William Stanley Jevons and the Rise of Mathematical Economics* Princeton, NJ: Princeton University Press.

Shepard R.N. 1981. Psychological complementarity. In *Perceptual Organization*, ed. M. Kubovy and J.R. Pomerantz, 279–342. Hillsdale, NJ: Lawrence Erlbaum Associates.

Shepard, R.N. 1990. *Mind Sights: Original Visual Illusions, Ambiguities, and Other Anomalies.* New York: W.H. Freeman and Company.

Stigler, George J. 1962. The economics of information. *Journal of Political Economy* 69 (June): 213–225.

Stigler, George J., and Gary S. Becker. 1977. De gustibus non est disputandum. *American Economic Review* 67 (2, March): 76–90.

Thaler, Richard H., and Cass R. Sunstein. 2008. *Nudge: Improving Decisions About Health, Wealth, and Happiness.* New Haven, CT: Yale University Press.

CHAPTER 4

Behavioral Economics, Evolution, and the Human Brain

Economists of different methodological persuasions have been at growing odds for a long time over the discipline's founding premise, its core concern, and its boundaries. Adam Smith elevated the role of self-interest (or selfishness or "self-love") in economic thinking, but he never pressed the view that people were exclusively self-interested, nor would he ever have entertained that people were, or could be, perfectly rational at all times.[1] Indeed, no serious, respectable economist has ever thought such was the case, at least from my reading of the literature on methodological thought. Even George Stigler and Gary Becker never suggested that perfect rationality was perfectly descriptive of human decision-making and, at times, made concessions that the rationality premise should probably be set aside in some areas of policy making (e.g., in proscribing a waiting period in cases of legalized suicide).[2] However, both generally adopted a stylized rationality premise for practical and modeling reasons grounded in economics. It was a founding premise that was not only "good enough," but also served its function well, at least better than any of the proposed alternative premises.

Even Milton Friedman, whose methodological perspective became ingrained in neoclassical (or conventional) microeconomics from the early 1950s, accepted the strained premise on practical, economic grounds: It had worked tolerably well (or better than other methods) in developing testable predictions. Friedman suggested, as Herbert Simon insisted, that optimizing and equilibrium analysis in classical economics could be a "valuable and powerful aid to thought" so long as its basic

R. B. McKenzie, *A Brain-Focused Foundation for Economic Science*,
https://doi.org/10.1007/978-3-319-76810-6_4

premise does not deviate so much from real-world conditions that its conclusions (predictions) are "vitiated."[3] However, Friedman and Simon differed, substantially, in the 1950s over the extent to which the discipline's basic premise had been, or would likely be, undermined.

As noted early in the book, Alfred Marshall restricted economic analysis to the commercial sphere, maybe concerned that its founding premise and stylized models (e.g., supply and demand) would not apply outside of people's business dealings. From Friedman's rare ventures in his own writings outside the economics of markets and applied government policies, and, of course, monetary theory and history, I have to suspect he worried about Stigler's and Becker's application of economic analytics to familial and social settings where market-type competition and feedback loops carried limited force, potentially causing predictions to be at least partially vitiated.

As shown later in this chapter, behavioral psychologists and economists and many neuroeconomists have declared open season on the rationality premise (in what economic journalist Michael Lewis has dubbed "the undoing project," at least with reference to Danial Kahneman and Amos Tversky's behavioral work[4]) over the last six or so decades, using psychology and neuroscience experimental and inductive methods, to show how far removed people's various actual behaviors and decisions are from dictates of perfect rationality. The behaviorists' demonstrations of irrationalities have become a form of good social science sport. Behavioral critics have piled up demonstrations that people's behaviors, in fact, deviate so much from predicted behavior (at least to their satisfaction, but not, most notably, to Becker's and Stigler's satisfaction as long as they were alive) that much neoclassical economic reasoning has been vitiated enough to suggest that the neoclassical approach could and should be strongly disputed and, if possible, revised. Some critics have suggested the premise should be discarded altogether.

Behaviorists' research has shown that, to one degree or another, people cannot be counted on to always (or even most of the time) equate at the margin, dutifully ignore sunk costs and consider opportunity costs, discount risks, and costs and benefits consistently and precisely over time, choose consistently, and so on. Therefore, behaviorists have largely shied from deductive reasoning in their pursuit of Robbins' treasured economic "generalizations." They have effectively argued that the neoclassical economic approach is no longer "good enough" (Friedman's turn of words). Generalizations can be inducted with greater confidence from what people do or say they would do in surveys and laboratory experiments, rather than from tested predictions based on models founded on what behaviorists believe to be a wildly unreal or other-worldly premise.

I have extensively and in some depth reviewed elsewhere the burgeoning behavioral economic literature, adding the details of the research studies, and critiquing them as I thought necessary.[5] Here, my purpose is to substantially advance the argument for continuing the use of neoclassical analytics, not to cover old ground on the behavioral literature. However, I understand many readers will not return to my earlier book or the sizable and rapidly growing library of behavioral economic texts that review, often in accessible ways, the behavioral literature that I repeatedly cite in this and the following chapters.[6] Hence, here, I will follow a middle course, briefly outlining behavioral arguments, with some updating. My goal is to give enough details of behavioral findings so that readers will understand the methodological context that gives value to my proposed revision of the discipline's core methodological foundation. Consider the following sampling of arguments and findings of behavioral economists and psychologists.

Behavioral Economics, a Brief Review

Behaviorists have, in general, concluded that the founding premise of neoclassical economics is simply wrongheaded, not worthy of being the core concern of any discipline that seeks to be deemed a "science." Casual observation of people's daily decisions alone, behaviorists suggest, substantiates their reluctance to start with economists' rationality premise, but, they recognize, only scientific findings will dislodge the stranglehold neoclassical economics has on the discipline's analytical future. For example, marketing researchers grounded in behaviorism write in their survey of the differences in approaches to research by people in marketing and economics:

> The weakest part [of "economists' theoretical edifice"] is surely the notion of utility-maximization by rational consumers. This is not only implausible as a general description of buyers' behavior but there are many instances in everyday experience of most people that seem to contradict it. Moreover, the work of psychologists and several psychological experiments have shown beyond any doubt that rationality and utility-maximization can hardly be considered as universal and ever-present traits of consumer behavior.[7]

Economic behaviorist Richard Thaler argued in the early 1990s that economists, especially theorists, had an allergy to data on how people make the decisions they do, preferring to rely on their economic models that are "elegant" and can generate "precise predictions," whereas behaviorists' theorizing is necessarily more "messy, with much vaguer predictions," but then he asks, "But, ... would you rather be elegant and precisely wrong, or messy and vaguely right?"[8] Thaler later joined with behavioral law professor Cass Sunstein to pile on mockery of neoclassical economics, primarily for its reliance on perfect rationality as its founding premise, drawing a contrast between "Humans" (real people replete with physical and mental weaknesses) and "Econs" (economists' imagined decision-makers who have superhuman physical and mental powers): "If you look at economics textbooks, you will learn that homo economicus [textbook authors' imagined Econ] can think like Albert Einstein, store as much memory as IBM's Big Blue, and exercise the will power of Mahatma Gandhi," whereas real Humans have trouble remembering their passwords, finding their keys, and avoiding temptations that make them obese and lazy, and leave them impoverished in their retirement.[9]

Behavioral psychologists Daniel Ariely argues that people are so consistently irrational (as judged by economists' construction of perfect rationality) that they are "predictably irrational," which should have long been expected because, after all, he quips, people are effectively "goslings," with, he suggests, more or less the same limited mental proclivities to follow their own life paths.[10]

Behavioral economists Colin Camerer and George Loewenstein argue they have a modest but simple goal: "At the core of behavioral economics is the conviction that increasing the realism of the psychological underpinnings of economic analysis will improve the field of economics *on its own terms*—generating theoretical insights, making better predictions of field phenomena, and suggesting better policy" (emphasis in the original).[11]

Consumer Choice Theory

Behaviorists have sought to undercut the validity of neoclassical economists' analytics by denying the validity of their most widely treasured and applied generalization, the law of demand, deduced from consumer choice theory that is grounded in the presumption that rational people will choose deliberately and consistently, making sure that the last marginal values of all goods purchased are the same. To help him discredit consumer choice theory, Thaler has deferred to Gary Becker who showed in the early 1960s that downward-sloping demand curves will emerge if consumers do no more than randomly pick their purchase combinations within their binding budget constraints.[12] If that's the case, Thaler asks, "What then is the economic theory of consumer?"[13] Since preferences can't be observed, there is no way to test whether or not people "equate price ratios to marginal rates of substitution." But, it should be noted again that Becker's budget-constraint argument for downward-sloping demand curves was challenged by Austrian economist Israel Kirzner in the early 1960s when Becker published his article under dispute.[14]

Daniel Ariely denies that demand curves can be counted on to be downward sloping, deferring to Mark Twain to make his point that there are behavioral reasons for believing demand curves can be upward sloping, "Tom had discovered a great law of human action, namely that in order to make a man covet a thing, it is only necessary to make it dear."[15] As do (almost) all behaviorists, Ariely insists that what people are willing to pay for a good depends on exactly how the pricing issue is "framed," even by seemingly extraneous and irrelevant factors.

For example, Ariely asked 55 MIT management students to write down the last two digits of their social security numbers, after which he asked them to give the highest price they would pay for a highly rated bottle of wine. The fifth of the students with the highest social security numbers gave prices for the wine that were 216–346% higher than the fifth of the class with the lowest social security numbers. (He makes no note of how a few students with low social security numbers could have provided high bids.) He found much the same results when students were asked to price other goods (keyboards, for example[16]), which caused him to conclude that people are not so much intent on optimizing their welfares, as neoclassical economists insist they do, but rather seek "arbitrary coherence," or a form of consistence between numbers recently considered, dubbed "anchors," and prices they are willing to pay.[17] (I hasten to point out that if "framing" is so important to decisions, then we must wonder how any generalizations can be devised with much confidence given that all decisions, even those made in strictly control laboratories, are made in the context of a multitude of different frames, with many of the differences in frames going unnoticed, partially because they are unobservable, mainly because, like numbers articulated, are mental constructs.)

Ariely also argues that the law of demand seems to break down totally at a price of zero, or so he found with a relatively simple (possibly simplistic) experiment. He reports setting up a table on the MIT campus, offering Lindt truffles and Hershey Kisses at half price, 15 cents and 1 cent, respectively. Seventy-three percent of the students who stopped at his table bought the truffles and 27%, the Kisses. When he lowered the price of each candy by a penny, to 14 cents and zero, respectively, the percentage breakdown of the students' purchases reversed: 69% "bought" the Kisses, which Ariely chalks up to "irrational excitement" (without noting whether or not more of the two candies were purchased). Zero prices pressed an "emotional hot button."[18] According to Ariely, the students were freely grabbing the Kisses, "not because they had made reasoned cost-benefit analysis before elbowing their way in, but simply because the Kisses were FREE!" (caps in the original), which can be attributed to people innate "loss aversion": No one must fear a loss at a price of zero, or so he contends.[19] (One has to wonder how Ariely was able to deduce, in any scientifically valid way from his experiment, that the changes in the purchase distribution could be attributable to "irrational excitement," perhaps an unprovable, and maybe fanciful, conclusion that stands apart from his quantitative findings from a loose experimental setting.)

Expected Utility Theory

Choices are rarely made between or among fully *known* options, but even with options with elements of gambles, rational decision-makers should be expected to choose the option with the higher *expected* value, after discounting for risk and time, if utility is to be maximized, as deduced under neoclassical economics. Variable and uncertain outcomes abound, which can mean that choosers must often gamble on their choices and can often make ill-advised and inconsistent choices, according to behaviorists. Daniel Kahneman and Amos Tversky gave 150 subjects a choice between a sure-thing option with a value of $240 and a gamble with an expected value of $250. Eighty-four percent of the subjects took the sure-thing, which had a lower expected value.[20] Similarly, when subjects were given a choice between a sure-thing option worth $3000 and a gamble with an 80% chance of receiving $4000 and a 20% chance of getting nothing (with an expected value of $3200), 80% took the sure-thing.[21] These are two among a number of cited cases in which subjects (supposedly) violated a central cannon of expected utility theory, even when money was not involved.[22] (In Chapter 5, I will critique another "prospect" problem that reveals, supposedly, the same sort of violation of neoclassical choice theory.)

Loss Aversion

A major generalization induced from behavioral economics (and psychology) is that people are inclined to be loss averse, which behaviorally means they should be expected to be more prone to gamble to avoid a loss than to gamble to obtain a gain of equal value. People's loss aversion shows up in their reluctance to sell stocks that have declined in price, which means they can be expected to hold onto losers longer than gainers, as has been found to be the case (for some percentage of subjects studied).[23] Similarly, homeowners whose houses have declined in market value have been found to be reluctant to price their house at their lower market value, with the result being that they end up delaying the sales of their houses and adding to their losses.[24]

Dominance, Invariance, and Framing

The principles of *dominance* and *invariance* are critical to neoclassical choice theory. The principle of *dominance* in decision-making means that option A, which is better than option B in at least one respect, should always be preferred to option B. The principle of *invariance* means that the choice between A and B should not be affected by the framing of the choice options, that is, by how the options are described or presented, as neoclassical economists argue (although I'm not so sure why neoclassical economists should not expect choices to be affected by their "frames," given the imprecision of the concept of frames and how many times the exact features of the frame, say, the buying setting, can be an important part of the "good" bought and consumed). What is important in choices, according to mainstream, neoclassical microeconomic theory, is the respective discounted value of the options, not so much the exact context of purchases or reference points, i.e., the choice frame.

For behaviorists, however, context matters a great deal. Sometimes even incidental considerations (consider the earlier example of subjects repeating the last digits of their social security numbers), as well as major, matters in choice contexts. Kahneman and Tversky found that when 152 subjects in a laboratory setting were told that the outbreak of an unusual influenza virus was expected to kill 600 people.[25] The subjects were then told there were two potential reaction programs: Program A could save 200 people and program B would yield a one-third probability that 600 people would be saved and a two-thirds probability that no one would be saved, making the expected lives saved 200. Nonetheless, 72% of the respondents chose program A.[26]

The problem was reframed for a different set of 155 subjects. They were told that if they chose program C, 400 people would die for certain. If they chose program D, one-third of 600 people would not die but two-thirds of the people would die. Seventy-eight percent of the subjects favored program D even though the two programs, C and D, would result in the same expected deaths. In short, as has been found in similar experiments. The subjects reversed their choice division between A/B and C/D, when in fact all four options are "indistinguishable in real terms" (that is, so long as variance in outcomes is ignored for choice purposes).[27]

Expected utility theory comes up short in other framing experiments, not the least of which involve immediate temptations for gratifications. A hundred adult students were asked to choose between three lifetime income paths that had the same total income over time with no discounting. The first income path had income starting high and declining. The second, income was constant over time, and the third path had increasing income. Obviously, even though the first path was superior of the three paths in terms of the present discounted value of the income streams and the second was superior to the third, 12% of the subjects chose the first path and 12% chose the second, meaning that the remaining subjects, 76%, chose the path with the lowest discounted value. Even after the discounting of income streams was explained to the students, they stuck with the third path by a substantial majority, 69%.[28] The explanation? Perhaps, again, loss aversion. Perhaps, choosers of a stream of benefits over time engage in "hyperbolic discounting," which to say that their discount rate declines into the future. Perhaps, most students are irrational (or, to put it less politely, are nuts).

At the same time, there are subtle findings within these results worthy of keeping in mind, even though behaviorists often sidestep them: Not all subjects in the experiments are "irrational" in behaviorists' terms. In dynamic markets (or other social settings) over time, the "rational" subjects/market participants (even when only a few) can provide "irrational" subjects with learning experiences, as Milton Friedman argued.

Also, the results show that subjects, as a group, do seem to respond the way neoclassical economists would predict *on the margin*: The percent of subjects taking the "irrational" course (which for a host of reasons not considered by the narrow confines of the behavioral experiments) goes down with explanations of the relative merits of the three paths. Economists greatest claims to scientific analysis have never come from their ability to identify exactly what people want, but from their predictions of how people will respond, given their wants and given changes in conditions, say, information and prices of choice options.

Mental Accounting and Framing

Two hundred subjects were told that they had spent $10 for movie tickets but discovered that they had lost their tickets when they arrived at the theater. When asked if they would buy another ticket at the theater, only 46% said they would, which may not sit well with neoclassical economists who assume that rational people will ignore sunk cost. The problem was framed differently for another set of 188 subjects. They were told that they had not bought tickets but had lost $10 on the way to the theater. Nevertheless, 88% of the subjects said they would go ahead and buy tickets.[29]

Supposedly, such findings bolster behaviorists' claim that people engage in *mental accounting*, which means that they compartmentalize categories of purchases in their minds. When the moviegoers lost their tickets, the suggestion that they buy another ticket doubled the price of seeing the show in their mental "entertainment account." When they had lost $10 before buying the ticket, the price of seeing the show was much lower, $10, as measured by the depletion of their entertainment account. The lost $10 might said to be unassigned to an account, or didn't necessarily come from their entertainment account, an inference that seems to require a form of mind reading.

Nevertheless, mental accounting can possibly help explain people's dieting and risk-taking problems. When people drink diet sodas, they "save" 180 calories, which can cause them to be more receptive to the temptation of later eating a sugary treat (which could have more than 180 calories). When people are required to wear helmets when biking, they might be expected to bike more recklessly, assuming they seek to use up their mental "budget" for recklessness.

Opportunity Cost

People are prone to be inconsistent in assessing opportunity costs in purchasing decisions, contrary to neoclassical economics, according to behaviorists. When 88 subjects were told that a hand calculator could be bought for $15 in one store and $10 in another store at some distance, 68% of the subjects said they would make the drive to save the $5. However, when another set of subjects were told that a hand calculator could be bought at $125 in one store and $120 at another store, with the distance between these two stores was the same as between the first two stores, only 29% said they would make the drive to save the $5 difference.[30]

Similarly, in another experiment, behaviorists found that buyers were not willing to expend more effort to save $15 on a $150 purchase than they were willing to spend to save $5 on a $50 purchase, presumably contrary to neoclassical economic wisdom.[31] In general, behaviorists have found that the value subjects put on the time cost of their buying decision is directly related to the prices of goods available for purchase. In neoclassical economics, opportunity cost is supposedly fixed by, say, the subjects' wage rate.[32]

Behaviorists have also found that MBA students "systematically prefer" projects that caused their firms to incur opportunity costs from the use of firms' resources than ones that required them to make out-of-pocket expenditures of the same amounts, which means that opportunity costs are not seen as equivalent to explicit expenditures, as should be the case for perfectly rational people. It also suggests that the MBAs would accept projects with lower rates of returns on projects with opportunity costs than those with explicit expenditures, which means they would not be maximizing their firms' profits (unless the subjects are thinking in terms of other associated costs not evident to researchers running the experiments).[33]

Again, behaviorists seem to consistently dismiss the value of "correct" choices of subjects in dynamic systems, when substantial economic gains and losses are at stake.

Choice Inconsistencies

Under neoclassical economics, a person who doesn't have a ticket to, say, a football game, but who is unwilling to pay $100 for one should be expected to sell the ticket for $100 if given. The person who refuses to pay $100 for the ticket is (presumably) revealing that she has something better to do with $100 than go to the game. When she has a ticket, she should still have something better to do with $100 than go to the game. Hence, she should sell. Presumably, she undercuts her potential welfare by not selling and going to the game.

However, behaviorists have found this line of neoclassical economic reasoning to be greatly flawed, yet again. Behaviorist Dan Ariely contacted a hundred Duke University students, all of whom had camped out to be able to join a lottery for tickets for a basketball game. Half of the students won the lottery and got tickets; the other half did not. Those students who did not get tickets gave prices for buying tickets that averaged $170. Those who got tickets gave an average selling price of $2400, with no student with a ticket willing to sell his or her ticket for as little as the highest price given for buying a ticket by any one student who did not get a ticket. Behaviorists argue that this finding is inconsistent with neoclassical economic reasoning but consistent with behaviorists finding that choice frames matter.[34]

Endowment Effect

The difference in the average buying and selling prices might be explained by the fact that the game tickets received by students produced a consequential "wealth effect," causing them to elevate their selling prices (which, if given the same added wealth in some other form, might have caused them to be willing to pay the higher prices, when not given tickets). Other behaviorists have sought to eliminate the wealth-effect explanation by offering students a good with little intrinsic worth and market value, a coffee mug. They gave half the students in an experimental group mugs and gave nothing to the rest. The "willing to buy" price given by those who didn't get mugs remained much lower than the "willing to sell" price, which caused the researchers to conclude that the wealth effect could not explain the gap.[35] Thaler offers what he calls a more "parsimonious" explanation for the reoccurring price gap, the *endowment effect*: people simply value the things they have more than the things they don't (which he suggests can be traced, again, to people's inherent loss aversion).[36]

However, it needs to be noted that this type of research rarely, if ever, shows that "people," as in "all people," in experiments exhibit the endowment effect. There are almost always some people who are not captured by behaviorists' all-inclusive conclusions. Some people choose as neoclassical economists might suggest they would—that is, don't exhibit an endowment effect—which, if noted, undercuts the generality of generalizations drawn from behaviorists' experiments. And the "non-conformists" can have powerful effects on how people's choices evolve over time.

Acquisition and Transaction Utility

Generally, neoclassical economists assess the value of a purchased good solely in terms of its intrinsic value to consumers, which leaves them groping for explanations for seasonal, and nonseasonal, sales (beyond the ready-made explanations: "demand curves slope downward" and "goods elasticities of demand change over the year"). Neoclassical economists have a few ready-made explanations for why people have various goods in their closets and garages they rarely or never use. Their purchases were mistakes. They later found better substitutes. They have no such ready-made explanation for why people have things in their closets and garages that don't have, and may never had, intrinsic values that are negative or lower than their prices.

Thaler has filled in the conceptual void in neoclassical economics. He argues there are two sources of consumer utility for buyers, "acquisition utility" and "transaction utility."[37] The former is the net consumer surplus in neoclassical theory. The latter is the "perceived value of the deal" itself that buyers get from an especially good price at the time of the purchase, or the added value derived from the "difference between the amount paid and the 'reference price' of the good."[38] The separation of these two utility sources can help explain a conundrum for neoclassical economists, why many (not all) people have closets and garages filled with unused, or rarely used, goods, for example, shirts, shoes, and tools. Especially good deals can cause people to buy goods when the transaction utility more than offsets the negative difference between the good's price and its acquisition utility (a line of argument that reintroduces a form of rational assessment in behavioral consumer theory).

Thaler has found that his subjects will indeed be more prone to buy goods with the sale price exceeds even high reference prices. He asked half his subjects to imagine that on a hot day at the beach, they could only buy beers at an expensive hotel. He told the others that they could only buy beers from a "small, run-down grocery store." He then asked the two groups for the maximum price they would pay for beer. The first group gave an average maximum price of $2.64 in 1984 dollars. The average given by the second group was $1.50 in 1984 prices.[39] (Note that no mention is made of the differences subjects imagined in the ambience (and maybe risks) of the two buying locations, and, also, not all subjects in the second group likely gave prices that were lower than the lowest prices given by subjects in the first group, a fact not mentioned in Thaler's report on the experiment for general audiences, which is understandable, but hardly inconsequential for inducing a truly *general* generalization.)

Sunk Costs

Neoclassical economists insist that sunk costs are dead costs, already incurred and gone forever. They are not really costs for current choices and, accordingly, should be ignored, or not considered in decisions (nothing can be done about them in current decisions). Behaviorists insist, sunk cost does matter, or at least people choose, in their experiments and surveys, as if they matter. Consider a study done in the late 1950s involving different levels of initiation demands for three groups of students wanting to join a discussion group[40]:

- The first group of students was put through a "severe" initiation (as judged, supposedly, by the standards of the era): They were required to read aloud sexually explicit material.
- The second group was given a "mild" initiation. They had to read aloud tamer materials.
- The third group did not face an initiation requirement involving reading aloud.

Students who endured the severe initiation reported enjoying the discussion group more than the other two groups, an experiment repeated with the same results by others.[41]

In another sunk-cost experiment, Lewis Broad ran an experiment at a pizza parlor, which charged $2.50 for all you can eat, an upfront price the researchers considered to be a sunk cost. Other customers, who were randomly selected on entering, were offered a free lunch. If people were unaffected by sunk costs, then the latter group would eat no more than the first group, as argued by Broad. But the first group consistently consumed more pizza than the control group, supposedly showing that sunk costs affect consumption.[42] Nevertheless, researchers have found that while sunk costs matter, the effect gradually wears off over time.[43] (This latter finding suggests that sunk costs may not matter at all when or if the time frame is sufficiently narrowed that subjects don't have a chance to recognize their mistakes, learn from others, and/or to economize over a sequence of such upfront purchases.)

Behavioral Finance

Behavioral finance scholars have produced a mountain of research seeking to disprove Eugene Fama's "efficient-market hypothesis." Fama argued in the early 1960s that all stock and real estate prices correctly reflected their underlying economic values, given all available, current and future, information on their values.[44] In this regard, market prices are "efficient." Consequently, even experienced investors, who seek to pick "winners" and discard "losers," have difficulty beating the rate of return for the market taken as a whole (as represented by, say, the S&P Index). This is because stock prices accurately reflected their underlying economic worth.[45] Prices are "information efficient." (No one should expect stock and real estate prices to reflect considerations that are unknown and can't be known at the time or information that, if potentially available, is not widely available and can't be except at estimated costs that exceed the estimated benefits of securing the information.)

It is also hard to predict stock prices because changes in them depend on *new* information, which, because it is *new*, could not be known in advance of its revelation. Ever-watchful rational investors would quickly force market prices to capture the new relevant information, if the information were readily and widely available. Behaviorists were initially skeptical of the Fama's hypothesis, and have remained so, mainly because market prices seem to move often without any apparent cause (to outside observers), or without some new information event, and often for seemingly unrelated events, such as weather events.

Much behavioral finance literature suggests that investors are often no more rational in their decision-making than consumers, and both investors and consumers are affected by a host of biases and conditions seemingly unrelated to financial markets, such as weather and the salience (or prominence) of information, new or old.[46] Moreover, investors have been found to be subject to "irrational exuberance" and "bubble thinking." Because stock prices have gone up in the past, investors might continue to buy, even without new information, because people could be captured by the same "bubble thinking" and believe in some "new economy story" that justifies price/earnings ratios moving away from their historical trends.[47] The realities of the stock market dot.com bubble in the late 1990s and the housing bubble and crash in the first decade of this century have understandably caused many finance researchers, especially newly minted PhDs, to retreat from research founded on the efficient-market hypothesis and to embrace research grounded in behavioral finance, and behavioral economics more generally.

The Growing Divide in Economics

Clearly, modern economists' inquiries (especially when behaviorists are included) now cover more areas than when Robbins declared that scarcity in the external world is the discipline's core unifying concern (especially since Robbins, his contemporaries, and his followers put psychology outside the "economic" domain). As I have noted, Robbins' observed in the early 1930s, "We all talk about the same things [generalizations], but we have not yet agreed what it is [at the methodological foundation of the discipline] we are talking about."[48] Today, whether we economists of different methodological stripes are talking about the same thing (or things) is not at all clear. Perhaps we are even talking at cross purposes, engaging in an intellectual struggle among competing methodological factions for professional dominance.

In challenging the rationality premise, many behaviorists have moved into the study of the brain and its decision-making capacity. That arena was largely off-limits, ignored, or overlooked in neoclassical economics—until relatively recently, surely partially in response to behaviorists' methodological and policy challenges.

However, the behaviorists have largely left behind their neoclassical economic analytics but, at the same time, have retained interest in topics that have economic dimensions, preferring to focus on the brain's demonstrated limited capacities and foibles. They have not in a formal way considered the brain as an economy unto itself, whose identified limitations and failures in behaviors have evolutionary and economic foundations, grounded in an efficient, rational approach to scarcity both within the brain itself and in the external world. Rather, behaviorists have encircled rational decision-making behind evolved "boundaries" (as in "bounded rationality"), found to be ever tighter through their growing array of findings from surveys and laboratory experiments. Their proscribed boundaries for human rationality are more or less given, fixed, and exogenous to their analytical methods (although many behaviorists might see the boundaries as growing with their discoveries of new biases, weaknesses, and limitations in decision-making.

In this chapter (and book), I seek to revive Robbins' quest to find a unifying theme in the ever-expanding breadth of economists' inquiries. I accept the behaviorists' position that neoclassical economics (without revisions) is no longer "good enough." However, in search of a "unified field theory," by which I mean a conceptual framework that brings coherence among insights developed in neoclassical economics and behavioral economics, I remain dedicated, to the extent that I can, to Robbins' scarcity paradigm (or his insistence that *scarcity*, or a form of it, is at the discipline's core). That is, I seek to retain all the trappings of neoclassical economic analytics, grounded in maximization, optimization, and equilibrium constructs, but with an important adjustment: *The scarcity in the external world intrinsic to the worldview of neoclassical economists is no longer the key unifying theme; rather, the ultimate but unheralded scarcity that can potentially unify neoclassical and behavioral economists is the internal scarcity of the human brain.*

More directly, I assert that the ultimate scarce resource for economists of all persuasions in the conduct of their analytics—as well as the analytics of their subjects (investors, producers, consumers—and even themselves as economic educators)—is the human brain. I use scarcity as involving the same pervasive type of conflict economists have always used: The brain must cope with the expansive demands placed on its limited neuronal and energy resources as best it can, which means as efficiently and rationally as it can within its evolved resource and process constraints. Below, I will comment further on the excessive demands the brain faces and on its limited resource constraints.

Recognizing the scarcity of humans' mental powers, including economists', I make the degree of actual human "rationality" in decision-making endogenous to a revised economic conception of the world, which requires reformulating economists' models: In my reconstruction of economics, I argue that many less-than-perfect and even wrong decisions in the use of external resources are not only expected, but are also efficient and rational. This means I imbue rationality with a more expansive and useful construction of economic life and methodology than heretofore appreciated. *Indeed, my proposed reformulation of the discipline's foundation leads to the conclusion that perfect rationality for human decisions (not for their brains), as normally conceived, is perfectly irrational from the perspective of the human brain's scarcity and maximizing, optimizing problems.*

Like all premises, my starting premise is a claim that, if not exactly true in all regards (attributable in part to high variability in all aspects of human life), is approximately true and workable or "good enough" (and far better than neoclassical economics provides) for deducing testable predictions and generalizations regarding the behavior of "representative people," or a sizable segment of people in their economic (especially commercial) spheres. Accordingly, my founding claim can be restated: *The human brain is efficient and rational, and, for clarity and ease of analysis in my reconstruction of the foundation of the discipline, the human brain is* perfectly *efficient and* perfectly *rational—and has evolved to be so constructed.* Thus, my premise is workably compatible with neoclassical and behavioral economics, although its relevance is limited to an underappreciated scarce resource that is a major step removed from all other external scarce resources that have been neoclassical economists' central concern.

However, do understand that I do not mean to suggest that the human brain is operating at all time at full capacity and full throttle, with complete precision and correctness in its own use of its resources (much less in the use of external resources). Its efficiency and rationality must be construed as optimal multifunctional relationships between the brain's use of its own internal resources and the value it receives from the decisions it makes, internally and externally, given the myriad of demands made on it. The human brain would not likely have evolved to always operate at full capacity and full throttle and with full precision and correctness. To do so, it would have increasingly wasted its scarce energy and neuronal and energy resources on progressively lower marginal values in use of its limited resources as it shifts toward full capacity and throttle, progressively depriving its host of larger developmental advantages in other parts of the body.

Rather, I am suggesting that the human brain always seeks to match appropriately, as best it can, given evolutionary constraints, the marginal costs, and benefits of its decision, knowing its own physical limitation and the limitations and deficiencies of the sensory data inflows. This means that, I posit, the brain's efficiency and rationality are different in different circumstances, meaning it is endogenous and variable to the brain's own economy, all else held constant. But I also posit that not all else has to be held constant, or ever will be. This is the case because by the brain's design, it has a capacity for learning (which I interpret as adjustments, most often, but not always, improvements, in its decision-making algorithms), and learning can reposition the multifunctional relationship I have described.

To be clear, I do not mean to suggest that the human brain ever goes into "idle," or goes to sleep, for much the same reasons that the heart never idles or goes into sleep mode, and can't because of the obvious deadly consequences. At the very least, the brain must have a standby mode, involving cross-circuit signaling, just to be ready to take action in fight-or-flight decisions, if nothing else. The brain must work with other parts of the body to keep them going and in sync with appropriate responses to ongoing internal and external sensory flows. Any lax time the brain has, such as when the brain's host is asleep (or just daydreaming), it can sort through (perhaps via dreams) experiences of the day, reconsidering, and making yet-noticed connections among them, fortifying memories of some and setting aside and dismissing others.

An efficient brain should not be expected to deal with all of its tasks in periods of high demand on it resources, simply because of the economics of its resource allocation problems. This means that in downtimes the brain can also undertake delayed maintenance set aside during times of intense demands on neuronal resources. It can clean out accumulated debris and repair neuronal connections, and it can make a multitude of decisions on which short-term memories are worthy of being shifted to long-term memory.

In addition, it can make calculated (cost/benefit) assessments regarding the discarding of unused or rarely used long-term memories. For example, the brain could decide to retain some unused or rarely used memories because the energy required to delete the memories is estimated to be greater than the energy required to leave the memory embedded.

Evolutionary (and economic) forces make my premise far more palatable to a wider range of analysts than now is the case for the perfect rationality premise in neoclassical economics and the deduced irrationality premise in behavioral economics, with both premises exogenous to both camps' economic investigations. Moreover, as I will show, my reconstruction of the discipline has powerful predictive power, which is no less so, and maybe more so, than neoclassical economics. It also has the significant advantage of being able to predict, or explain, many behavioral findings on flawed decision-making.

I propose scarcities at two levels, first and foremost, at the level of the human brain that has its own internal economy founded on the scarcity of its own resources as it copes with the complex interacting and competing demands of the body and external environment and its own internal physical processes. Of course, the brain must use its scarce resources to optimize its efforts even as it optimizes the second level of scarcity, that in the external world, the usual domain of economic analysis. This unheralded but ongoing dual optimization effort necessarily complicates processes of optimization/maximization of human wants.

Equilibrium processes are also complicated because of the interactions of the two scarcities on decision-making. I hasten to add that I employ equilibrium only as a conceptual/analytical device for thinking (a framework too often not acknowledged, with equilibrium represented something real of market forces in real life). Equilibrium is not something that exists "out there," nor is it something desirable, to be sought after, and it need not have ever been achieved or achievable in real-world markets, as critics of economic analytics seem to believe to be its purpose for neoclassical economists. Again equilibrium is an analytical construct that serves an analytical purpose, which is to reduce the immense complexity of analysis of human behaviors within markets (or other spheres in which human interactions are ongoing) to manageable proportions within the confines of economists' mental resources.

Behaviorists tout their laboratory experiments—most notably, "gambles"—as the analytical equivalent of "fruit flies" that allow them, as scientists, to test the effects of isolated changes in problems presented to subjects in their confined laboratory spaces to assess their relative responses and effects, yielding, effectively, "snapshots" of fruit fly behavior, or, rather, human behavior.[49] Equilibrium in neoclassical economics remains an analytical means of taking conceptual snapshots of the central tendency of markets (or whatever other institutional setting is under study), given the expansive array of extant conditions and changes in them, which is a perplexing and elusive process that, like all processes, are subject to evolutionary constraints of their own.

More concretely, equilibrium in supply-and-demand-curve analysis permits economists to take analytics one step at a time. Demand is first derived and introduced in the "model." Supply follows. The central tendency of introduced competition can then be assessed, with equilibrium as being the conceptual central tendency then easily conceptualized, maybe only as a reference point, one that is relevant only when some change in market conditions is considered, and then another and another. Equilibrium in such models mainly has meaning as a central tendency, given each set of specified conditions. But its importance stems from the facts that the construct enables analysts to work within their limited abilities, which is the case of gambles concocted for study as "fruit flies." Both analytical methods are necessarily deficient in their separate ways in seeking the "truth" of human decision-making and behavior. Both methods are abstract, but only in the sense that only a few important relationships have been isolated from the complex real world in which decisions must be made.

As we will see, the brain's own scarcity problem ensures that real people's decision-making and behaviors will not match many predictions grounded in the perfect rational decision-making of neoclassical economics. At the same time, my approach shows how many (not necessarily all) declared-to-be "irrationalities" are likely to be deemed rational (potentially at least) for the brain itself as well as its human host because they enable the brain to operate more efficiently and to make decisions that are more welfare-enhancing in the real world than would otherwise be possible. My approach also helps to explain why economists' pursuit of science through divergent methodologies, neoclassical and behavioral, necessarily proceeds the way it does, using simplified models for complex realities that people face (a path I also must follow in this effort to found the discipline on the economy of the brain).

In effect, I seek to initiate here the development of an economic theory of the human brain that is largely grounded in neoclassical economic analytics (with unavoidable twists), but that explains, *and* even predicts, many of the behaviorists' findings of what behaviorists tout as irrationalities. My approach helps to explain the many ways people fall short of perfect rationality, conventionally conceived, in their observable decisions and behaviors. Indeed, my proposed reconstruction of economics' founding premise and methodology leads initially at least to something of a counterintuitive, maybe puzzling, conclusion: *A perfectly rational human brain, even when operating with perfect efficiency and guided by its own form of perfect rationality, will make decisions and engage in behaviors that often will fall far short of the usual implications of perfect rationality, as behaviorists have found.*

However, my approach leads to a perspective on the implications of scarcity not recognized by neoclassical economists and behaviorists and explains an important point of behaviorists: As conventionally conceived, perfectly rational human decision-making (if it were to exist, which it can't) is suboptimal. That is, human welfare would be lower if people were ever to attempt to be perfectly rational rather than make less-than-perfect decisions, including intentional outright mistakes, within their limited evolved brains. This is because by allowing less-than-accurate and even incorrect decisions (a point that others have made, albeit in different ways[50]), decisions' costs within the brain are lowered. This is to say that economics must be grounded in evolutionary biological forces as they have played out, not as we might wish them to be (a perspective that Thorsten Veblen posited more than a century ago[51]).

From my perspective, specialization and trade improve welfare in the widely appreciated ways in neoclassical economics, through better allocation of scarce external resources. But they also improve human welfare in an underappreciated way: They enable the brain to economize on its own resources, which improves the brain's efficiency and allows people to be more rational than they could and would otherwise be. In turn, people are more efficient in their work and external endeavors than they otherwise would be.

That is, the human brain has a hardwired bias toward seeking or just taking advantage of opportunities for specialization of resources, external and internal to the brain, and mutually beneficial trade. Adam Smith was right on target (more than he could have documented in the late eighteenth) when he observed in the second chapter of his *The Wealth of Nations*:

> This division of labour, from which so many advantages are derived, is not originally the effect of any human wisdom, which foresees and intends that general opulence to which it gives occasion. It is the necessary, though very slow and gradual consequence of a certain propensity in human nature which has in view no such extensive utility; the propensity to truck, barter, and exchange one thing for another.[52]

Smith doesn't explain the origins of his "certain propensity." I offer at least a suggestion for Smith's "certain propensity" and its prevalence within human societies across all regions and cultures in the world.

In developing such points, I understand that I am building on others' insights and positions.[53] Indeed, I accept the many important claims, arguments, and findings of behaviorists from Herbert Simon to the more contemporary economists, that people are subject to "bounded rationality" or that the extent of their rationality is contained to something less-than-perfect rationality by available reliable information, imperfect senses, cognitive resources, and limited time for decision-making.[54]

My contribution to my proposed shift in the foundations of economic science comes mainly in my reframing past discussions of the human brain's limitations in order to treat the human brain as an economy unto itself that has evolved to optimize on the use of its own limited resources. I will show in the following chapter how my reconstruction of the essential scarcity in the discipline could lead to a host of predictions, not all of which are covered by neoclassical and behavioral economics. Throughout, I occasionally show how my reconstruction alters how economics education must be revised and how economic inquiries are conducted. I start my reconstruction with a review, in skeleton form, of how evolutionary forces through millennia have shaped the size, operations, and limits of the human brain. I then discuss the implications of the brain's evolved size, structure, and operations and people's decision-making capacities and proclivities.

In describing my reconstruction of the foundations of economics, I seek to accommodate those who have no more than a nodding acquaintance with evolutionary biology and psychology, neuroscience and, for that matter, behavioral economics (or who may have forgotten much of what they studied years ago). At the same time, I seek to introduce enough relevant details of these noneconomic disciplines to convince readers that I have consistent and coherent reasons, grounded in soft and hard science, for pressing for a repositioning of economics' scarcity foundation.

Evolutionary Constraints on the Human Brain

In his *Origins of the Species*, Charles Darwin's essential thesis is as elegant and relevant to economics today as it caused a monumental paradigm shift in biology in the late 1800s: All species of plants, insects, and animals—including humans, of course—evolved over an extraordinarily long period of time through "natural [and sexual] selection," a competitive process in which species struggle against each other for survival and the opportunity to propagate. Variations (even at the DNA level, which was only identified long after Darwin's death) are endemic to the life of species, and those variations of a given species that better fit their local environments throughout evolutionary history had a selective advantage, which increased their odds of survival and, hence, propagation.[55] Darwin mused (surely with his own interest in breeding pigeons in mind):

> Under domestication, it may be truly said that the whole organization [of the natural world] becomes in some degree plastic...Can it then be said, be thought improbable seeing that variations useful to man have undoubtedly occurred that other variations useful in some way to each being in the great and complex battle of life, should sometimes occur in the course of thousands of generations? If such do occur, can we doubt (remembering that many more individuals are born than possibly survive) that individuals having any advantage, however slight, over others, would have the best chance of surviving and procreating their kind? On the other hand, we may feel sure that any variation in the least degree injurious would be rigidly destroyed. (Darwin 1859, p. 130)

Energy Demands of the Human Brain

Through the eons of evolution, the serious struggle of all life forms has been to obtain the next meal and, thus, secure sufficient energy to power existence until another meal could be found, and between meals, to escape becoming a meal for predators. That struggle may have been particularly acute for humans who have had to rely on their mental faculties, not physical prowess and strength, to find the energy required for their large brains (relative to body size). Indeed, the scarcity of energy was probably one of a number of nonconsequential driving forces behind the growth in the human brain.[56] If energy had been less scarce than it was, humans with relatively larger brains may have had less selective (relative) success because people with smaller brains (and less cunning) could have been able to survive and propagate with greater frequency.

A widely recognized limit on the growth in the human brain was its co-evolution with human reproduction and births. Babies with large brains could have been thwarted at the starting gate, or the birth canal, given that the larger human brain could have caused the death of their mothers and babies. Therefore, the size of the human brain and the birth canal had to coevolve. Moreover, because the growing size of babies' brains required that they be born "prematurely," or largely helpless, parents had to evolve a proclivity to take care of their offspring for a long period of time, more than any other species.

Economic Limits of Brain Development

However, human brain size and decision-making prowess just as surely had economic limits. A larger human brain demands additional energy, a scarce commodity, which implies unavoidable cost/benefit comparisons on the margin in the mental development of the brain through evolutionary time. (Today, the modern human brain consumes about a fifth of all energy ingested to do its work, including maintaining all bodily functions.) Beyond some point, increases in brain size and decision-making prowess could have become a survival and propagation *dis*advantage: Not only would the larger brain challenge the limits of the birth canal, the energy cost to maintain a larger brain would likely at some point exceed the value of more precise, sophisticated decision-making. Moreover, more energy diverted to a larger, more capable brain would have checked the development and efficiency of other parts of the body, such as those allowing early humans to speedily escape the clutches of predators.

When survival depended on obtaining the next meal, our ancestors, each with local information unavailable to others, understandably developed a decision-making bias for satisfying their own immediate needs and survival goals (or tended to pursue their own "self-interest," as economists have broadly defined that motivation). That is, a narrow focus and pursuit of self-interest at some level had obvious selective advantages: Individuals (at least adults) are understandably prone to know with greater clarity their own interests over the interests of others, which should give rise to a bias, on mental energy grounds, for pursuit of one's own interest over those of even close relevant other (understanding the interests of others is simply more energy demanding than understanding one's own interests).

Those individuals concerned about their own advantage in decisions (up to a point) were more likely to survive and propagate for a number of reasons, not the least of which can be mental energy conservation. Accordingly, psychologists have found—unsurprisingly—in a series of studies that people surveyed approved of autonomous vehicles (driverless cars) with built-in algorithms that permit the sacrifice of themselves and their passengers to save the lives of pedestrians, but they would avoid riding in such vehicles "at all costs."[57]

Nonetheless, without some (not exclusive) focus on a basic, narrow goal like self-interest to guide a multitude of daily choices (say, what foods to seek, where to sleep and socialize), our ancestors would likely have expended much scarce energy in contemplating whose interests would be best served. A focus on self-interest surely could lead to decision mistakes, but the issue must have been whether the costs of mistakes would be more than offset by the value of the energy saved in not having to figure out the motivation for each of a multitude of daily choices. Even attempts to reduce decision mistakes from decision biases could have undercut early humans' survival and propagation chances. Natural selection would be expected to have favored decision biases that optimized decision mistakes or came tolerably close.[58]

Evolved Altruism

However, this doesn't mean that all humans along our evolutionary course did not have (or do not now have) an interest in being altruistic, either out of straightforward selflessness or selfishness. After all, for most of evolutionary history human beings have lived in small groups or tribes for good reasons: protection from predators, including other human groups, and for predation against other species.[59] Sharing for the sake of others' interests must have been a critically important attribute with a selective advantage, a form of group self-insurance. For instance, an individual hunter's success over space and time would likely have varied more than the success of a collective of hunters.

No one should be surprised that modern humans tend to favor the rule of tit for tat in their interactions with others and to favor those within the protective bounds of their groups and tribes, as psychologists and experimental economists have found.[60] Even when individuals are today in "large" groups, in which monitoring is costly, we might expect them to have a bias toward working for group ends, at least up to a point. Surely eons of living in small groups should have engrained concern that "someone" (maybe God) is watching with the intent of enforcing group rules, a predisposition that could be self-reinforcing. If groups have common interests and receive collective benefits from all contributing to the development of the collective good, even when individual contributions are inconsequential, then a tragedy of the commons can emerge—that is, in the absence of an enforcer. With the presumption of the existence of an enforcer (God) with punishment powers in this life and/or the next, then all might contribute to the collective good, and not being able to attribute the added collective value to anyone, all may give credit to the enforcer.[61]

Selfish Genes

Evolutionary biologist Richard Dawkins advanced in the 1970s a theory of sharing and cooperation founded in genetics.[62] He posited a "selfish-gene" theory of evolutionary success grounded in genetic competition for survival and propagation. He built his theory on the premise that genes control what their human hosts think and do, with or without awareness, and genes are controlled principally, if not exclusively, by the drive to maximize their own chances of, effectively, being immortal.

Dawkins and other evolutionary biologists (before and after the appearance of Dawkins' book) have argued that even selfish genes should be expected to have an interest in pursuing, to some extent, the interests of relevant others.[63] After all, genes that promote sharing and cooperation with others (at least, up to some limit) are likely to be more evolutionarily successful. For instance, where opportunities for divisions of labor exist, the fruits of team members' efforts can be enhanced, enabling all to secure larger pieces of an enlarged economic pie, which can result in a higher chance of survival and propagation. In addition, cooperative team (group) efforts, even when driven by genes, also can provide a form of social security insurance and welfare gain, again because variations in individual efforts will likely be greater than those in team efforts. Moreover, teamwork allows for specialization of labor and knowledge, then the brains of all can specialize the use of their own mental resources and operate more efficiently and rationally than otherwise, because they are able to make use of their mental comparative advantages. In Dawkins' words:

> Another aspect of the particulateness of the gene is that it does not grow senile; it is no more likely to die when it is a million years old than when it is only a hundred. It leaps from body to body down the generations, manipulating body after body in its own way and for its own ends, abandoning a succession of mortal bodies before they sink into senility and death.[64]

I should note in passing that by pressing their human hosts to search out opportunities for specialization and trade, genes' chances for survival and propagation are increased in two ways: First, there is the economic effect Smith held dear available external resources would be more efficiently allocated, with an increase in income, which can reduce the controlling force on the survival of subsistence earnings. Second, which emerges from my brain-focused perspective, human brains can reduce the demands on their resources, which can lead to more efficient and rational decisions, and fewer decision mistakes. Improved decisions can further increase incomes, which can add an advantage to the genes' goal of surviving and propagating.

Another way a selfish gene can maximize its own chances of surviving and being passed on to future generations is to exercise a bias toward sharing with those people—specifically, kin—who have the same genes (a perspective dubbed "kin sharing"). Such a predisposition also is intended to provide a form of insurance to individual selfish genes, and the closer the kinship, the greater the likely sharing. Therefore, the selfish gene is more likely to be helpful to its hosts' siblings or children than to the hosts' first cousins, which the selfish gene would be more motivated to help than second and third cousins, and so on.[65]

Dawkins' theory reinforces the presumption for a self-interest bias at individuals' decision level, pressed by their selfish genes. Individuals have a 100% of their own genes, of course, a point I make only to stress that all other's (parents, siblings, cousins, etc.) have a smaller fraction. All humans share many genes as an identifiable species, which means we all should have some genetic-induced interests in others, but that interest is not likely to be as strong as the interest and attention we give to the survival and propagation of our own genes (or put another way, to be genetically induced to help unrelated or distantly related others would require many more others be served by what we do than when we pursue our own interests).[66]

Loss Aversion, Again

For genetic reasons, real people today are unlikely to be as exclusively focused on their own direct selfish ends, narrowly defined, as many neoclassical economists assume is the case for subjects in their models (maybe only for simplification of analytics). While Smith wrote that "we are not ready to suspect any person of being defective in selfishness"[67] and stressed the dominance of "self-love" in economic decision-making, he also recognized a role for "beneficence" (and other virtues), as well as for the rule of tit for tat in helping others.[68] Nonetheless, any charity toward others cannot necessarily be construed as pure altruism (or disinterested concern for one's own well-being).

There are good economic reasons to believe that the scarcity of food caused early humans to be inclined to value losses more than equal gains, which behavioral economists have made a core principle in their economic theorizing.[69] Risks from predators, diseases, weather, and accidents and their associated economic losses abounded eons ago (far more so than today, an obvious observation), which surely caused early humans to evolve a built-in ability, albeit imperfect, to cope with risks. (Plants with no known brains have been found to cope with risks associated with variability in soil nutrients.[70]) Many risks were then a matter of life and death, which suggests a high variance in outcomes in many situations. Early humans existed on or close to a razor's edge of survival, and losses could, and often did, spell death. Beyond some point, progressively larger losses could be expected to progressively increase the chances of death, which suggests that the expected internal value of losses likely rose faster than the losses themselves. For example, $100 in losses might be evaluated at $110, but $200 in losses could be evaluated at $250, and so on. This effect is implied by the preeminent importance of survival and propagation in Darwinian theory.

Moreover, progressively greater gains, *beyond some point*, would lessen the chance that the added gains would increase survival chances or even improve early humans' subsistence standard of living. Early humans had few means of saving their added gains for future consumption, and of course, modern conveniences such as refrigeration, savings accounts, and insurance policies were far in the future (although they surely took some advantage, when they could, of, say, ice packs or desert dooms for food preservation). Also, an upward trend in living standards was likely to be unrecognized among early humans who had very short lifespans (and no measured and known economic records of significant economic improvement over time) and, no doubt, had an understandable built-in reluctance to make long-term investments (far more so than today), especially those with an array of risks and uncertainties attached. Current and progressively larger investments could be expected, beyond some point, to undercut their own current survival chances and the opportunity to pass their genes to following generations. Thus, over the eons, a sizable segment of humans likely evolved brains that became biased toward risk aversion, which we see played out today as people tend to give more weight to prospective losses in their decisions than to prospective gains (a consistent finding at the foundation of Kahneman and Tversky's "S-curve").[71]

Gains and Losses

Today, people should be expected to seek prospective gains that are greater than the prospective losses, and no one should be surprised if people tend to demand higher prices for items they have than they would offer to pay for the same items when they don't have it, as noted, a finding behaviorists have dubbed the "endowment effect." Such behavior doesn't square with perfectly rational decisions, conventionally conceived, but does square with a fully rational brain making efficient decisions *within its own evolved resource constraints*.[72] With stringent living conditions and the urgency of survival way back when humans were likely prone to live by the creed (or heuristic) that "a bird in the hand is worth two [or more] in the bush." What they had (in hand) was known with high confidence; what they didn't have was not as well known, and could not be, given the risks and uncertainties, however slight, that exist before an item is in "hand," physically possessed and experienced.[73] This point may be weakly applicable to goods as simple as coffee mugs which can be thought to be more or less uniform. Surely the point is strongly relevant to more complex goods, say, basketball tickets and steaks, cooked or uncooked with far greater variation in a far greater number of perceived attributes.

According to this line of argument, we can expect modern humans to take more risks than early humans even without a change in risk aversion over the eons (although their risk aversion may have also evolved somewhat). This is likely the case because today modern humans have an array of opportunities to spread and deflate individual risks associated with individual decisions as well as opportunities of greater rewards from their safer diversified portfolios of riskier investments, with the overall risk of their portfolios being modulated by intermediate and longer-term investments that harbor a greater likelihood of added payoffs from economic growth. And, I should note, the prevalence of developed markets today effectively increase people's portfolios of goods and services available to them, which can reduce some forms of consumption risks and people's inclinations to be more risk averse than otherwise.

Of course, we also should not be surprised that any restrictions on future growth and greater rewards can cause risk aversion to rise through a decline in long-term investments in real and human capital in many people's decision-making, which can undercut future growth. (Welcome to the Watts riots of the 1960s and the Venezuela food riots in recent years.) With their far greater income today, which means they can buy a much larger portfolio of goods, modern humans can be expected in many cases to buy, at times, riskier purchases, for the same reasons they can expand the risks of their investments portfolios with greater wealth, which can translate into even larger portfolios and greater wealth. This is to suggest that while loss aversion likely remains hardwired in people's psychic, no one should be surprised if research showed a relaxation of loss aversion over the eons (admittedly, such a research project would prove challenging).

Life Expectancy and Investment

Early humans' short life expectancies, maybe no more than thirty years, surely had a profound effect on their outlook for the future, the evolution of the human brain, and our decision-making practices today. Behaviorists have found that people today are not generally (without training) as adept as economists presume at denying temptations that yield immediate benefits but have long-term cost. In other words, modern humans face some difficulty in appropriately discounting intermediate and distant gains and costs—for example, in their assessments of the pains and gains from smoking and overeating or of payday loans and advanced education, and their propensity to save for retirement.[74]

Long ago there was far less need for and value in making such cost/benefit calculations and comparisons for what we (and apparently, behaviorists) consider the "long run." Developing the skill level to make precise calculations and comparisons over months or years would have been economic nonsense. Indeed, such long-term cost/benefit calculations would have been a waste of energy because proto humans would have had low probabilities of living into what we might today consider to be intermediate futures, much less distant futures. Beyond some point, the calculations themselves would have shortened even their relatively short futures because of the demands such calculations would make on their brains amid a scarcity of brain energy.

Again, we should not be surprised if many people today have difficulty avoiding "misusing," by economists' standards, credit cards with high interest rates and buying more house than they can afford in the long-run with the availability of thirty-year mortgages, especially ones with introductory "teaser interest rates." Also, people's innate ability to resist temptations may have improved, given that their longer life expectancies would cause them to consider more carefully the longer-term costs associated with, say, eating sugary foods. However, people today can still face an "obesity crisis" because the temptations to eat have outpaced the improvements in their ability to resist. (As economist Dwight Lee has stressed to me, "Long ago, humans had a successful hunt after days of stalking and downing a woolly mammoth. Today, they can be said to have had a successful hunt when they pass a vending machine, now ubiquitous.")

The Efficiency of the Human Brain

From an evolutionary perspective, there is no reason to assume that the human brain today is anything less-than-*efficient* (or as efficient as evolutionary forces have allowed) in the use of available resources, a key one being energy to power decision-making through the brain's neurons, supported by glia cells (which, in addition to their duties maintaining neurons, also process information, greatly increasing the brain's processing capacity, but also increasing its energy requirements).[75] If a more efficient design for the human brain were possible amid evolutionary-settled constraints at each point along the eons-long evolutionary timeline, such a design would (likely) have had a selective advantage. Humans with that advantage would have propagated relatively more successfully—assuming a more efficient design was not repeatedly wiped out by, say, volcano eruptions or plagues (but even such catastrophes were a part of the evolutionary constraints through time on the brain's development).

Evolution, it must be noted, is a process driven by within- and cross-species competition without intention. The evolutionary process relies on chance variations in species with relatively more rapid propagation going to those variations that are *relatively* more fit for their immediate circumstances or more able to adapt to their circumstances. Over evolutionary time in relevant geographical locations, the capabilities and capacities of people's brains must have varied along many vectors, most notably the count of neurons and overall size and speed of decision-making processes, key dimensions of people's mental capacities and capabilities. With time and competitive selection, these variations caused the mental capacities of humans to build on top of the more limited brain power structures previously developed.

The brain of modern humans is now something of a *kluge*, or a structure that *could possibly* be redesign for better performance *if*—and the "if" is a very big one—somehow the brain could be reconstructed from scratch, which never has been an option (although the brain is, within limits, "plastic," which means its processes can be improved, again, within limits, through daily challenges and education).[76] But our analyses of human decision-making and behaviors must start with what humans currently have in brain size, structure, and processes, and we must develop our analyses and make predictions based on that reality and not on what we might imagine *could have been* long ago or *could be* today.

As an undirected competitive process, the brain's evolution has always confronted an economic problem: Larger brains with a greater count of neurons, greater volume, greater decision-making precision, and decision-making speed place progressively greater demands on available internal energy resources, which again, were largely in very short supply when the brain was evolving long ago. Even if the human brain had been able to determine its own size and capabilities, it likely would have checked its own growth at the point where increased size undercut the energy available for development of other body parts necessary for survival and propagation—a long time ago, not now.

Of course, the growing cheapness of food and energy over the last two or three millennials and in computer processing and storage capability over the last half-century may very well have already had evolutionary effects on the size and operation of the human brain. No one knows how much time is needed for evolution to make detectible adaptions, especially in complex biological systems (and there is no reason for adaptions to have been made smoothly over time). Many modern humans now have greater concern over ingesting too much energy, and getting heavy, than in ingesting too little. Others must worry more about computers taking their jobs than learning to spell.

Maybe small adaptions already have been underway. If so, they have been made in record time, and maybe the full effects of adaptions may still take centuries, if not millennia. No one can now say for sure. However, evolutionary biologists who once thought evolution could only occur at glacial speed (as Darwin, and maybe even Dawkins, thought) have begun to find evidence in nonhuman species (e.g., pigeons) that significant adaptions, even at the genetic level, have occurred within the time frame of the rise of modern cities.[77] Other researchers have more recently found that the Everglades-based population of snail kites, birds with curved beaks, rapidly dwindled through 2007. This was the case because the bird's main menu item, small snails, was being overtaken by an invasion of much larger snails. However, within a decade or so, the kites have evolved larger beaks for extracting the larger snails from their shells.[78]

The Human Brain on Chess

Chess is played in a confined space according to a few simple rules governing how a small set of pieces may be moved on a game board. The game is greatly simplified by the fact that the pieces don't have minds of their own (something players might never want them to have because the pieces would be unlikely to see the entire chessboard and communicate with each other, which means that players can lose a measure of control over wins and a measure of pride in winning).

Nevertheless, even though chess is a simplified setting, a player's alternative moves at any point can be voluminous and exceedingly complex, because moves lead to counter moves that introduce a sequence of consequences that are not readily predictable at any point throughout the game (a good reason chess games don't always end in draws). Mastering chess is a formidable mental challenge, and modern chess players spend years (and even decades) honing their skills for understanding and evaluating the full range of alternative move sequences available under ever-changing game circumstances and sequence of opponents. Nevertheless, chess players rely—and must rely—on heuristics, devised from experience, to select strategies and moves to stay within proscribed time limits.

The human brain did not evolve long ago to play chess instinctively well (or to play a multitude of other yet-to-be-conceived games), but rather the invention of chess must have followed the evolutionary development of the brain. The demands of mastering chess through a set of preprogrammed responses to all possible alternative moves from various opponents would have far outstripped the brain's limited resources. Such an evolutionary path might have soaked up enough of the brain's neuronal and energy resources to have stymied the brain's development through natural selection, which, ironically, could have meant human brains may never have been sufficiently advanced to invent the game of chess in the first place! Instead, to play chess (and other games), humans had to have developed the capacity to *evaluate*, albeit imperfectly, the alternative moves and their likely sequential consequences, to compare the alternative evaluations, and then to *choose* among them.

Life for humans is played out in a far less confined space with far more players and far more alternative choice sequences than exist in a chess game. The growth in the human brain greatly expanded human's purview of alternative courses of action, making for an ever-more complex world with which it had to cope. To be successful in the game of life as in the game of chess, the brain needs skills of *evaluation* to cope with a multitude of alternative choices and to discriminate among them. Therefore, the ever-enlarging human brain must have evolved to have the capability for making real *choices*, which is to say that many (if not most, but hardly all) decisions and actions are not, and cannot be, preprogrammed. At one level or another, decisions and actions must be organized around the brain's capability of digesting available germane, often local, information on alternatives without fixed, predetermined responses.

To one degree or another, the brain's responses may be either novel, when conditions warrant, or drawn from similar past decisions made under similar conditions—a form of freedom of decision-making. Species with much smaller brains, or only a nervous system—say bacteria, earthworms, and maybe chickens—may never have gotten beyond automatic responses to stimuli in their relevant environments, which were contained by what their brains could conceptualize. They could not have evolved, and had no need to have evolved, a capacity to make real choices. They just couldn't conceptualize that many options for their behaviors, which might be best described as "responses." Genes might supplement the brain's capacity to make preprogrammed decisions in response to given circumstances, but the ever-changing complexity of environments can also overwhelm the limited count, maybe 25,000, of human genes and their capability to cope with the demands of environments. Then again, genes that facilitated choices would have a selective advantage in complex environments.

To expand on the title of philosopher Daniel Dennett's book, *Freedom Evolves*, some level of freedom of choice (or some such approximation of freedom) and the human brain's ability to make real (even novel) choices must have evolved for good economic reasons.

For the brain to make only fully determined decisions, it seems to me that the task would have required preprogramming the brain with automatic responses to a myriad of local conditions (possibly outnumbering the count of atoms in the universe), which surely would have required an enormous brain capacity and energy usage.

In contrast, having the capacity to make real *choices* even with attendant imperfections and biases must have provided humans with a welfare and fitness advantage, because freedom of choice would free up energy to deal with constantly changing circumstances and interactions and other bodily needs.[79] Dennett fully recognized that human behaviors are extensively determined by genes, the environment, and nurture, although the ever-present prospects of chance and luck abound, which by definition are not determined (or maybe determined only in some weird sense, but are not predictable, given humans' limited knowledge). Thus, the prospect remains that human assessment of options and choices must be, at least to a degree, independent of determining forces (or, maybe better put, "influencing forces"). Many choices might be soaked in an array of biases, miscalculations, and outright mistakes (as behaviorists have found), but these "errors" can be reflections of the brain's evolved efficiency, as we will see.[80] But, then, can these types of "errors" be construed to be what they are called?

To make choices among alternative options with different choice sequences and different ends, the brain also must have evolved a capacity to apply a common denominator with which to compare options. Economists have conventionally considered "utility" or "money" as proxies for whatever common denominator the brain uses. The point is that the brain must resort to a common denominator to avoid the demands of preprogramming all responses to all possible decisions and courses of action, and to make comparative decisions that conserve resources. In evolutionary terms, a brain that developed an evaluative system, anchored by a common denominator, would have had a selective advantage, or so I would argue must have been the case.

In a chess game, the common denominator can be a single marker, how moves affect players' chances of winning games (or become grandmasters). Even then, chess players don't even try to process all possible sequences of chess moves at every point in the game, and wouldn't try if they could—just too taxing (and energy costly) on their brains. Such players would likely wear down mentally before their games were over, insuring a greater frequency of defeats. Rather, they draw on—and must draw on—brain-rational heuristics from their experience to ease the move decisions, a good reason for why grandmasters must dedicate many years of play before being able to move up to the top ranks of chess players.

In the game of life, the denominator will likely be more general than in the game of chess because so many games will be played in life more or less simultaneously, such as how various categories of decisions contribute to the players' chances of survival and propagation. Even then, players' chances of survival and propagation can be affected by a consideration that affects their survival and propagation as they move among the "games" they play, their individual welfares.

Now, we must add some details on the scarcity conflict within the human brain. If I am wrong in asserting a perfectly efficient, rational human brain as a founding premise, I can retreat, I think, to more solid ground underneath my position, which is Friedman's methodological escape hatch, that "perfect rationality" in decisions is "good enough" for economic modeling. If the premise I adopt is close enough to how the brain must work, with *net* attendant gains in simplifying the analytics, then a multitude of implications for human rationality, economic education, and even public policies should be borne out in real-world examinations of people's decisions and behaviors. I already have noted how a number of key behaviorists' findings are consistent with predictions made from a brain-focused view of economic thinking.

Findings in Evolutionary Psychology

While many human choices may not be predetermined or preprogrammed, choices are surely bounded or influenced by genetics that is passed down. Also guiding human choices and preferences for goods and services—their preference functions—are reasonably construed propensities, guided by long-ago evolutionary forces. The human brain obviously has built-in predilections, often "hardwired" in connected clusters of neurons, although these can be overridden and redirected, at least within limits. For example (and the evidence on evolved predilections is abundant), modern humans are overwhelmingly predisposed to heterosexuality, which has an obvious propagation advantage over a homosexual orientation. Women are more predisposed than men to be more selective in their choice of sexual partners because of the extra cost they bear. The nine-month human gestation period provides them with a limited capacity to have children and imposes costs on women for sexual activity that can't be shared completely by men, not directly at least. On the other hand, men may seek to impregnate many women and produce any number of children within nine months. Therefore, they have an evolved propensity, evolutionary biologists argue, to be less sexually selective than women because males who successfully impregnate multiple females pass along their genes with greater frequency[81] (which Dawkins would argue reflects male's selfish genes at work).

Evolutionary biologists have found many other presumably evolutionarily "hardwired" propensities. For example, eons ago (maybe a half-million years or more), when the brain made evolutionary leaps in size and mental power, pregnancy was debilitating, indeed, a life-and-death matter for women. Until as recent as 1900, women had a shorter life expectancy than men partially because of deaths during childbirth. Women also needed support and resources for themselves and their babies both pre- and post-partum, and physical protection from the threat of rape, enslavement, and other dangers. Evolutionary psychologists have found that modern women across regions of the globe, cultures, ethnic groups, and religions tend to seek (obviously, not always successfully) males who are willing and able to make credible commitments of requisite short- and long-term support and protection. Accordingly, women across the planet tend to favor men who are (other attributes being similar) three to four inches taller than they and have a measure of "social status," as evolutionary psychologists David Buss, his colleagues, and other researchers have shown in a small library of studies (with some of the details of their findings relegated to an endnote for space purposes).[82]

People today have demonstrated a propensity to cooperate with one another, especially in small groups of say, 25–150, and to a degree, with kinship being important for group cohesion and cooperation. We also tend to adhere to rules of quid pro quo and reciprocity for largely evolutionary reasons.[83] Economist Paul Rubin summarized a mountain of research in evolutionary psychology, behavioral biology, and the newly emerging subdiscipline in economics dubbed "bioeconomics" when he wrote:

> The groups formed by more cooperative players will do better than groups with less cooperative members, and members of the cooperative group will have more offspring. As a result, the degree of cooperativeness can grow in the population over time. This assortment by cooperativeness has another

> interesting feature. Everyone (cooperator or cheater) would prefer to deal with a cooperator. Therefore, individuals will have an incentive to appear to be cooperators even if they are not.[84]

The prospect of some people pretending to be cooperators means that humans (especially women) have evolved skills to deceive and to detect deception and cheating in their dealings with relevant others (which can mean that the noncooperators must elevate their deception skills with cooperators doing the same for their detection skills, and so forth).[85]

Criminologist James Wilson has argued that most modern people have a "moral sense," which can show up in their willingness to forgo individual advantage (or opportunities to shirk) for the good of the group (or firm). Wilson argued that those individuals who developed a moral sense (which can make them more trusting and trustworthy) and were inclined to cooperate had a selective advantage. The individuals could work together more effectively as a cohesive collective to down prey and fend off predators than individuals or less cohesive groups. Individuals not inclined to cooperate, who simply decided to outrun danger, say, the charge of a sabretooth tiger, could be picked off one by one by tiger.[86] As noted, people's moral sense could have been fortified by those who believed in a higher all-knowing and all-powerful God, who may or may not have had a temper but who was surely believed to be deadset on enforcing rules of behavior ("thy shall not steal, cheat, murder" and so forth), backed by threats or the actuality of serious punishments. Such religious beliefs might have enabled believers to incur lower monitoring costs, which increased their welfare and survival and propagation chances.

Moreover, experimental economists have shown people will be more likely to cooperate when the shares of whatever is being divided are more or less equal, with women more inclined to favor "equal shares" than men.[87] People are willing to extend favors in cooperative ventures in the knowledge that the favor will be returned.[88] Experiments have shown not only that people are willing to cooperate to a degree, but that some are willing to go a step further and devote some of their own resources to punish shirkers and cheaters, which suggests some form of evolved hardwiring.[89] Cooperation is more likely when people are allowed to communicate with one another and made to feel as though they are members of the relevant group.[90] Also, neuroscientists have suggested that human touch (or more generally, human nurturing), in, say, the form of hugs, is important in children's development and in later adult life because touch promotes the release of oxytocin, a chemical released in the brain that encourages those who hug to become (with variation) more trusting and trustworthy should the situation warrant it.[91]

The central point that emerges from the evolutionary psychology literature is that rationality today, as well as the goods and services people seek, is bounded to one degree or another on many sides by the evolutionary forces that have been at work through human history, not just by current external resource constraints. Choices can never be open, at least not fully, and my brain-focused construction of the discipline allows for conceptual connections among the interests, methods, and findings of a number of disciplines adjacent to economics and economic analytics. For example, a link can be drawn, as has been drawn between brain chemistry, activated by human touch and credible commitments, to human decision-making, trust/trustworthiness, transaction costs, trade, and economic growth (all of which can have reverberating effects on trade and trade policies).[92]

Hardwired Choice Responses and the Brain's Efficiency

With many "automated" (or semi-automated) decisions and behaviors operating outside the scope of consciousness, and often ahead of awareness of the relevant sensory information and responses, the brain is free to focus its limited cognitive resources and efforts on other matters with greater efficiency and rationality, which increases the chances of a rise in people's welfare, survival, and propagation, individually and collectively.

Also, the brain has evolved a capacity through learning to automate, or just speed up, many decisions and actions, which can improve current welfare and survival and propagation chances. When individuals first learn to drive, they often do not look over their shoulders when changing lanes. They initially have to use their cognitive capacities to remember to glance over their shoulders, but with practice (and close calls), the cautionary move can become routine or even habitual, often with lower costs and without or before awareness. Basketball players spend hours practicing their jump shots, at first thinking carefully about how to square off before attempting the shot and then how to add the proper spin on the ball as it is released. With perseverance, the required neuronal operations, including communications among neurons and various body parts, become at least partially offloaded from the brain's limited cognitive resources to "muscle memory," which again releases neuronal (memory) resources for other duties that muscles can't perform, improving player performance in other aspects of their games, following the dictates of proscribed plays. Eventually, and often, athletes cannot explain exactly how they perform at the level they do under ever-changing external conditions.

Similarly, seasoned economists steeped in a long sequence of applications of economic theory who see just a hint of overt and hidden price changes on consumption (such as the increased use of paper towels when people are confident that the discarded towels will be recycled or reports of greater pain experienced when cash is used for purchases instead of credit cards[93]) will think "demand curves," often within milliseconds, close to requiring no thought at all. When they are also asked about opportunity and sunk costs, they will point (with very limited thought) to frequently missed opportunities for business people to make greater profit through recognizing full costs and then equating all costs and all benefits at their respective margins, a well-honed rule (heuristic) for maximizing profits and welfare. Early humans were unlikely to have been pressed to hone such basic analytical skills when so many decisions involved life-and-death (or 0/1) outcomes, although marginal decision-making was surely common when outcomes were not 0/1. When economic heuristics become well-honed, they can, again, release cognitive resources to advance the level of analysis, and this can be the case even when the heuristics result sometimes in mistaken thinking.

Still, even with many decisions more or less automated, the brain is left with substantial spheres of cognitive responsibility and influence. Hence, the brain must economize and optimize within the constraints of its available resources, structure, and mental processes that evolved in pursuit of the organizing goal of all living things: survival with procreation through natural and sexual selection. So far, the brain with its current resources, architecture, and processes have passed the survival test, which means that through time the brain has had a central tendency to evolve in ways that optimize (not perfect) its use of available internal energy to maximize the chances of survival and procreation.[94] Those early humans who honed their mental optimizing processes and skills likely had a fitness advantage.

However, evolution was unlikely to leave modern humans with little to no capacity to shift automated decisions to cognitive ones through learning "new tricks," which could mean developing new and improved alternative ways of thinking and enhanced decision-making—but only when economical. Therefore, as the ever-enlarging brain sought to efficiently employ its limited but growing neuronal resources, the capacity to learn likely had a selective advantage. Those early humans who developed roughly the economic way of thinking often had fitness advantages. However, as evident by current thinking deficiencies of economic students, perfecting (or even widely adopting) the economic way of thinking probably didn't make evolutionary and economic sense. But then, perfection is never a viable option in evolutionary biology and economics. There are good evolutionary reasons that today students (and maybe all other noneconomists) have built-in resistance to adopting *homo economicus* being a behavioral model to be emulated. It's hard for them to recognize him in others or themselves, and understandably, given their evolved current predilections in making many decisions with heuristics that have been widely adopted because they do not always yield correct decisions.

The Interconnectedness of Specialization and Trade and the Size and Efficiency of the Human Brain

In our discussion to this point, we have followed how the human brain can be expected to seek out avenues for specialization and trade to economize on its own and external resources, making for greater brain efficiency and welfare through more rational decision-making. However, we must note before closing this chapter that the efficiency gains from specialization and trade can come to the release of resources the brain would otherwise need to use to advance other bodily functions. This can mean that long stretches of evolutionary time, specialization and trade can affect, say, the size of the human brain. Interestingly, evolutionary biologists have found that when early humans began gradually moving from societies of hunter-gatherer and farmers and herders, maybe 50,000 years, the human brain began to contract somewhat in size, perhaps, partially *because* of the greater opportunities for specialization and trade in agricultural societies.[95] This suggests that specialization and trade can give rise to a greater urgency to find means of specialization so that humans could stay within the shrinking limits of their mental resources. Even Smith decried the effects of growing specialization of production tasks in the then growing modern manufacturing firms.

He stressed how specialization of labor in factories could corrode workers' mental faculties:

> He naturally loses, therefore, the habit of such exertion, and generally becomes as stupid and ignorant as it is possible for a human creature to become. The torpor of his mind renders him not only incapable of relishing or bearing a part in any rational conversation, but of conceiving any generous, noble, or tender sentiment, and consequently of forming any just judgment concerning many even of the ordinary duties of private life.[96]

Concluding Comments

Lionel Robbins in the early 1930s explained how economists, then undertaking myriad and disparate inquiries, could find unity of purpose and methods by recognizing the simple the fact of *scarcity* in all of life, the unavoidable conflict between limits of means in consumption and production and the virtually unbounded demands on those means. In the next chapter, I extend my efforts to find unity of purpose and methods by rethinking the scarcity foundation of the now sparing camps of behavioral and neoclassical economists. I point to the human brain as the ultimate scarce resource with which economists must cope, with that essential scarcity showing up in the constraints on their subjects' decision-making and in their own capacity to think through the complex decision-making processes of their subjects. It is also the best candidate we have for a source of human decisions that are optimally efficient and rational, which will necessarily result in some level of decision errors.

Notes

1. Adam Smith wrote: "How selfish so ever man may be supposed, there are evidently some principles in his nature, which interest him in the fortune of others, and render their happiness necessary to him though he derives nothing from it, except the pleasure of seeing it…The greatest ruffian, the most hardened violator of the laws of society, is not altogether without it" (Smith 1759, pp. 193–194).
2. For example, Becker argued that suicide could be discussed in cost/benefit terms, leading him to conclude that suicide should be a legal way of life termination, but he recognized that in policy deliberations due consideration should be given to the fact that people may not always commit

suicide in strictly rational terms: "Although I support the right to suicide, ideally it is best to have a cooling off period to make sure that a suicide is not attempted in a moment of great agitation that will pass before long. For example, a teenage boy may hang himself because he is bluntly rejected by his girlfriend. If his hanging were prevented, he would likely have realized in a few months that he will be attracted to other girls as much or more than to the one who rejected him. He would be ashamed that he was so upset by her rejection" (Gary Becker, Becker-Posner Blog, February 5, 2012).

3. See Simon (1957), Friedman (1966, Chapter 1).
4. Lewis (2016).
5. See McKenzie (2010, mainly Chapters 6 and 10).
6. See Ariely (2008), Kahneman (2011), Thaler (1991, 1993), and Thaler and Sunstein (2009).
7. Skouras et al. (2005, p. 362).
8. Thaler (1992, p. 198).
9. Thaler and Sunstein (2008, pp. 6–7).
10. Ariely (2008, p. 28).
11. Camerer and Loewenstein (2004, p. 3).
12. Becker (1962, 1971, Chapter 2).
13. Thaler (1991, p. xiii).
14. See Becker (1962, 1963, 1971), and Kirzner (1962, 1963).
15. Ariely (2008, p. 25).
16. Ariely (2008, pp. 26–29).
17. Ariely (2008, p. 26).
18. Ariely (2008, pp. 51–53).
19. Ariely (2008, pp. 53, 54).
20. Kahneman and Tversky (2000a, p. 6).
21. Kahneman and Tversky (2000b, p. 21), citing Allais (1953).
22. Kahneman and Tversky (2000b, p. 21).
23. Weber and Camerer (1998).
24. Genesove and Mayer (2001).
25. Kahneman and Tversky (1979).
26. See Tversky and Kahneman (1981).
27. Kahneman and Tversky (2000a, p. 5).
28. Loewenstein and Sicherman (1991).
29. Kahneman and Tversky (2000a).
30. Kahneman and Tversky (2000a, p. 12).
31. Pratt et al. (1979).
32. Leclerc et al. (1995).
33. Thaler (2000b, p. 274).
34. Ariely (2008, pp. 129–133).

35. Kahneman et al. (1990, p. 1325).
36. Thaler (2000b, pp. 273–276).
37. Thaler (2000a, pp. 248–249).
38. Thaler (2000a, p. 248).
39. Thaler (2000a, p. 248).
40. Aronson and Mills (1959).
41. Gerard and Mathewson (1966).
42. As reported by Jones and Cullis (2000, pp. 75–76).
43. See Arkes and Blumer (1985), Gourville and Soman (1998).
44. Fama (1965a, b).
45. See the early work of Cowles and Jones (1937).
46. For an array of behavioral finance studies, see Thaler (1993, 2005).
47. Shiller (2005, 2008).
48. Robbins (1935, p. 1).
49. See Kahneman and Tversky (2000a, p. 3).
50. Gigerenzer et al. (1999a, b), Gigerenzer (2008).
51. See Veblen (1898).
52. Smith (1776, I.2.1).
53. I freely acknowledge that my methodological perspective developed here is built on the work of others whose work was mainly covered in the last chapter, most notably, Herbert Simon, Daniel Kahneman and Amos Tversky, Richard Thaler and Gerd Gigerenzer, all of whom made the limitations of the human brain central to their academic and public policy work. However, these and other scholars have largely attended to explaining why the complexity of the human condition and the limited capacity of the observed human brain does not comport with the behavioral implications of perfect rationality, or anything approximate, through inductive science. That is, these scholars have been mainly concerned with asserting some fixed and unspecified limit on human decision-making and then uncovering the gaps between observed behavior and predictions of economic models grounded in perfect rationality. They have not sought, as I understand their works, to posit an efficient, rational human brain on which to build predictions of imperfect decision-making on the part of real people. They have been inclined to see imperfections in decision-making as mistakes in need of corrections through, for example, guidance by others (e.g., through their proposed array corrective "nudges" to alter behaviors). See Gigerenzer (2008), Gigerenzer et al. (1999a, b).
54. Simon wrote, in his first known use of "bounded rationality,"

    The alternative approach employed in these papers is based on what I shall call the principle of bounded rationality: The

> capacity of the human mind for formulating and solving complex problems is very small compared with the size of the problems whose solution is required for objectively rational behavior in the real world — or even for a reasonable approximation to such objective rationality. (Simon 1957, pp. 198, 202)

55. Darwin 1979 (first published 1859).
56. Anthropologists have offered a number of explanations for why the human brain tripled over the last eight to six million years, since humans and chimpanzees took divergent evolutionary paths from their common ancestor, for example:

    - Humans developed genes that diverted energy (glucose) from muscle to brain building, leaving humans far less powerful than chimpanzees. At the same time, with progressively more energy going to their brains, humans were able to develop far larger brains. Modern humans now deploy about 20% of their energy and oxygen intake to their brains, whereas other modern primates' brains use only 7–8% of their energy intake (with all primates today consuming daily about the same number of calories) (Aiello and Wheeler 1995; Fedrigo et al. 2011; Leonard et al. 2003).
    - Early humans evolved agile hands with fingers and opposing thumbs and the ability to walk upright, which likely meant that they could take on more complex, brain-challenging tasks than other species, increasing their predatory successes and affording them more energy for larger brains. Those with larger brains had a selective advantage (Wilson 2012, p. 45).
    - Early humans faced the challenge of a series of ice ages over the last two or three million years, during which the polar ice caps extended into Africa, increasing the continent's aridity. Those who were smart enough to find ways of enduring radical climate changes had a selective advantage (Holmes 2009).
    - Early humans were never endowed with the physical prowess or the raw killing power of big cats or even chimpanzees and baboons. The advancement of their mental power was likely a compensating selective advantage, as it proved to be through their invention of tools, including the development of weapons that improved their predation (and their defenses against predators). Tools facilitated they're obtaining the energy they needed to power their growing brains (Lakatos and Janka 2008).
    - Early humans learned to use fire for cooking, which made meat, an energy-laden food, more digestible. The greater energy enabled the

growth of humans' brains and gave those who developed relatively larger brains a selective advantage (Adler 2013).

- Early humans evolved to be able to communicate verbally, enabling them to organize themselves into progressively larger groups. The growing complexity of group interactions probably afforded a selective advantage for members with relatively larger brains (Dunbar 1998).

57. Bonnefon et al. (2016). However, it is worth emphasizing that any engrained bias toward pursuit of self-interest narrowly defined by economists need not have been controlling, and likely would not have been, given the complexity of human environments that required a human discretion in deciding whose interest should be served to most effectively be served in pursuit of survival and propagation, with such discretion consuming energy and placing another economic limit of decision-making.
58. Neuroscientists James Fallon has reminded me that deviants, such as psychopaths, within the human populations can have positive effects of the rest of the population who, because of the prospects of deviants, must hone their survival skills, which can include remaining alert to deviant, perverse behaviors that seem destructive to the human specie.
59. Similarly, and for much the same economic and survival reasons, brain nuclei often cluster for the purpose of sharing inputs, outputs, and functions, contributing to the brain's efficiency and rationality.
60. Thaler (1992, Chapter 2), citing Marwell and Ames (1981), Kim and Walker (1984), and Isaac et al. (1984, 1985).
61. I developed this economic perspective of God several decades ago (1977).
62. Dawkins (1978).
63. See Hamilton (1963, 1964), and Smith (1964).
64. Dawkins (1978, p. 34).
65. Dawkins (1978).
66. Of course, another way genes' survival chances could have been improved is through shared memes that cause people to differentiate others as relevant "insiders" and "outsiders" from groups, tribes, and countries.
67. Smith continues,

> This is by no means the weak side of human nature, or the failing of which we are apt to be suspicious. If we could really believe, however, of any man, that, was it not from a regard to his family and friends, he would not take that proper care of his health, his life, or his fortune, to which self-preservation alone ought to be sufficient to prompt him, it would

undoubtedly be a failing, though one of those amiable failings, which render a person rather the object of pity than of contempt or hatred. It would still, however, somewhat diminish the dignity and respectableness of his character. Carelessness and want of oeconomy are universally disapproved of, not, however, as proceeding from a want of benevolence, but from a want of the proper attention to the objects of self-interest. (Smith 1759, ¶ VII.II.87)

68. Adam Smith (1759, ¶ 19) wrote in *The Theory of Moral Sentiment*:

> Of all the persons, however, whom nature points out for our peculiar beneficence, there are none to whom it seems more properly directed than to those whose beneficence we have ourselves already experienced. Nature, which formed men for that mutual kindness, so necessary for their happiness, renders every man the peculiar object of kindness, to the persons to whom he himself has been kind. Though their gratitude should not always correspond to his beneficence, yet the sense of his merit, the sympathetic gratitude of the impartial spectator, will always correspond to it. The general indignation of other people, against the baseness of their ingratitude, will even, sometimes, increase the general sense of his merit. No benevolent man ever lost altogether the fruits of his benevolence. If he does not always gather them from the persons from whom he ought to have gathered them, he seldom fails to gather them, and with a tenfold increase, from other people. Kindness is the parent of kindness; and if to be beloved by our brethren be the great object of our ambition, the surest way of obtaining it is, by our conduct to show that we really love them.

69. See Kahneman and Tversky (1979, p. 279). See also Smith (2008, p. 153), citing Plott and Zeiler (2005), Berg et al. (2005), and Isaac and James (2000).
70. Scientists have grown pea plants with half their roots directed toward a pot with a constant level of nutrients and the other half directed toward a pot with variable nutrients. At high levels of nutrients in both pots, the roots in the two pots grew at about the same rate. When the researchers lowered the level of nutrients going to both pots, but kept the nutrients variable in one pot, the plants grew more roots in the variable-nutrient

pot, presumably as its means of coping with the risk of not getting enough nutrients (as reported by Klien 2016).

71. See Kahneman and Tversky (1979, p. 279).
72. See Castro et al. (2003).
73. I understand that behaviorists have found that their subjects will pay less for a coffee cup than one they have. The assumption of the researchers is that the cups are exactly the same, but not necessarily to the subjects themselves, which is what their buy and sell price suggest just as easily as the two different prices suggest that people's preferences are inconsistent in such cases. But as noted in the last chapter, behaviorists have emphasized the extent to which "framing" can affect decisions, and buy and sell decisions are necessarily in different frames, one is held and the other can be potentially held and may not, on close inspection be exactly the same in form and use. In laboratory settings, the researchers may think the cups are the same, but as with the case of the perception of time, choices are truly relative and must be when subjective values are involved. A truly astounding finding would be that the sell and buy prices were consistently the same.
74. As estimated by Castro et al. (2003).
75. Granted, as Gould (1990) has argued, evolution does not necessarily, or always, result in "progress" by selecting the "best" variation in specie available through time. "Mistakes" are likely, given the complexity of evolutionary process for the multitude of species. Evolution does not (generally) have the option to start anew within improved initial designs, which could allow for greater improvements with time. Evolution must always work with and build with current designs and alter them in marginal ways.
76. See Marcus (2008). He defines a "kluge" as "a clumsy or inelegant – yet surprisingly effective – solution to a problem" (p. 2).
77. For a brief survey report of the growing evidence on the speed of evolutionary adaptions of several species, see Schilthuizen (2016).
78. Cattau et al. (2018).
79. Dennett (2003). He writes, "We live in a world that is subjectively open. And we are designed by evolution to be 'informavores', epistemically hungry seekers of information, in an endless quest to improve our purchase on the world, the better to make decisions about our subjectively open future."
80. Admittedly, I find Dennett hardly easy to follow, especially what he means about freedom of choices. If so, I have no problem staking out an independent position: the argument that I have representative as Dennett's is one I wish I had originated, and maybe have. I can rely on my own introspection and deduced assertion that I can, within limits, make real

choices that possibly no one else would make in identical circumstances. I won't debate further the issue of free will/no free will on the grounds that it is an epistemological quagmire where I need not venture for my limited purposes. Real choices within limits for me are real, period.

81. Buss (1986, 1989, 2003), Buss and Barnes (1986), and Buss et al. (1990).
82. See Buss (1986, 1989, 2003), Buss and Barnes (1986), and Buss et al. (1990). Sexual preferences are often obscure and can be surprising. For example, females' receptiveness to sexual advances has been found to vary through their menstrual cycles, peaking when they are ovulating at mid-cycle and are most fertile. During that phase, unattached and attached females are far more likely to go to bars and other venues where males gravitate and are also inclined to show more skin in their dress, supposedly, to show their relatively greater accessibility (and perhaps fertility, as gauged by skin tone, with the presence or lack of blemishes, which can be a partial explanation for wearing makeup). On the other hand, females also have been found to favor males based on bodily odors, which contain pheromones that indicate skin chemistry that is most favorable for conception (see Wedekind et al. 1995).

    Males, who have a far greater reproductive capacity, *if* they can gain access to females, have an incentive, and inclination apparently hardwired in their brains, to spread their "seeds"—and their genes—by impregnating as many females as feasible (and economical). Accordingly, males across the globe have been found to be more inclined to take risks of all kinds than females, perhaps because risky behaviors carry relatively higher rates of (monetary and sexual) returns. When such behaviors pay off, men are able to acquire relatively greater resources, greater access to females, and more progenies carrying their genes and their female partners' genes into future generations (Rubin and Paul 1979).

    Men, on the other hand, have been shown to be attracted to women who are, well, "attractive," with overt physical features obviously influencing their selection. However, researchers have found that "attractive" is significantly defined (unknowingly to most men) by signals from women that indicate their relatively high fertility. Women's health, in itself, is an obvious direct signal of fertility (given the physical demands of childbirth), but also has potential interactive effects of attractiveness on fertility and vice versa. For example, evolutionary psychologists have found that men universally tend to find women with a waist-to-hip ratio of 70% most attractive (which also is the typical ratio for models in *Playboy* magazine). Maybe surprisingly, women's fertility tends to peak at that ratio (see Singh 1993, 1994; Marlowe et al. 2005; Buss 1989; Elder 1969; Taylor and Glenn 1976; Udry and Eckland 1984).

83. Hoffman et al. (1998), and Dawkins (1978).
84. Rubin (2002, pp. 60–61).
85. Trivers (1971, 1985), Frank (2009), and Cosmides et al. (1992).
86. Wilson (1993).
87. Knauft (1991), and Boehm (1993).
88. Trivers (1971), Steiner et al. (1999), and Gintis (2000a, b).
89. McCabe and Smith (1999).
90. Thaler (1992), Ledyard (1995), and Hoffman et al. (1998).
91. Zak (2012).
92. Zak (2012).
93. As reported by Korkki (2016).
94. Darwin (1859).
95. See for example, McAuliffe (2011) where links to several related articles can be found.
96. Smith expounds on his concerns for how specialization can undermine workers' mental and physical capacities:

> In the progress of the division of labour, the employment of the far greater part of those who live by labour, that is, of the great body of the people, comes to be confined to a few very simple operations, frequently to one or two. But the understandings of the greater part of men are necessarily formed by their ordinary employments. The man whose whole life is spent in performing a few simple operations, of which the effects are perhaps always the same, or very nearly the same, has no occasion to exert his understanding or to exercise his invention in finding out expedients for removing difficulties which never occur. He naturally loses, therefore, the habit of such exertion, and generally becomes as stupid and ignorant as it is possible for a human creature to become. The torpor of his mind renders him not only incapable of relishing or bearing a part in any rational conversation, but of conceiving any generous, noble, or tender sentiment, and consequently of forming any just judgment concerning many even of the ordinary duties of private life. Of the great and extensive interests of his country he is altogether incapable of judging, and unless very particular pains have been taken to render him otherwise, he is equally incapable of defending his country in war. The uniformity of his stationary life naturally corrupts the courage of his mind, and makes him regard with abhorrence the irregular, uncertain, and adventurous life of a soldier. It corrupts even the activity of his body, and renders him incapable

of exerting his strength with vigour and perseverance in any other employment than that to which he has been bred. His dexterity at his own particular trade seems, in this manner, to be acquired at the expence of his intellectual, social, and martial virtues. But in every improved and civilized society this is the state into which the labouring poor, that is, the great body of the people, must necessarily fall, unless government takes some pains to prevent it. (1776, ¶ V.1.1.178)

References

Adler, Jerry. 2013. Why fire makes us human. *Smithsonian Magazine*, June.

Aiello, L., and P. Wheeler. 1995. The expensive-tissue hypothesis: The brain and the digestive system in human and primate evolution. *Current Anthropology* 36: 199–221.

Allais, M. 1953. Le comportement del'homme rationnel devant le risqué, critique des postulats et axioms de l'ecole Americaine. *Econometrics* 21: 503–546.

Ariely, Dan. 2008. *Predictably Irrational: The Hidden Forces That Shape Our Decisions.* York: HarperCollins.

Arkes, Hal R., and Catherine Blumer. 1985. The psychology of sunk cost. *Organizational Behavior and Human Decision Processes* 35 (February): 124–140.

Aronson, E., and J. Mills. 1959. The effects of the severity of the initiation on liking for a group. *Journal of Abnormal and Social Psychology* 59: 177–181.

Becker, Gary S. 1962. Irrational behavior and economic theory. *Journal of Political Economy* 70 (1, February): 1–13.

Becker, Gary S. 1963. A reply to Israel Kirzner. *Journal of Political Economy* 71 (February): 82–83.

Becker, Gary S. 1971. *The Economics of Discrimination.* Chicago: University of Chicago Press (originally published in 1957).

Berg, J., J. Dickhaut, and K. McCabe. 2005. Rick preference instability across institutions: A dilemma. *Proceedings National Academy of Sciences* 102: 4209–4214.

Boehm, Christopher. 1993. Egalitarian behavior and reverse dominance hierarchy. *Current Anthropology* 14: 227–254.

Bonnefon, Jean-François, Azim Shariff, and Iyad Rahwan. 2016. The social dilemma of autonomous vehicles. *Science* 352 (6291): 1573–1576.

Buss, David M. 1986. Human mate selection. *American Scientist* 73: 47–51.

Buss, David M. 1989. Sex differences in human mate preferences: Evolutionary hypotheses tested in 37 cultures. *Behavioral and Brain Sciences* 12: 1–14.

Buss, David M., and Michael F. Barnes. 1986. Preferences in human mate selection. *Journal of Personality and Social Psychology* 50: 559–570.
Buss, David M., et al. 1990. International preferences in selecting mates: A study of 37 societies. *Journal of Cross-Cultural Psychology* 21: 5–47.
Buss, David M. 2003. *The Evolution of Desire: Strategies of Human Mating*. New York: Basic Books.
Camerer, Colin F., and George Loewenstein. 2004. Behavioral economics: Past, present, and future. In *Advances in Behavioral Economics*, ed. Colin F. Camerer, George Loewenstein, and Matthew Rabin. Princeton, NJ: Princeton University Press.
Castro, J.M. Bermúdez de, M. Martinón Tores, S. Sarmiento, M. Lozano, J.L. Arsuaga, and E. Carbonell. 2003. Rates of anterior tooth wear in middle Pleistocene hominines from Sima de Los Huesos (Sierra de Atapuerca, Spain). *PNAS* 100 (21, October 14): 11992–11996.
Cattau, Christopher E., et al. 2018. Rapid morphological change of a top predator with the invasion of novel prey. *Nature Ecology and Evolution* 2 (1, November 27): 108–115.
Cosmides, Leda, John Tooby, and Jerome H. Barkow. 1992. Introduction: Evolutionary psychology and conceptual integration. In *The Adapted Mind: Evolutionary Psychology and the Generation of Culture*, ed. Jerome H. Barkow, Leda Cosmides, and John Tooby, 3–18. New York: Oxford University Press.
Cowles, Alfred, and H. Jones. 1937. Some posteriori probabilities in stock market action. *Econometrica* 5: 280–294.
Darwin, Charles. 1859. *Origins of the Species by Means of Natural Selection*. New York: Random House (republished 1979).
Dawkins, Richard. 1978. *The Selfish Gene*. Oxford, UK: Oxford University Press (paperback).
Dennett, Daniel C. 2003. *Freedom Evolves*. New York: Viking Adult.
Dunbar, Robin. 1998. The social brain hypothesis. *Evolutionary Anthropology* 6: 178–190.
Elder, Glen H. 1969. Appearance and education in marriage mobility. *American Sociological Review* 34 (4): 519–533.
Fama, Eugene F. 1965a. The behavior of stock market prices. *Journal of Business* 38: 34–105.
Fama, Eugene F. 1965b. Random walks in stock market prices. *Financial Analysts Journal* 21 (5, September/October): 55–59.
Fedrigo, O., A. Pfefferle, et al. 2011. A potential role for glucose transporters in the evolution of human brain size. *Brain, Behavior and Evolution* 78: 315–326.
Frank, Steven A. 2009. Evolutionary foundations of cooperation and group cohesion. In *Games, Groups, and the Global Good*, ed. Simon A. Levin. Heidelberg: Springer.

Friedman, Milton. 1966. *Essays in Positive Economics*. New York: University of Chicago Press.

Genesove, David, and Christopher Mayer. 2001. Loss aversion and seller behavior: Evidence from the housing market. *Quarterly Journal of Economics* 116 (4, November): 1233–1260.

Gerard, H.B., and G.C. Mathewson. 1966. The effects of severity of initiation on liking for a group: A replication. *Journal of Experimental Social Psychology* 2 (July): 278–287.

Gigerenzer, Gerd. 2008. *Rationality for Mortals: How People Cope with Uncertainty*. New York: Oxford University Press.

Gigerenzer, Gerd, Peter M. Todd, and the ABC Research Group (eds.). 1999a. *Simple Heuristics That Make Us Smart*. Oxford, UK: Oxford University Press.

Gigerenzer, Gerd, and Peter M. Todd. 1999b. Fast and frugal heuristics: The adaptive toolbox. In *Simple Heuristics That Make Us Smart*, ed. Gigerenzer, Gerd, Peter M. Todd, and the ABC Research Group, 1–18. Oxford, UK: Oxford University Press.

Gintis, Herbert. 2000a. *Game Theory Evolving*. Princeton, NJ: Princeton University Press.

Gintis, Herbert. 2000b. Strong reciprocity and human sociality. *Journal of Theoretical Biology* 211: 169–179.

Gould, Stephen Jay. 1990. *Wonderful Life: Burgess Shale and the Nature of History*. New York: W. W. Norton.

Gourville, John T., and Dilip Soman. 1998. Payment depreciation: The effects of temporally separating payments from consumption. *Journal of Consumer Research* 25 (September): 160–174.

Hamilton, W.D. 1963. The evolution of altruistic behavior. *American Naturalist* 97 (896): 354–356.

Hamilton, W.D. 1964. The genetical evolution of social behaviour. *Journal of Theoretical Biology* 7 (1): 1–16.

Hoffman, Elizabeth, Kevin A. McCabe, and Vernon L. Smith. 1998. Behavioral foundations of reciprocity: Experimental economics and evolutionary psychology. *Economic Inquiry* 36: 335–352.

Holmes, Bob. 2009. Did the ice age boost human brain size? *New Scientist*, July 29.

Isaac, R. Mark, and D. James. 2000. Just who are you calling risk averse. *Journal of Risk and Uncertainty* 20: 177–187.

Isaac, R. Mark, James M. Walker, and Susan H. Thomas. 1984. Divergent evidence on free riding: An experimental examination and possible explanation. *Public Choice* 43: 113–149.

Isaac, R. Mark, Kenneth F. McCue, and Charles Plott. 1985. Public goods provision in an experimental environment. *Journal of Public Economics* 26: 51–74.

Jones, Philip, and John Cullis. 2000. Individual failure: And the analytics of social policy. *Journal of Social Policy* 29 (1): 73–93.
Kahneman, Daniel, and Amos Tversky. 1979. Prospect theory: An analysis of decisions under risk. *Econometrica* 47: 313–327.
Kahneman, Daniel. 2011. *Thinking, Fast and Slow*. New York: Farrar, Straus and Giroux.
Kahneman, Daniel, and Amos Tversky. 2000a. Choices, values, and frames, as reprinted in *Choices, Values, and Frames*, ed. Daniel Kahneman and Amos Tversky, 1–16. Cambridge, UK: Cambridge University Press.
Kahneman, Daniel, and Amos Tversky. 2000b. Prospect theory: An analysis of decision under risk, as reprinted in *Choices, Values, and Frames*, ed. Daniel Kahneman and Amos Tversky, 17–43. Cambridge, UK: Cambridge University Press.
Kahneman, Daniel, J. Knetsch, and Richard H. Thaler. 1990. Experimental tests of the endowment and the Coase theorem. *Journal of Political Economy* 98 (6): 1325–1348.
Kim, Oliver, and Mark Walker. 1984. The free rider problem: Experimental evidence. *Public Choice* 43: 3–24.
Kirzner, Israel M. 1962. Rational action and economic theory. *Journal of Political Economy* 70 (August): 380–385.
Kirzner, Israel M. 1963. Rejoinder. *Journal of Political Economy* 71 (August): 82–83.
Klein, Joanna. 2016. Lacking brains, plants can still make good judgements about risks. *New York Times*, June 30.
Knauft, Bruce. 1991. Violence and sociality in human evolution. *Current Anthropology* 32: 391–428.
Korkki, Phyllis. 2016. Paying with cash hurts. That's also why it feels so good. *New York Times*, July 16. Available online from https://www.nytimes.com/2016/07/17/business/paying-with-cash-hurts-thats-also-why-itfeels-so-good.html.
Lakatos, L., and Z. Janka. 2008. Evolution of human brain and intelligence. *PubMed.gov*, July 30.
Leclerc, France, Berndt Schmitt, and Laurette Dubé. 1995. Is time like money? Decision making and waiting time. *Journal of Consumer Research* 22: 110–119.
Ledyard, John O. 1995. Public goods: A survey of experimental research. In *Handbook of Experimental Economics*, ed. John H. Kager and Alvin E. Roth. Princeton, NJ: Princeton University Press.
Leonard, W., M. Robertson, et al. 2003. Metabolic correlates of hominid brain evolution. *Comparative Biochemistry and Physiology Part A: Molecular & Integrative Physiology* 136: 5–15.
Lewis, Michael. 2016. *The Undoing Project: A Friendship That Changed Our Minds*. New York: W.W. Norton.

Loewenstein, George, and Nachum Sicherman. 1991. Do workers prefer increasing wage profiles? *Journal of Labor Economics* 9 (1): 67–84.

Marcus, Gary. 2008. *Kluge: The Haphazard Evolution of the Human Mind.* Boston: Mariner Books.

Marlowe, Frank, Coren Apicella, and Dorian Reed. 2005. Men's preferences for women's profile waist-to-hip ratio in two societies. *Evolution and Human Behavior* 26: 458–468.

Marwell, Gerald, and Ruth Ames. 1981. Economists free ride: Does anyone else? *Journal of Public Economics* 15: 295–310.

McAuliffe, Kathleen. 2011. If modern humans are so smart, why are our brains shrinking? *Discover*, January 20.

McCabe, K., and V.L. Smith. 1999. A comparison of naive and sophisticated subject behavior with game theoretic predictions. *Proceedings of the National Academy of Sciences of the USA* 97: 3777–3781.

McKenzie, Richard B. 2010. Predictably irrational or predictably rational? *Library of Economics and Liberty.*

Plott, Charles, and K. Zeiler. 2005. The willingness to pay/willingness to accept gap, the endowment effect. Subject misconceptions and experimental procedures for eliciting valuations. *American Economic Review* 95 (3): 530–545.

Pratt, John W., David A. Wise, and Richard Zeckhauser. 1979. Price differences in almost competitive markets. *Quarterly Journal of Economics* 93 (2): 189–211.

Robbins, Lionel. 1935. *An Essay on the Nature and Significance of Economic Science.* Auburn, Al: Ludwig von Misses Institute (first published in 1932 and revised and reissued in 2007).

Rubin, Paul H. 2002. *Darwinian Politics: The Evolutionary Origin of Freedom.* New Brunswick, NJ: Rutgers University Press.

Rubin, Paul H., and Chris Paul. 1979. An evolutionary model of taste for risk. *Economic Inquiry* 17: 585–596.

Schilthuizen, Menno. 2016. Evolution is happening faster than we thought. *New York Times*, July 23.

Shiller, Robert J. 2005. *Irrational Exuberance*, 2nd ed. Princeton, NJ: Princeton University Press.

Shiller, Robert J. 2008. *The Subprime Solution: How Today's Global Financial Crisis Happened and What to Do About It.* Princeton, NJ: Princeton University Press.

Simon, Herbert. 1957. *Models of Man.* New York: Wiley.

Singh, Devendra. 1993. Adaptive significance of waist-to-hip ratio and female physical attractiveness. *Journal of Personality and Social Psychology* 65: 293–307.

Singh, Devendra. 1994. Is thin really beautiful and good: Relationship between waist-to-hip ration (WHR) and female attractiveness. *Personality and Individual Differences* 16: 123–132.

Skouras, Thanos, George J. Avlonitis, and Kostis A. Indounas. 2005. Economics and marketing on pricing: How and why do they differ. *Journal of Product and Brand Management* 14 (6): 362–374.

Smith, Adam. 1759. *The Theory of Moral Sentiments*, ed. D.D. Raphael and A.L. Macfie, vol. I of the Glasgow Edition of the Works and Correspondence of Adam Smith. Indianapolis: Liberty Fund (1982).

Smith, Adam. 1776 (reprinted 1904). An Inquiry into the Nature and Causes of the Wealth of Nations. In *Library of Economics and Liberty*, ed. Edwin Cannan. London, UK: Methuen and Co., Ltd. Available online from http://www.econlib.org/library/Smith/smWN1.html.

Smith, J. Maynard. 1964. Group selection and kin selection. *Nature* 201 (4924): 1145–1147.

Smith, Vernon L. 2008. *Rationality in Economics: Constructivist and Ecological Forms*. Cambridge, UK: Cambridge University Press.

Steiner, Mary C., Natalie D. Munro, Todd A. Surovell, Eitan Tchernov, and Ofer Bar-Yosef. 1999. Paleolithic population growth pulses evidenced by small animal exploitation, *Science* 283 (5399, September 25): 190–194.

Taylor, Patricia A., and Norval D. Glenn. 1976. The utility of education and attractiveness for female status attainment through marriage. *American Sociological Review* 41: 484–498.

Thaler, Richard H. 1991. *Quasi Rational Economics*. New York: Russell Sage Foundation.

Thaler, Richard H. 1992. *The Winner's Curse: Paradoxes and Anomalies of Economic Life*. New York: Free Press.

Thaler, Richard H. (ed.). 1993. *Advances in Behavioral Finance*. New York: Russell Sage Foundation.

Thaler, Richard H. 2000a. Mental accounting matters. As reprinted in *Choices, Values, and Frames*, ed. by Daniel Kahneman and Amos Tversky. Cambridge, U.K.: Cambridge University Press, 2000, pp. 241–268.

Thaler, Richard H. 2000b. Toward a positive theory of consumer choice, as reprinted in *Choices, Values, and Frames*, ed. by Daniel Kahneman and Amos Tversky. Cambridge, U.K.: Cambridge University Press, 2000, pp. 269–287.

Thaler, Richard H. (ed.). 2005. *Advances in Behavioral Finance*. Princeton, NJ: Princeton University Press.

Thaler, Richard H., and Cass R. Sunstein. 2008. *Nudge: Improving Decisions About Health, Wealth, and Happiness*. New Haven, CT: Yale University Press.

Thaler, Richard H., and Cass R. Sunstein. 2009. *Nudge: Improving Decisions About Health, Wealth, and Happiness*. New York: Penguin Books.

Trivers, Robert L. 1971. The evolution of reciprocal altruism. *Quarterly Review of Biology* 46: 35–57.

Trivers, Robert L. 1985. *Social Evolution*. Menlo Park, CA: Benjamin-Cummings.

Tversky, Amos, and Daniel Kahneman. 1981. The framing of decisions and the psychology of choice. *Science* 211 (4481): 453–458.

Udry, J. Richard, and Bruce K. Eckland. 1984. Benefits of being attractive: Differential payoffs for men and women. *Psychological Reports* 54: 47–56.

Veblen, Thorsten. 1898. Why is economics not an evolutionary science? *Quarterly Journal of Economics* 12 (4): 373–397, also available online with an introduction by Jean Boulton. 2010. *E:CO Issue* 12 (2): 41–69.

Weber, Martin, and Colin F. Camerer. 1998. The disposition effect in securities trading: An experimental analysis. *Journal of Economic Behavior & Organization* 33 (2): 167–184.

Wedekind, C., T. Seebeck, F. Bettens, and A.J. Paepke. 1995. MHC-dependent mate preferences in humans. *Proceedings of the Royal Society, London* 260: 245–249.

Wilson, Edward O. 2012. *The Social Conquest of Earth*. New York: Liveright.

Wilson, James Q. 1993. *The Moral Sense*. New York: Free Press.

Zak, Paul. 2012. *The Moral Molecule: The Source of Love and Prosperity*. Boston: Dutton.

CHAPTER 5

The Human Brain: The Ultimate Scarce, Efficient, and Rational Resource

Maybe I repeat to the point ad nausea, although I see the repetition as made advisable by the new perspective I seek to expound, which is likely to be more of a challenge to my cohorts in neoclassical economics than in behavioral economics (whom I am sure will have concerns of their own over how my thesis will play out for them): Recognition of scarcity as the controlling force in economics must begin with the ultimate scarcity of resources intrinsic in the human brain. Granted, as noted, much human behavior can be tied to and guided by genes, which can relieve some of the pressure on the brain to "learn" everything from scratch and to come up with (efficient and rational) decisions on everything it confronts in the complex world. Nevertheless, moment by moment the brain faces extraordinary external and internal demands that buck up against its limited (especially, cognitive) resources and the constraints of the brain's evolved biological architecture and processes. Before people can efficiently, and rationally, consider economists' conventional conception of scarcity in the external world, their brains must carefully allocate their own scarce resources. Brains can be viewed as making their allocation decisions in many of the same ways that neoclassical economists have viewed people making allocation decisions for external resources.

R. B. McKenzie, *A Brain-Focused Foundation for Economic Science*,
https://doi.org/10.1007/978-3-319-76810-6_5

Demands on the Human Brain

As all economic scholars have long acknowledged, the external world contains an enormous, complex amount of *potentially* relevant sensory information to which people must apply their mental powers to digest as they pursue their economic interests. Much potentially relevant information for human decision-making is not always obvious, or even readily available, and access to it comes only with an exploration of a range of information sources and their relevant linkages. Even so, information may or may not be relevant, which means the human brain must be predisposed to gamble, and often does, on which potential information to access and evaluate. Moreover, as behaviorists posit, outright uncertainties are ever-present in any effort to access and use competing information inflows that inevitably change as people interact with each other in their continually, if not constantly, shifting local environments. A lot of potential information is simply noise, and weeding out the potentially irrelevant information from the relevant imposes a substantial demand on the brain.

When uncertainties abound in physical and social environments, people must explore. It's the only way uncertainties in decision and behavioral options can be converted to risks, and much exploration may not appear to involve allocation decisions that are rational in neoclassical terms, but they can still be purposive.

The mere existence of probabilities, uncertainties, and noise in information flows ensures that humans will fall short of *perfect* decision-making, or perfect rationality, both of which could not have passed evolutionary tests. Consciously or not, the brain must stop its evaluation of available data well before perfection can be attained because the drain on the brain's scarce energy resources would exceed its benefits, even if neuronal resources were not the constraint they are. The brain itself is subject to accepted "laws" in economics, not the least of which include the law of diminishing marginal returns and increasing marginal costs and diminishing marginal utility.

Separately or together, perfect decision-making and perfect rationality are evolutionary nonstarters. From the standpoint of the human brain, perfect rationality is perfectly irrational. Of course, such cost/benefit calculations presuppose that evolutionary forces have endowed the brain with a capacity to assign values with a common denominator on the benefits and costs of information inflows at the margins (imperfectly, of course). Otherwise, the brain would have no basis for efficiently allocating its limited energy and other resources.

Limitations of the Senses

As everyone knows, the brain accesses the external world through five senses: sight (vision), touch (tactile stimulation), hearing (audition), taste (gustation), and smell (olfaction), with additional information coming from the sense of balance and movement (vestibular) and the sense of determining one's place in the environment (proprioception). These senses have their own limited capabilities, which we must assume have been, to date, as well optimized as possible through evolution.

Obviously, human sight cannot access more than a minor portion of the broad electromagnetic spectrum. Humans don't have anywhere near the visual acuity of hawks. Nor do we have the olfactory capability of dogs and many other animals. Moreover, individual human beings differ, sometimes significantly, in sensory capabilities, and human senses deteriorate with age and circumstances, with the changes affecting assessments of the potential relevance of various information inflows. First and foremost, humans' varying less-than-perfect sensory capabilities constrain the brain's abilities to make decisions with perfection, or even make the same decisions with the same assessments of choice options. People can and do differ, for example, on the value of large ultra HD televisions for many reasons, with differences in incomes and "preferences" being two conventionally identified causes of the differences, but preference differences can also be related to differences in, say, visual acuity (with colorblindness an obvious extreme limitation), which means different people could be experiencing, effectively, (slightly or largely) different "goods" as they watch the same television programs.

Small and Large Daily Decisions

People make an enormous number of small and large decisions in their daily lives. Buying a car may be a sizable decision for most people, but it involves many small decisions: Gas or electric? Color and water-absorbency of floor mats? The combination of a variety of electronic options? And so forth.

People's days are obviously filled with other small, ordinary decisions that are largely independent of one another: Should I awake at six or eight? Should I eat cereal and toast or bacon and eggs (at home or in a restaurant), and then how much of each and how should the meals be prepared and with what? Should I get dressed now or later, and what should I wear? Should I park in a space at the mall twenty feet from the entrance or go ten more feet and pull through, eliminating the need to back out of the space on leaving? Even, should I use the bathroom now or later, which often reduces to the question of when can I most economically interrupt what I am doing, with due respect for bladder limitations?

Most such decisions made during the day must be addressed with incomplete and imperfect information, which requires the human brain to devote its resources to evaluating the information options before determining and evaluating alternatives in choices.

With so many daily decisions (not to mention yearly decisions) that imperfect people are called upon to make, less-than-perfect—even seemingly irrational—choices are guaranteed, simply as a matter of mathematical probabilities and uncertainties (which often are undetected until after decisions are revealed). And as is true of all biological and mechanical systems, human brains have built-in error rates. If these problems did not exist, human beings would not have evolved to be as smart, efficient, rational, and as capable in myriad ways as we are. Indeed, we might not have survived for as long as we have.

Sensory Information Inflows and the Discovery of Decision Imperfections

The behaviorists' half-century hunt to find less-than-perfect decision-making—an unbelievable low bar for any scientific endeavor—was bound to have met with success, especially in their largely artificial (and, at times, other worldly) laboratory environments, intentionally divorced from real-world context in which people under study must operate daily before and after their laboratory experiences. Often, experimental subjects must find laboratory conditions novel in myriad ways. Subjects may only have very roughly constructed algorithms for such decision settings, with the prospects of built-in decision errors, and these settings can be, and often are, devoid of continuing feedback loops that prompt subjects to make corrections. And even if there were feedback loops made available in laboratory settings, those loops would not likely mirror the feedback loops found in the subjects' real-world settings, which have different boundaries and involve different people with different interests and incentives. Such differences are bound to affect decisions at multiple levels. After all, again, behaviorists have found and then taught that the "frames" (including lab settings) for decisions can be inconsequential at times, but they can also be highly influential (unless behaviorists are willing to concede that "frames" are not as important as they have insisted).

Although no one (to my knowledge) has sought to estimate even roughly the amount of potentially relevant information the human senses provide daily, no one doubts the number is overwhelming, beyond the brain's considerable but limited processing and storage capabilities. As a decidedly second-best hint at the size of the brain's information problem—or, more accurately, its information-overload problem—one two-hour ultra HD movie can require more than 42 gigabytes of hard disk storage. Just a full day of movies, one played after the other, could easily overload many memory-endowed laptop computers.

Now consider that the brain's information problems are hardly limited to data from the two senses—sight and sound—used to enjoy an ultra HD movie. Behavioral economist Robert Nease has roughly estimated that a person confronts at every moment ten million bits of information and is aware of just a trivial number, maybe as few as fifty bits (perhaps, partially limited by the brain's processing power but also by its internal heuristics or algorithms that have been honed imperfectly from experience and that tell the brain to ignore a substantial majority of the millions of bits of incoming information, because they are not likely to add value to its internal allocation decisions and/or to the choices made among external options).[1]

In addition, the sensory inflows we confront daily are hardly as simple as single signals sent in one narrow band over a computer's circuitry. On the contrary, sensory inflows contain data that vary in "quality," such as the substance, intensity, tone, depth, validity, and integrity of the information, which the brain must assess using stored experiences, heuristics, and algorithms.

A substantial portion of daily human experiences involves all five (or seven) senses, with the sensory information intermingling in experiences in both the outer and inner worlds of the brain. For example, the sense of taste evolved with the senses of sight and hearing. Perceptions entering are often blended and integrated by the brain to make an accurate assessment of the different information sources, generating another information "output" with which the brain must cope. The exact timing of the information inflows coming from different senses plus the brain's own output flows can make the assessment even more complicated. For instance, when a person touches his nose, his brain must cope with the signals coming from both the nose and finger (as well as from the ears and eyes). The tactile information coming from the finger will reach the brain slightly later than that from the nose (or eyes) because of the greater distance the signal must travel from the finger. Even this slight (maybe better, minuscule) delay complicates the brain's task of integrating the sensory information. Of course, from time to time, if not often, the human brain will fail to integrate the information or misinterpret the data from the various information sources. For example, with eyes closed, subjects can confuse hot and cold touches, a repeatedly confirmed experimental finding (but how many people in the outside world intentionally and blindly touch surfaces they are told could be hot or cold?).

Needless to say, the limitations of the senses to access, assess, and admit some subset of the enormous amount of available surrounding information represents another serious limitation on the human brain's own decision-making capacity and capability, guaranteeing various less-than-perfect actual internal and external decisions and external behaviors.

Conscious and Subconscious Decision-Making

Another challenge to the brain's scarcity problems is the fact that the brain doesn't make a simple decision either to cognitively handle sensory information or completely ignore it, or consider only preliminarily, and then discard the information. Apparently, the brain can use sensory information in noncognitive ways, below consciousness, with some form of parallel processing at work. Michael Polanyi argued that we have "tacit knowledge" from the sensory information that is not directed to the prefrontal cortex for conscious decision-making, but is stored in other parts of the brain without our conscious awareness. There, the information remains available to be processed in conscious and unconscious decisions. According to Polanyi, we often "know more than we can tell."[2] For example, we might not be able to describe a person's face in sufficient detail for someone else to recognize the person, yet we can immediately recognize (albeit it with established errors) the person when we see him or her. Art experts can pick out forgeries (with greater accuracy than nonexperts) of, say, Rembrandt's works when they "see" them, but can't articulate exactly how they identify fakes.

Thus, we make decisions by intermingling what we "know" at some conscious level and what we "don't know" we know, with the same level of clarity outside the conscious domain. No wonder many people give credence to intuition in decision-making and often may not understand how they (we) make as many correct decisions as they (we) do.[3]

In addition to external sensory stimuli, the brain also must cope with a constant flow of information from within the human body, including within the human brain itself. For example, the brain works behind consciousness to keep the heart pumping through approximately 800 million beats over the course of the average human lifespan. It also must control a multitude of complex human activities, such as maintaining the body's balance while navigating ever-changing and uneven terrain, a major challenge for very smart academic researchers seeking to develop autonomous robots that use advanced computers and communication systems. These researchers to date have not been able to create the required feedback loops between the robots' "brains" (computers) and their "limbs" for smooth, error-free movements. As a result, the robots frequently have jerky movements and often fall (or fall more frequently than their human creators) because they are not able to recover when encountering a rock in their paths or some other anomaly not included in their navigation programs (defects that may be eventually corrected, after maybe decades of intense research and experimentation). In contrast, the human brain makes maintaining balance while walking or jogging across uneven surfaces seem relatively effortless and seamless, so much so that stumbles and falls are relatively infrequent, if not rare, for most people (although aging does take its toll on people's balance).

Some decisions—ones involving survival, for example—must be made literally in a flash, even before we, or our brains, are consciously aware of the demands on the brain's resources (so-called flight-or-fight decisions). When survival is at stake, conscious, deliberate decisions are a waste of energy, given the dire consequences of not acting in short order. Indeed, devoting cognitive resources to the issue of "fight-or-flight" could jeopardize the prospects of survival. Other decisions, such as the dilation or closing of the iris in the eye, are fully outside of conscious control. The lack of conscious control for such systems can, however, be a boon to the brain's efficiency and rationality, freeing up scarce neurons in the prefrontal cortex, the center of thoughtful (cost-benefit) calculations and decisions.

Despite the efficiency of these unconscious activities, the brain contributes to its own information-overload problems. When encountering new or old information, the brain can recall, with more or less precision and completeness, related memories that add to the relevant information, although these memories may be reconstructed or even false when pulled back into use. For example, the mere sight or smell of a chocolate cake (even a picture of one) can trigger retrieval of stored images, tastes, and perhaps tactile sensory data of a chocolate cake. Repeated retrieval of the data can affect the strength and durability of the stored memories. The brain's efforts to intermingle, maybe millisecond by millisecond, new sensory information with memory-based information (as well as tacit knowledge drawn from elsewhere in the brain) can limit the brain's capacity to make correct and informed decisions, a limitation that nevertheless can be efficient and rational from the perspective of the brain.

Algorithms and Heuristics as Decision-Making Relief

Guided by the overarching goals of survival and propagation and their derivative day-to-day pursuits, the brain seeks ever more efficient ways of conserving its available energy and resources and to improve the individual human being's welfare. The brain develops information feedback loops, involving an assessment of the available information to make the best decision and then an evaluation of the correctness or appropriateness of the decisions made, as well as its processes for making the decisions. The brain must evaluate alternative decisions on alternative courses of action through what can best be imagined as "algorithms," which, very roughly speaking, are biologic counterparts to changeable computer-based multivariate estimating equations. These algorithms must be continually revised—when economical, which often means when experiences deviate "significantly" from experiences embedded in working algorithms that can set off a release of dopamine, which, in turn, can direct attention to the deviations for possible revisions in algorithms—to account for information feedback from prior decisions and from new data from changing circumstances, including the interactions and decisions of other relevant persons.

Given that algorithms are fortified with repeated reference and use, not all algorithms should be expected to be equal, and equally referenced. Indeed, no one should be surprised if there is a hierarchy of algorithms, some of which are more frequently referenced than others—possibly because they are more useful and used in more decision situations (with the involved neuronal networks having more connections), maybe because they are "cheaper" to employ and/or can be employed with greater confidence. Science seems to be a process of enshrining and elevating rules of logic and testing in people's hierarchy of algorithms through repeated tests against real-world experience or hard evidence (and the harder—more observable and measurable absent subjective judgment—the evidence, the better).

Relatively Absolute Absolutes

The late University of Chicago economist/philosopher Frank Knight insisted in his classes that there may be no *absolutes* in the form of claims about the social world (aside for that statement), but there can be, and should be and must be, *relatively absolute absolutes*, meaning rules for thinking (call them algorithms) that have been tested repeatedly for so long to good effect that they can be treated, more or less, as *absolutes*, or deferred to as being solidly right (making them something close to "laws" in the identified discipline) until evidence piles up that undermine practitioners' confidence in them (causing another dopamine release).[4]

Neoclassical economists have been prone to treat, for example, rationality (even perfect rationality) and the law of demand on par with Knight's relatively absolute absolutes. Behavioral economists, so it seems abundantly clear to me, have collectively been hard at work seeking to undermine the relatively absolute status of rationality within neoclassical economics, and to good effect (or else the driving purpose of this book would evaporate). Dan Ariely and other behaviorists have challenged the exalted status of the law of demand (the most firmly held of relatively absolute absolutes in economic neoclassical analysis).[5]

Nevertheless, many neoclassical economists can be expected to hold onto the status that rationality and the law of demand have in their analytics for some time, possibly because they have not yet considered the behavioral literature or believe the behavioral evidence is sufficiently strong and convincing for them to discard their long-held and productive (to them) premise, or they don't yet see a viable alternative analytical paradigm that works better than what they use (and behavioral economics is hardly without its own methodological problems, as I argue later in this chapter and at greater length elsewhere[6]). I am here seeking a way to move them and behaviorists (if only somewhat) in their methodologies in hope that they will both see some common ground in finding a common theoretical foundation, and maybe the "unity of purpose" Lionel Robbins sought in the 1930s.

For me, while I have found a way to adjust my thinking on rationality, the law of demand retains its status of my all-time favorite and most productive relatively absolute absolute, my go-to principle that, in spite of some behaviorists' efforts to relegate it to the dustbin of economic inquiry, I still find it to be widely (not perfectly) useful, with minimal demands on mental thinking. From my newly adopted methodological way of thinking, if I am wrong at times in the quick application of the law of demand, my portfolio of applications can provide me (and many other economists) with welfare and even rationality gains, on balance (which in an imperfect world, replete with scarcities of resources, is an analytical goal hard to surpass).

The Brain's Structure and Decision-Making

The brain's physical structure also complicates decision-making problems. Generally speaking, information is received from all senses through the limbic system, which encompasses several structures of neurons below the cerebral cortex and above the brain stem, most notably, the amygdalae (two almond-size structures at the base of the limbic system) and the thalamus. (Daniel Kahneman appears to have had the limbic system in mind when writing about people "thinking fast" under what he dubbed "System 1."[7]) Without the individual's conscious awareness, these structures can activate emotional responses almost automatically (in milliseconds), as well as "choose" to send the information to the pre frontal cortex for more considered cognitive evaluation (the seedbed of Kahneman's "System 2," encompassing "thinking slow"). As a result, the brain is structured to give people a built-in bias toward quick emotional judgments, especially when time for cognitive thought is scarce (but even when urgency is not a factor). This bias will likely translate often into emotion-controlled responses when alternative responses are judged to be more or less even, or are a tossup.

Hence, when confronted with videos of deprived children living in squalid conditions with a single mother who makes only the federal minimum wage ($7.25 an hour at this writing), many viewers may have a proclivity to favor immediately helping the family with a mandated pay raise, rather than to think through (as many economist advise) the mentally demanding abstract and distant negative employment effects of a minimum-wage hike. This bias toward thinking fast suggests that economists have to overcome evolutionary obstructions in the structure of the human brain if they are to help individuals understand and appreciate predictions of economic models. The more abstract the economic models and the more detached from emotion-laden stories, with well-honed mental associations, and the less frequent people employ economic principles and models, the greater difficulty people with only general interests in economics will likely have in absorbing and remembering for long economic tenets and models. But economists can take some solace from the fact that the brain has a scarcity problem and understandably seeks improved, even more economical, ways of thinking through complex issues.

The Brain's Scarcity Problem and Economic Education

The brain's scarcity problem can, in effect, give economic education a purpose, which is to cause students to slow down their reactions to many information inflows, to direct some inflows to the prefrontal cortex for analysis, and to offer heuristics for thinking through at reduced costs the consequences of what might otherwise be immediate emotional reactions. With a perfect-rationality premise, improvements in decision-making are effectively assumed away.

From my perspective, the brain can be trained, if the instruction appeals to the interests of students' brains, and has an internal economic incentive to be trained, but only for so long as the training is economically relevant. Humans may indeed miss considering opportunity costs and consider sunk concepts, but maybe because the brain has not yet seen their relevance. Repeated instruction on the concepts' relevance for improving decisions in utility and profit terms and for easing and speeding up thinking can cause the concepts to be embedded in the brain's algorithms, at least for as long as their use has net benefits.

Richard Thaler has serious reservations that students can be taught to think better, or more rationally or more profitably. Sure, he tells us, conventional economics may be right that a profit-maximizing firm should equate marginal cost with marginal revenue, but he seems to doubt that students (even working MBAs) have the mental capacity or proclivity (maybe because they are locked into their choice biases) to see the value of economic instruction on such deduced principles.[8] But why not? There are net gains (profits for businesses) to be had, as Thaler suggests is the case, by firms following that rule, which, in turn, suggests a source of incentives for firms to pay their employees for learning and applying that rule, as well as many other rules (e.g., ignore sunk costs and consider opportunity costs). He certainly has found an incentive to understand economic principles (and to dispute their value). But maybe he sees himself with thinking capacities not shared by others, which is likely true, but only to a degree, I suspect. I must worry that Thaler is resistant to the prospects of student learning economic principles because acceptance of such learning impairments makes the case for "nudges" by him and other "choice architects" all the more appealing. But "choice architects" will likely be drawn from the human race, and they will have a decided disadvantage: they will not know the fullness of the circumstances of all others (or their frames), which has to make Thaler and others inspired by the attraction of correcting other people's behaviors pause on assuming such choice authority.

And choice architects can simply be wrong on their proposed nudges, misled by misconstructions of the "frames" for their experiments, from which they devise their nudges. Or, given the potential multitude of ways experiments can be framed, their nudges don't work as deduced for all covered people by the imposition of their proposed nudges. And experiments can be contradicted or proven flat-out wrong in later experiments undertaken under the same or different frames, as has been found to be the case with most hard and social science empirical studies.[9]

For example, food researchers Brian Wansink and Koert van Ittersum created something of a stir within the nutrition and diet industries when they found in 2006 that plate and bowl sizes affect the portions of food people consumed, and, of course, calorie intake and weight.[10] Campers given larger bowls at a camp were found to consume 22% more cereal than their cohorts given smaller bowls, although they thought they had consumed 7% less.[11] Apparently, the researchers found, people seek an aesthetically pleasing amount of white space in their bowls and on their plates, which means they add more food when given larger dishware. Others succumb to an optical illusion, with a given portion looking smaller on a larger plate than on smaller ones.

As a consequence of this line of research, food gurus energetically began recommending surefire weight-loss nudges: people should reduce their bowl and plate sizes, except when they want to encourage the consumption of vegetables. Dishware manufacturers began offering specially designed plates to appeal to people who accepted claims that dieting-by-plate-size worked, and did so broadly.

A nice-sounding argument, right? No apparent downside, right? Maybe a confident "yes" would now be warranted to those questions, *if* the initial research were validated, or not contradicted, with repeat studies—which has not been the case. In a review of a dozen studies published after 2006, other researchers have found in a "meta-analysis" that the widely touted positive relationship between plate and bowl size and food portion consumed existed, but it was weak: "Evidence to date does not show that dishware size has a consistent effect on food intake, so recommendations surrounding the use of smaller plates/dishware to improve public health may be premature." Again, the impact of dishware size was positive but small and, as might have been expected, varied widely across sample groups under study.[12]

Even if a positive relationship were found to be statistically significant, and maybe substantial, as initially claimed, I must pause because of a quip a sociology colleague relayed to me three decades ago: "The first law of sociology is almost everywhere applicable: 'Some do and some don't.'" It's almost guaranteed that larger plates can induce some people to heap larger portions on their plates than they would if they had smaller plates. However, it's also a sure thing that other people can control their portions, no matter their plate sizes, while still others with small plates compensate for the "plate effect" by going back for second helpings. And, of course, behaviorists who take Thaler's mental accounting seriously must worry that some people who use larger plates and take larger portions compensate by curbing their calorie intake or expending more calories elsewhere. Variability in people's decision-making is a clear enemy in formulating nudges of all kind, appropriate for some, or many, but not so much for others.

Brain's Scarcity Problem and Increasing Choices

In neoclassical economics, an increase in the range of people's choices is generally considered a "good thing," an alleviation of scarcity, which is *the* all-pervasive and ever-present economic problem that puts satiation far beyond the reach of the vast majority of people (excluding, maybe, multibillionaires). Additional choices, in much neoclassical analyses necessarily translate into welfare improvements even when many existing choices are too poor or pricey to be viable, much less selected. A greater range of choices can imply a greater welfare for consumers and producers, at least potentially.

But based on what we know about the human brain, more choices may serve only to tighten the grip of the fundamental brain-based scarcity problem, potentially undercutting human welfare as people's brains attempt to cope with the demands of the onslaught of sensory information emanating from the widening range of choices, whether from a greater variety of goods and services or ever-expanding product characteristics. Beyond some point, growth in the array of choices can have neoclassical-type economic consequences, as psychologist psychologists Barry Swartz has stressed, summarizing a relatively new plight of wealthy societies:

> When people have no choice, life is almost unbearable. As the number of available choices increases, as it has in our consumer culture, the autonomy, control, and liberation this variety brings are powerful and positive. But as the number of choices keeps growing, negative aspects of having a multitude of options begin to appear. As the number of choices grows further, the negatives escalates until we become overloaded. At this point, choice no longer liberates, but debilitates. It might even be said to tyrannize.[13]

Faced with a prospective and escalating growth in choices (a familiar plight in contemporary times), people can be expected to devise methods (at economical cost to brain resources, of course) to limit their relevant choices simply to make them manageable and to improve the welfare gained from choices made. They may put on blinders to some options as they seek to be more efficient and rational in their decision-making that would be impaired if they remained completely open to all possible choices.[14] And outright avoidance of some choice opportunities (even with minimal thought) can be efficient and rational—for the human brain—even when some choices that are not recognized or avoided *could* at times enhance welfare if considered (or even when marketers exploit people's tendencies to narrow, consciously and subconsciously, their range of choices). The trick the brain must pull off is to optimize through containing the choices considered while being able to alter the methods for closing off choices when feedback sensory evidence warrants corrections—a nontrivial problem, to say the least. Remaining open to new choices has its rewards, but it also requires energy for neurons; therefore, "closed-mindedness" has its rewards, too—at least within limits and under some circumstances. In turn, such decisions can be quite rational from the perspective of a brain-focused economics, although some behaviorists and others who use the neoclassical economics perspective of rationality may (and very likely will) disagree.

From a brain-centered perspective of scarcity, people who restrict their choice of clothing by brand (Lauren Conrad) or outlets (Costco or J. Jill) or material (all cotton) or price (with price equated with quality) can be making perfectly sensible and economical—rational—decisions. Some buyers (me included) favor Amazon as a first "portal" for purchases because of the ease of discovering choice options and finalizing purchase: "1-click" and done! In spite of encountering occasional "buyer's remorse" and misfits on apparel, requiring returns, my portfolio of Amazon 1-clicks has me pleased that the company has become a retail juggernaut (and has forced the closure of any number of brick-and-mortar choice options).

Behaviorists have made much of the role of "salience" in decision-making, and with an abundance of choice options, no one should be surprised if salience were now a prominent choice determinant. After all, buyers' brains should be expected to economize on their limited resources, which can be expected to result in not all choice options being given the same attention. Option prominence has an advantage of likely reducing somewhat buyers' search and decision costs. However, salience need not always blindly determine purchases, with no thought at all expended, as seems to be intimated in behaviorists' commentaries on salience. After all, buyers can recognize their weakness to the display prominence of products in making choice. Many buyers succumb to saliences, but sure enough, many people pass on choice options they confront on entering stores and checkout lines. There is a good reason that the brain will want to be guarded and devise a decision rule that could be dubbed "rational salience," which can cause adoptees to explore to varying degree (depending on mental and other resource cost) choice options. They can be expected to be wary, to an economical degree, of ever-present temptations to take prominent choice options, but also wary of the costs of conducting extensive searches, especially when the expenditures are minor. We might predict with greater confidence that with a marked increase in choice options, and associated greater mental costs in making choices (a seeming transparent fact of commercial life in advanced countries over the last century), we would expect the importance of salience in affecting buyer choices to have risen in importance.

Many people who are reluctant to listen to expert advice from, say, behaviorists on how their choices are suboptimal (or stupid) or could be improved by their proposed nudges, can be exercising the type of rational thinking behaviorists spurn as irrational. Indeed, in recommending an array of nudges, behaviorists could be inadvertently proposing curbs in the welfare of the people they seek to save from their own irrationalities, as behaviorists construe irrationalities.[15] They don't seem to realize that people's choices are intrinsic to particular environments, which are far more numerous (and even unknowable to outside observers, or "choice architects") than behaviorists are willing to admit. Many behaviorists don't seem to recognize that they too are beset with all the mental/decision frailties they have uncovered for their "Humans," as well as "Econs."

Of course, neoclassical and behavioral economists in their analytics may also put on methodological blinders to alternative ways of thinking through, say, policy problems. The past productivity of their methods can be a key reason for them to resist switching methods. Besides, analytical alternatives abound, which means they face an "analytical dilemma" that is on par with the widely recognized "innovator's dilemma" in business.[16] Most supposed innovations are proven losers; a few, winners. The dilemma comes from the fact that firms can go broke chasing every proposed innovation and every proposal to "reengineer" companies. Economists face much the same dilemma, which means methodological change is likely to come slowly, especially in academe, which is hardly meant as a criticism.

The Brain and Algorithms

Behaviorists argue that their choice experiments involving gambles expose a major defect in people's rationality. When given a one-time choice between a sure-thing option—say, \$800—and a "gamble" option with an expected value of \$850 (which has, in a single draw, an 85% chance of being worth \$1000 and a 15% chance of being worth nothing), 80% or so of the subjects choose the sure-thing, which, behaviorists declare, violates a canon of neoclassical economics.

This is to say, truly rational/maximizing subjects are expected to choose consistently the option with the higher expected value.

Obviously, most subjects (most often, students) do not, as I've learned from my own testing of this key behavioral finding. I have repeatedly given this choice problem to my own business-experienced MBA students at the start of their microeconomics courses, usually on the first day of class, which means before I've taken up key concepts, for example, rational behavior. Sure enough, 75–85% of my students in different classes have chosen the sure-thing. (This choice division has held up even when I have delayed presenting the problem until after I have discussed economists' meaning of rationality and its many implications.)

Nonetheless, I have been critical on several grounds of behaviorists' quick conclusion that the typical choice division in this problem demonstrates conclusively (or anything close) that a premise of perfect rationality, even as an analytical device, is flawed, maybe fatally so. First, long before behavioral economics cohered into a distinct subdiscipline (or maybe a distinct discipline), Dwight Lee, a solid neoclassical economist, stressed in the late 1960s that people's choices must surely be affected by the variance of the choice options, which has been shown to be the case.[17] The sure-thing option in the problem as posed has no variance, which can be understood to indicate no associated risk. The gamble has substantial variance in outcomes, from no payoff to a payoff of $1000, indicating a much greater risk factor. The high variance of the gamble in the experiment could easily have had a negative value that was greater than the monetary difference between the expected values of the two options, which could have made the sure-thing a "rational" choice for a substantial majority of the subjects in a one-off experiment. If the variance of the gamble (or the value of the sure-thing) had been lower, a higher percentage of the subjects would be expected to choose the gamble (at least beyond some point in lowering value of the sure-thing or the variance of the gamble).

And, it should be remembered that the primary goal of assuming rational/maximizing behavior is not to predict which option will be taken in what percentages, but to predict marginal adjustments made by people when presented with changes in constraints, in this case, the relative values of the two options, a sure thing and a gamble.

When I gave my students a choice between an $800 sure-thing and an option to draw multiple "tickets" that had lower individual values, but with the expected value remaining at $850, which lowered the variance in outcomes associated with the gamble, a greater percentage of students did, in fact, take the gamble, as predicted.[18] A reduction in the value of the sure-thing option to below $800 (say, $750 or $650), while holding the gamble to the original terms, had the same predicted effect, a smaller percentage of my students took the sure-thing.

I also have criticized the sure-thing/gamble choice experiment on grounds that the researchers didn't give the subjects the summary results of their choices and didn't allow them time to consider and recover the obvious "money being left on the table" ($50 in the original problem) by their supposed "irrational" choices. I gave my students the summary findings of their choices and then assigned them to teams to develop team papers that focused on two questions:

1. Is there money being left on the table, given the choice distribution within the class?
2. If there is money left on the table, are there means your team members can devise to pick up the money?

More than three-quarters of the student teams came up with workable solutions: Several teams said that they would offer students choosing the sure-thing option insurance, at a price, of course (but at less than $50). Other teams said they would join students in cooperative efforts (cartels of sorts), encouraging all to choose the gamble and then dividing evenly the total take. (Every now and then a team would even recognize the potential free-rider and strategic-bargaining problems inherent in such a proposed cooperative/collective action.)

Several teams realized that those students choosing the sure-thing could be bought off, if they were given an offer of more than $800 to choose the gamble, say, $801 or more, and to hand the payoff from their draws over to the buyer. A handful of teams realized that several teams would emerge with this solution, which means that the surplus value, $50, would cause teams to bid up the price paid to those who were initially inclined to choose the sure-thing. Therefore, much of the $50 difference between the options' expected values might end up going largely to the supposed "risk-averse" students. Several teams, even when they had to write the assigned paper during the first week of the course, noted that the risks of the buyers of the options was lower than the risks faced by individual students choosing alone, because of the numbers of tickets bought and the diminished variance in their net payoffs (although the point was not so precisely made in their papers).

If behaviorists were truly intent solely on laying out the extent of people's irrationalities, they could have dispensed with the complications of pitting a sure-thing against a gamble. Instead, they could have asked subjects: Which would you choose, sure-thing option A worth $800 in cash or sure-thing option B worth $900 in cash (or even $801)? If a sizable majority chose option A, we could unequivocally conclude that something is remiss with a rationality premise at any level. Does anyone believe that 80-plus percent of MBA students would choose this option A?

Behavioral researchers who present the type of division-of-choice findings just covered often focus their analytical attention exclusively on the sizable majority (75–85%) of the subjects who make the "wrong" or "irrational" choices. Such majorities enable the researchers to condemn neoclassical economic theory as being fundamentally flawed at its core, after which they all too often, in follow-up discussions and writings, smoothly move from noting the choices of the errant majorities to discussing the findings in more general terms, such as "people" (sometimes, if not often, implying "all people") make wrongheaded and irrational decisions. Little, if any, attention may be subsequently given to the finding that the "wrong" or "irrational" choice was hardly universally made. The relatively small percentage (which could, at times, approach a fourth, or a third, or close to half in different behavioral studies, not just sure-thing/gamble experiments) of all subjects made the "right" or "rational" choice are easily overlooked or set aside, leaving the impression that their choices are inconsequential or irrelevant to what may subsequently transpire among all subjects in sequential and evolving real-world choice environments. The fact that 75–85% of subjects made "wrong" decisions will hardly be overlooked or set aside by entrepreneurs (and the larger the percentage of "wrong" choice, the better for them). The fact that 25–15% of the subjects chose "right" could be quite consequential over time as subjects making "wrong" choices discover that they could have made mistakes in that their gains, over a sequence of choices, grow by less than the gains of those who chose "right" initially and cause reconsiderations of the relative merits of the choices. In short, minorities in given choice circumstances can teach majorities a thing or two, causing "wrong" choices to be self-correcting, at least partially—making "irrationality" a less pervasive human flaw than might initially appear to be the case from isolated laboratory/classroom "experiments." By providing the options as noted, giving no feedback information on subject choices, ruling out corrective choices, and constraining the time period for choices to a matter of minutes at most, the behavioral researchers have *framed* their experiments to get exactly what they, and I, would have predicted—given the economy of the brain.

For a real-world example of how learning can occur in markets (if not allowed in classroom experiments), consider a report from the *New York Times* in mid-2016 about how early adopters of solar panels for home electricity production had begun to learn that their solar investments, which could run upwards of $20,000, had minimal or no payoffs in terms of reductions in their monthly electricity bills. They learned the hard way from their mistakes. Some early adopters were beginning to ask for their money back. Probably far more non-adopters were also learning from the bad experience of the adopters. They simply didn't get suckered in by the solar hype. Sales of solar panels had begun to fall, even with government subsidies.[19] To offset the effects of the informational and learning feedback loops, the government would have had to increase subsidies.

Looking at the behaviorists' A–B choice problems from a brain-focused perspective offers yet another avenue for such experiments. As noted, the brain must make choices based on something approximating an ever-adjusting algorithm (perhaps multiple algorithms operating in parallel), based partially, maybe extensively, on past experiences. When the A–B options were presented in my classes, many students might have seen the options as novel, outside of their past experiences, and many were likely unprepared for the in-class experiment. Prior to class I had never mentioned that I would present them with the options I did, or any options at all. Also, the options were artificial, concocted from the needs of the behavioral researchers' and my experimental needs, rather than being "natural," emerging from the students' normal daily activities. The options were also presented in a fabricated, somewhat strange lab (classroom) environment over which students had no control.

In other words, the choices did not spring from what experimental economist Vernon Smith has called "ecologically adaptive environments" in which subjects and their choices coevolve within their environment. In such choice environments, students might have some input into construction of the options, at least on the local level, and the choices themselves could have emerged from and be integrated into their past choice experiences—and could have been integrated into their brains' decision algorithms.

In many experiments, researchers construct the laboratory environment without input at all from the subjects themselves (at least, I've never read of the options presented being collaboratively developed by researchers and subjects). Indeed, the researchers seek to sterilize, to the extent possible, their laboratories of all (potentially relevant) behavioral and decision-making variables that are of no interest to them, the researchers, but may have significant "ecological validity" to the subjects' workaday worlds in which they normally make decisions. The researchers' goal is to so construct their experiments in such a way that their favored key elements can be isolated from all other elements.

Subjects are often given a one-shot choice with no feedback, which is hardly how people encounter most choices in the real world. Moreover, many laboratory experiments include no real-world competitive pressures with meaningful short-term, much less long-term, rewards at stake that might induce subjects to devote the requisite mental resources to hone their decision-making skills (and refine their brains' decision-making algorithms), and in turn make improved decisions (in terms of the subjects' preferences, not the researchers' goals).

Experiments are mostly short-term, offering immediate rewards, if any, although most "natural" decisions are made to gain rewards extending over a much longer time frame. For example, summer interns may work for nothing, without a guarantee that their experience will involve anything more than stapling documents, because they seek future rewards from their acquired experience (and maybe a line on their short resumes), which might only be watching and working with people in business settings where profit-seeking can be an important controlling force. Hence, in discounted terms, their hourly pay for their work can easily be above zero, and could be as high or higher than they ever earn in later life.

In addition, many subjects are likely befuddled to some extent by the totality of the choice setting, and may expend much mental energy, with limited time to do so, just trying to absorb the new sensory information from the odd environment and from other subjects whom they likely have never met and with whom they have no working relationship. More to the point, choice decisions made in an experimental/laboratory/classroom context by subjects with no history of making such choices must require the subjects to spend time and mental energy to send new information to the prefrontal cortex for cognitive processing and to draw on mental decision algorithms that they were born with and/or created from past experiences in their workaday worlds. Might the experimental settings have been devise, albeit inadvertently, with the findings a sure outcome?

Had the students been given repeated experiences with similar choice situations and the opportunity to create feedback loops through communications with researchers and other subjects—as my students were allowed to do in their paper assignments—most students might very well have revised their decision algorithms. No one should expect anything approaching consistent rational choices (as the researchers might define them) from inexperienced subjects in novel environments (which challenges the very definition of what it means to be "rational"). The human brain simply does not work the way behaviorists demand in their concocted sterilized laboratory experiments (or surveys). But then, one of the behaviorists' goal has likely been to demonstrate that the human brain does not and cannot work the way neoclassical economists assume either (but the same could be said of behaviorists' inductive research). I have to agree, and I suspect Milton Friedman, Gary Becker, and George Stigler would concur.

I do not mean to imply that given time and experience with particular choices and particular choice environments, people will make "perfectly rational" and consistent choices through time, according to researchers' definitions. No one should expect them to do so. As I have argued, perfectly rational choices through time is an evolutionary nonstarter under the best of conditions because of the energy and resource economics inside the brain. Moreover, from a brain-focused perspective, the supposed "wrong" ("irrational") choices in these experiments may have been every bit deliberate—even fully rational, but short of perfectly rational—because within the constrained laboratory circumstances, the subjects optimized use of their brain's energy, and neuronal resources with tolerably efficiency, based on their past experiences and the known costs and benefits of cognitively considering the presented choices.

On the other hand, some subjects' decisions may not have been at all rationally deliberate, in the sense that they drew in a significant way on their limited cognitive resources—perhaps understandably so. As we have seen, sensory information arrives in the brain through the limbic system that is wired to make largely quick responses (sometimes emotion-laden) with a bias for saving the brain's scarce energy and neuronal resources (especially when confronted with unfamiliar subject matter). I suspect that many students were not given time to think more than, "Ah, the sure-thing option will cover rent (or beer) for a month! Then, again, I can play games with my professor with my low-cost response: Check the box for the sure-thing, the one with the lower expected value." Again, the researchers may not have intended for the students to have time to think carefully (use their "System 2s") about the specified options, and may not have offered any (or adequate) incentive to engage their exceedingly scarce cognitive resources to do so. My students weren't given more than a minute or two (and surely got less than five minutes) before I asked them to mark their answers. Even when I didn't put any time pressure on students to make their selections, many took no more time to make their decision than to read the options and then check their choices. In class, I never offered a payoff of any kind for deliberate consideration of the problem (and doubt that I could have offered many students as much as their opportunity wage rates, given that the students were self-selected from middle and upper corporate management ranks and a handful were medical doctors).

In one class I incorrectly specified the terms of the A/B choice. I correctly specified the sure-thing's worth at $800, but told my students that the gamble involved a 75% chance of drawing $1000 and a 25% chance of drawing nothing, which had an expected value of just $750. Yet, the percent of students who chose the gamble was higher than in any other experiments I ran over several years! The students choosing the gamble may have been certified nutcases, but I suspect they had neither the time nor incentive to waste brain energy and neurons on sending the details of the choice options to their prefrontal cortex for a few seconds of good old-fashioned thought. (I wouldn't be surprised if several students rationally decided to demonstrate their irrationality by their "perverse" choices, and several students may have thought, "There's got to be a trick here. The sure thing looks to me to be the best option, so I am going to assume that option is wrong and go with the gamble," a response I've had students give me after getting wrong a series of policy questions because the answers were counterintuitive.)

Simply put, subjects' brains need time and repeated experience with choice situations to adjust their algorithms, and they need a reason to figure out the "right choices" for their particular circumstances. If students had been told to take whatever time they needed to explore the merits of the options over the following week (which suggests something might be amiss in their immediate, quick responses) and to employ their full cognitive capacities (including adjusting their decision algorithms to override immediate emotional reactions), no one would be surprised if the distribution of the choices changed substantially. In fact, that is what happened when my MBA students were given the choice problem as a class assignment. When their grades were at risk, their studied responses were far "more rational" than their initial responses might suggest (and their choices in their student teams possibly had the added vantage of thinking through the problem with other students, which increased the likelihood that their collective choices were "improved," or more consistent with the dictates of rational thinking). When people are asked to make immediate, quick responses in novel circumstances, so-called irrationalities are inevitable, and of little value in a world in which less-than-perfect (or optimal) rationality is part and parcel of evolution and our energy-constrained mental and behavioral/decision-making *processes* brimming with feedback loops that need an economic motivation for activation.

The main take away? Many supposed "irrationalities" can be construed as (tolerably) rational—*if* we construct economics as a discipline founded on the innate problem of coping with controlling scarcity within the human brain. Rationality appears to be a variable, dependent on circumstances, costs and rewards, to name two of probably many factors, which means people's assessed rationality can be manipulated. Such potential variability and manipulation is assumed away in neoclassical economics but seemingly used repeatedly in behavioral economics.

There is no reason to expect people to operate their cars at the same speed, or efficiency. Scarce resources would obviously be wasted, misused, misallocated. Similarly, there is no reason to expect the brain to devote the same cognitive resources to achieve the same degree of rationality in all situations. It might do that, at times, but only in situations where the correctness or rightness of decisions have a more-than-offsetting benefit, and casually devised classroom experiments guided by the purposes of researchers, not subjects, do not meet the implied test for the brain to treat the choice options presented in class with the same seriousness and rationality as choice options in the real world where far more is at stake.

Diet Cokes, Brain-Focused Economics, and Decision-Portfolio Management

Harvard behavioral economist Sendhil Mullainathan confessed in a 2017 *New York Times* commentary that he has long succumbed to a disturbing choice "failure," drinking a carton of Diet Cokes daily and never even trying an another "equivalent," although cheaper, diet cola. He expressed confidence that he *should* correct his failure for financial reasons: "As a frugal economist, I'm well aware that switching to a generic brand would save me money, not just once but daily, for weeks and years to come. Yet I only drink Diet Coke. I've never even sampled generic soda."[20]

Mullainathan explained that he had not corrected is errant choice ways because the money saved would be "inconsequential" and he could well "afford" to stick with "this little extravagance." Still, he insists, "I'm clearly making an error, one that reveals a deeper decision-making "bias" whose cumulative cost is sizable: "Like most people, I conduct relatively few experiments in my personal life, in both small and big things."[21]

Mullainathan believes he has found yet another choice "bias," but has he? His declarations don't seem to make a lot of sense (to me, maybe because I'm too steeped in neoclassical thinking). But maybe not, if the critically scarce resource is the human brain, which understandably seeks to optimize on the allocation of its own internal resources.

Rationality and Habitual Choices

Mullainathan assures readers that his own and other's added choice experimentation would clearly be rational and welfare enhancing, because the "downside" is "limited," "while the potential gains are disproportionately large." As support, he notes that close to half of consumer choices are much like his, "habitual," and misguided.

Researchers may have discovered that people often stick with their choices. Some habits may not make any more sense than Mullainathan's. But tagging all frequently repeated choices as "habitual" is a leap in judgment, given that "habitual" suggests an absence of rational, cost-benefit calculations. He adds, "[M]any people persist in buying branded products even when equivalent generics are available."[22] Habits may result in decisions without contemplation and errors, but *habit formation* need not be an irrational (or nonrational) decision process (just as shooting heroine may result in an uncontrollable compulsion, whereas the choice to start heroine use can be a rational decision, as Gary Becker and Kevin Murphy argued in the 1980s.[23]

As evidence of his presumption that people are prone to be irrationally locked into choices, Mullainathan points to findings from a "natural experiment," involving the then recent closure of several London subway stations during a 48-hour strike, which forced commuters to find alternative routes.[24] On their new routes, commuters reduced their commute times by an average of 6.7 minutes, deemed to be a "valuable" time saving.

Nevertheless, when the strike ended, only 5% of commuters stayed with their new routes, "suboptimal behavior" according to the study's authors.[25] Mullainathan concluded the commuters' choice failures occurred because change is "painful" and people are "overconfident," just as he had been "unduly certain," of the value of the alternatives, "even though I haven't tried them."[26]

Scarcity and Brain-Focused Economics

I report on Mullainathan's commentary because it reflects problems that seem to crop up in much behavioral research. The commentary also offers me a chance to suggest, yet again, how a brain-centered foundation for economics—organized around the premise that the human brain rationally seeks to optimize use of its own internal scarce resources in pursuit of its own goals—can help economists, both neoclassical and behavioral, to understand better people's choices other than through the lens of "biases" or "irrationalities" (if not stupidities).

Consider several responses. First, is there any reason not to believe that across a broad swath of people's product choices that some people, in any given snapshot-type research, will be caught making undeniable choice errors, even repeated ones? All biological and mechanical systems have built-in errors, partially for old-fashion economic reasons behaviorists often dispute. Maybe errors are assumed away from the perspective of neoclassical economists' premise of perfect rationality (which, again, is an evolutionary nonstarter) but surely not from a brain-focused perspective: The brain simply does not have, as behaviorists (and I) contend, the capacity to deal with all demands on its limited resources all the time without error. The brain can only be expected to economize on its resources partially by adopting decision rules (algorithms and heuristics), knowing that errors will be a product of the rules—and yet still make economic sense to neoclassical, if not also to many behavioral, economists.

Second, Mullainathan claims that his choice bias indicates a general problem of people not experimenting broadly. But does his claim have *general* validity (especially when he professed to have never experimented with alternative diet sodas, although he seems to know different sodas' relative merits)?

Experimentation abounds in nature. Honey bees and hummingbirds spend their lives "experimenting," with their survival often hanging in the balance of their optimizing risk and search costs in search of food and mates. Human's hunter-gatherer ancestors surely did much the same, leaving following generations with a predisposition to forage (a form of experimentation). When people go shopping, they appear engrossed in forms of experimentation, for example, feeling the fabric of various clothing items and accepting squirts of different lotions. Many experiment in dating. People even think through alternative ways conversations can unfold before they have them.

Indeed, one of the reasons for experimentation has to be uncertainties that behaviorists insist abound, with the experimentation often reducing uncertainties. One reason for malls and department stores within malls is not only to reduce search costs for known goods, but also, as already noted, to lower experimentation costs, thereby converting many uncertainties to manageable risks.

As reported in the last chapter, Richard Thaler has argued that the transactional utility people get from buying "bargains" (as determined by some preset mental reference price) helps explain why people have so many rarely used and unused goods in their closets and garages, even some goods that are not worth their prices. Well, many of those "excess" goods can likely be chalked up to buyers' prior experimentation, which can have a rational foundation, at least in part. Buyers often try a variety of goods within categories (say, shirts, biking gloves, and laptop computers) and find many of them disappointing, sufficiently so not to use them as frequently as planned, or at all. Other goods purchased might have met expectations, but are now held in storage because the buyers later found other superior replacements. Still, the utility of retaining the first-purchased goods in storage can more than cover their storage costs. Behaviorists might see the stored and unused goods as persistent decision mistakes, hardwired into mental biases and unchecked and uncorrected by feedback loops and rational thinking. Neoclassical economists might suggest an experiment to determine if rational thinking is absent: see what happens to the volume of stored and unused goods across different regions of the country with different storage costs or when the price of storage jumps by a significant amount in any given area. I suspect the neoclassicists' implied predictions would likely be supported by empirical tests, suggesting a form of rationality involved in keeping unused goods, but I would add that both the experimentation and storage processes are guided by the brain seeking to rationalize its own internal resources before dealing with choice problems in the external world: holding excess goods in storage can ease future decisions regarding matching different goods with future, not-fully-known needs, releasing neurons for other uses, and for making decisions not necessarily related purchases of goods more rational than otherwise could be the case.

If people were as uninclined to experiment as Mullainathan suggests he and all others are, it is hard to explain the sizable worldwide fashion industry that constantly churns the styles, colors, textures, and skimpiness of clothing lines. The electronics industry is similarly involved in continually upgrading (and downgrading) a multitude of variations in their products. Over 300,000 traditionally published books (excluding more than twice as many self-published books) are published each year in the United States, with a substantial majority being market failures. The advertising industry spends nearly $200 billion annually in the United States, partially on the presumption that many consumers can be persuaded to "experiment."

Firms convert some market uncertainties to manageable risks by developing portfolios of products, knowing some products will fail. The human brain does much the same with decision portfolios, bounded by its evolved resource and process constraints and by decisions budgets (or what Thaler calls "mental accounts,"[27] which can curb spur-of-the-moment decision-making).

No one, especially not behaviorists, should expect consumers, operating within rationality limits of their brains, to be totally flexible in their choices, trying every new product line that is launched. But it doesn't follow that Mullainathan has identified another broad-based choice and market failure, which undercuts welfare. Indeed, the opposite can be the consequence.

The relevant issue for firms is not whether they have product failures, but whether their portfolios of products are, on balance, profitable, and to what extent their portfolios should be, and can be, adjusted over time. (And doesn't the process of portfolio management involve a form, or forms, of continual experimentation?) Similarly, the relevant issue for consumers is not whether they make mistaken choices or even miss undertaking experiments that could lead to improved purchases. The relevant issue is, when scarcity constraints prevail on decisions, whether their brains' decision *portfolios* across a vast number of decisions (including product choices) are, on balance, more competitive, beneficial, and economical than achievable alternative portfolios.

Third, Mullainathan probably doesn't know as much about consumer choices, and their resistance to change, as he intimates. As noted, he insisted that consumers, in general, stay with their choices even when "equivalent generic options are available." "Equivalent"? I don't see how he can speak for anyone other than himself on what goods are "equivalent." Drawing equivalence on products' subjective values requires clairvoyance, a capability I am not willing to cede him (at least, not in scientific discussions).

Drawing equivalence among goods is also a strong claim coming from a behaviorist who likely agrees that "frames" (and "anchors") are endemic to choices and surely vary substantially over a large number of people and their particular circumstances. Obviously, many people drink *different generic* diet sodas, given that Coke and Pepsi have less than half the US market—and that all sodas have declined by more than a fourth over the past dozen years, in favor of water and tea. Might Mullainathan's choice failure be far less general and more understandable than he suggests—from the perspective of the brain's limited resources?

Fourth, Mullainathan insisted that the high percentage of commuters who returned to their old routes, were choosing irrationally, forgoing a "valuable" time saving. Again, Mullainathan claims too much. After all, the commuters took their alternative routes for only *two* days, hardly long enough to accurately assess expected commute times in the future. An unreported number of commuters likely didn't take the time (or brain energy) to accurately assess their time saving. No doubt, the time saved by commuters varied, above and below the mean. Surely, an unreported number of commuters' new routes required longer commutes, which made their return to their old routes fully sensible.

Even those commuters who returned to longer commutes could have concluded that attributes of travel by their old routes were superior to those on their shorter alternatives. Some commuters may have driven during the strike and returned to their old train routes because

- they could work on the train (with a net time saving),
- their train rides were more pleasant, and/or
- their money outlays on their new routes exceeded the value of their time saving.

Most likely, commuters had a multitude of individual reasons, not capable of being known by academic researchers. Might Mullainathan's choice recommendation make many commuters worse off, especially since he admits to serious errors in his own choices?

Fifth, Mullainathan seems to have concluded that consumers who report following habits in their purchases amounts to a bias, which, from his perspective, is tantamount to a choice failure, and yet another form of irrationality. He appears to believe habits cause people to do what he professes he has done with his persistent Diet Coke purchases, decrease welfare. Not necessarily so from my brain-focused perspective for consumer-choice theory. If the brain's resources were unlimited, habits might not make sense. However, with scarce resources, the brain should be expected to try to relieve its heavy decision-making burden by automating some repetitive decisions, especially "inconsequential" ones, and then honing habits' usefulness, and efficiency, over time with feedback sensory information.

As noted, putting some choices on automatic pilot can free up neurons and energy to be used in weighing more carefully a multitude of other, more important bodily and external decisions. Hence, habits can enhance the efficiency and rationality of the brain's decision-making, both internal and external, and can add, on balance, in many unseen ways to human welfare—and this can be the case even when habits lead occasionally, or even often, to decision errors.

Again, the brain needs to be considered through the lens of a decision-portfolio manager. From that perspective, many (not all) "mistakes" and "bad decisions" can be welfare enhancing, just as "losers" in stock portfolios can contribute to an increase in the portfolios' market value. The absence of erroneous stock picks in portfolios could suggest a sub-optimal (overly safe and wealth-reducing) portfolio.

From a brain-centered view of the commuting-choice problem, the commuters' propensity to stay with their old route becomes more understandable (intelligible and rational) for two major reasons: Commuters' brains have limited resources and simply may not be willing—rationally so—to be actively involved in all choices on products and experiments, and it can't be. The riders may have decided to apply their scarce mental resources, including decision-making time, to an array of goods that are not within the purview of Mullainathan's observations and experimental research.

In addition, because of the brain's scarcity of neurons and energy, it is unlikely to waste its time on trivial (or "inconsequential") differences in costs and benefits of particular decisions when it has an array of other decisions with the prospects of greater net gains. Proof that a new route saves time is hardly proof that the brain has, on balance, made mistakes across its many allocation decisions. In short, the human brain is unlikely to consider many decisions in isolation, as Mullainathan seems to suggest it should.

Concluding Comments

The chief lesson? Behaviorists often lay out the evidence on the brain's "bounded rationality," but report research decisions in isolation from one another, say, the choice of sodas or travel routes. That perspective should cause behaviorists to pause before declaring findings from isolated experiments to be "biases," "errors," or "irrationalities." Maybe so, when neoclassical economists' premise of perfect rationality in human decision-making is the standard for judgment, but not so when the brain's own internal level of rationality is optimized, given its evolved resource and process constraints.

Behavioral economists point to all the decision errors human brains make. Neoclassical economists assume them away. I suggest an improved perspective is to accept that the human brain is an evolved defective biological system (or collection of systems)—indeed, it is an evolved kluge, with components effectively "bolted," imperfectly, on top of one another—and then to consider the extent to which human's evolved mental resources and processes and rational capacity, whether innate or inculcated, along which institutions (such as markets), reduce decision errors.

Notes

1. Nease (2016). Unfortunately, Nease makes no attempt to explain how or where he got his estimate of the information bits encountered and considered.
2. Polanyi (2009, pp. xi and 108).
3. For an overview subconscious decision-making and conscious awareness of decisions that have been made, see Bear (2016).

4. Knights conception of "relatively absolute absolutes" was pressed on me by my mentor James M. Buchanan, one of Knight's students in the late 1940s.
5. Ariely (2008). See Becker (1962, 1975).
6. See McKenzie (2010, Chapter 10).
7. Kahneman (2011).
8. Thaler (1991, p. xiii).
9. See Freedman (2010).
10. See Wansink (2007).
11. Wansink et al. (2006).
12. Robinson et al. (2014).
13. Swartz (2005, p. 2).
14. For a discussion of the extent to which a growing array of choices taxes people mental capacities, see Swartz (2005).
15. In their work as analysts, even economists steeped in one school of thought or another, consciously and subconsciously put blinders on to the methods and findings of other schools of thought, because of the mental economies involved. Many neoclassical economists remain unaware of what behavioral economists have been doing for the past half-century. Behavioral economists often know little about Austrian economics, and vice versa. Economists schooled in the economics of mandated minimum wages, conventionally presented with supply and demand curves, will ignore (or when considered, dismiss) new theories and findings that show minimum-wage hikes have inconsequential labor-market effects, possibly because employers find ways of muting or negating, through increases in work demands or cuts in fringe benefits. They will continue to tout the count of jobs lost through wage hikes, without acknowledging that the job losses are a trivial percentage of total jobs in the studied labor-market segment. Such professional behaviors might be chalked up to "cognitive dissonance" by psychologists. However, cognitive dissonance can have economic roots when considered from a brain-focused perspective: by remaining tied to a single theory or set of theories, they might rightfully reason that they can be more productive within some time frame than they would be if they constantly tried to stay abreast of the theories and findings of all, or just a number, of schools of thought and remained flexible in moving among theories and schools of thought. The trick for academics is to pursue their work with some doggedness with a single orientation, but at the same time to remain open to switching to new perspectives, theories, and schools of thought when mounting evidence warrants shifts. (I would be the first to admit that my brain-focused perspective of the discipline could meet with professional resistance precisely for reasons embedded in the economics of the brain that I am seeking to lay out.)

16. Christensen (1997).
17. Lee (1969).
18. I have covered these arguments in McKenzie (2010, Chapter 10).
19. As reported for the *New York Times* by Segal (2016).
20. Mullainathan (2017).
21. Mullainathan (2017).
22. Mullainathan (2017).
23. Becker and Murphy (1988).
24. Mullainathan cites Larcom et al. (2017).
25. Larcom et al. (2017).
26. Mullainathan (2017).
27. Thaler (1990).

References

Ariely, Dan. 2008. *Predictably Irrational: The Hidden Forces That Shape Our Decisions.* New York: HarperCollins.

Bear, Adam, 2016. What neuroscience says about free will. *Scientific American*, June 16.

Becker, Gary S. 1962. Irrational behavior and economic theory. *Journal of Political Economy* 70 (1, February): 1–13.

Becker, Gary S., and Kevin M. Murphy. 1988. A theory of rational addiction. *Journal of Political Economy* 96 (August): 675–700.

Christensen, Clayton. 1997. *Innovator's Dilemma: When New Technologies Cause Great Firms to Fail.* New York: Harper Business.

Freedman, David H. 2010. *Why Experts Keep Failing Us and How to Know When Not to Trust Them.* New York: Little Brown.

Kahneman, Daniel. 2011. *Thinking, Fast and Slow.* New York: Farrar, Straus and Giroux.

Larcom, Shaun, Ferdinand Rauch, and Tim Willems. 2017. The benefits of forced experimentation: Striking evidence from the London underground network. *Quarterly Journal of Economics* 132 (4, November): 2019–2055.

Lee, Dwight. 1969. Utility analysis and repetitive gambling. *American Economist* 13 (2): 87–91.

McKenzie, Richard B. 2010. *Predictably Rational? In Search of Defenses for Rational Behavior in Economics.* Heidelberg: Springer.

Mullainathan, Sendhill. 2017. Why trying new things is so hard to do. *New York Times*, December 1.

Nease, Robert. 2016. *The Power of Fifty Bits: The New Science of Turning Good Intentions into Positive Results.* New York: Harper Business.

Polanyi, Michael. 2009. *The Tacit Dimension* (revised edition). Chicago: University of Chicago Press.

Robinson, E., et al. 2014. Will smaller plates lead to smaller waists? A systematic review and meta-analysis of the effect that experimental manipulation of dishware size has on energy consumption. *Obesity Review*, July.

Segal, David. 2016. Solar snare: Spend thousands and cut power bills by $9 a month. *New York Times*, August 13.

Swartz, Barry. 2005. *The Paradox of Choice*. New York: Harper Perennial.

Thaler, Richard H. 1990. Anomalies: Saving, fungibility, and mental accounts. *Journal of Economic Perspectives* 4 (1): 193–2005.

Thaler, Richard H. 1991. *Quasi Rational Economics*. New York: Russell Sage Foundation.

Wansink, Brian. 2007. *Mindless Eating: Why We Eat More Than We Think*. New York: Bantam.

Wansink, Brian, and Koert van Ittersum. 2006. The visual illusions of food: Why plates, bowls, and spoons can vias consumption volume. *FASEB Journal* 20: A618.

CHAPTER 6

A Brain-Focused Neoclassical Microeconomics

The previous and this chapter have been wide ranging, necessarily so. I have sought to develop a largely new perspective of the core concern of economics as a discipline, shifting the focus from the rationality of people facing external scarcity constraints to the rationality of the human brain facing its own internal scarcity constraints, with the external and internal scarcities inextricably intertwined in its own internal resource allocation decisions and in its decisions relating to external allocation, all made as economically as possible. In the process, I have tried to assimilate and integrate, in preliminary ways, theoretical aspects and findings of evolutionary biology and psychology, behavioral and cognitive psychology, neuroscience and neuroeconomics, behavioral economics, and neoclassical economics. In this last chapter, I seek to refine these points, perspectives, and findings.

The Economic Problem Recast

Scarcity should and must remain at the foundation of the economics disciple. Scarcity gives boundaries to what economists do and how they do it. And scarcity provides a foundation for the employment of logic and deductive thinking. However, the focus of *the* scarcity problem must be markedly recast to focus on the brain's own internal fundamental scarcity problem. After all, the brain's limited abilities and capacities in decision-making is at the core of behaviorists' challenge to neoclassical economics, widely grounded in perfect rationality.

R. B. McKenzie, *A Brain-Focused Foundation for Economic Science*,
https://doi.org/10.1007/978-3-319-76810-6_6

Not only must the brain cope with data supplied through senses which have limitations and frailties, but it also must work within its own evolutionarily limited computing and storing capacities, contained in three pounds of gray matter with between 80 and 100 billion neurons (depending on the source of the estimate). Each neuron has the ability to develop up to 100,000 dendrites (along with axons), or extensions and connections. According to one recent estimate, each of the connectors between neurons, or synapses, can hold about 4.7 bits of information, which means that at maximum the brain can store the equivalent of 4.7 billion average-size books (ten times the previous estimate of the brain's storage capacity).[1] Obviously, in absolute terms, the human brain has a substantial capacity for work. However, it faces daunting demands on its capacity and hardly works error free, or even close, which should never be expected of simple, much less complex, biological systems.

Through electrical and chemical signals sent across synapses, these dendrites connect neurons with each other, typically in their local vicinity. In this way, the brain and nervous system can communicate over an internet-type network with the potential for parallel processing, often within milliseconds, to evaluate sensory information, make decisions, direct actions, and create and store memories, as well as determine how well prior evaluations and decisions have worked and, when economical, adjust its developed algorithms to make better future decisions.

The brain's collaborative communication network includes an enormous number of connections among neurons (maybe several hundred trillion) with the connecting "wiring" estimated to be long enough in a twenty-year-old male to stretch around the globe at the equator four and a half times.[2] Because the network is biology based and densely packed, opportunities for misfires or miss-wirings, short circuits, miscommunications, and poor or just less-than-perfect decisions (in speed, precision, and reliability) are ever-present (and substantial when excessive alcohol or recreational drugs bathe the neurons), given the enormous count of large and small decisions made daily. *Problems* in decision-making (if "problems" is the right word) also may have both biological ***and*** economic sources, with the latter the more underappreciated, especially among economists who labor in both neoclassical and behavioral economics.

The brain's overwhelming economic problem is self-evident, grounded in the fact that the demands placed on it far exceed its capacity to handle them fully, with complete care, precision, and consistency in decision-making. The brain is involved in the continuous operation and maintenance of all physiological functions, including its own. Therefore, the brain can draw *directly* on only a minor portion of all neurons gathered in the prefrontal cortex for its cognitive and decision-making work, although it does draw *indirectly*, at one level or another, on neurons in just about every corner of its mass (as well as biological resources embedded in the "gut" and "heart").

The brain can never be fully at rest, but there is no reason to expect it to operate at full capacity at all times, for biological and economic reasons. Then, very few natural organs or man-made machines work most efficiently at full throttle, with all available resources being used to their absolute maximum, again, for biological and economic reasons. Costs can escalate as "full throttle" is approached (as is true of combustion engines), making any added processing beyond some point questionable (except in exceptional cases, say, when survival is at stake). The economic goal for any survival machine, facing scarcity constraints, is optimization of resource use. "Experts" in any discipline, including economists, hone their thinking skills, and thinking algorithms, to reduce neuronal resource use and to increases their efficiency in use, which, by the way, seems to be descriptive of what economists seek to do in their courses in developing for their students "the economic way of thinking," usually presented in simplified graphical and mathematical models.

Indeed, the brain's conscious decision-making capacity is largely proscribed by the prefrontal cortex, which covers only the top one-quarter inch or so of the brain's surface just beneath the forehead, and accounts for maybe no more than 1% of the brain's total neuron count. The prefrontal cortex includes the brain's "executive functions," which connect past experiences with current sensory data, orchestrate the development of alternative decision algorithms, assess relative merits and values for alternative actions, and make decisions and send out instructions on behaviors to be taken. The brain obviously draws on other parts of the brain for interpretations of sensory and other data flows and for storage and retrieval of short- and long-term memories.

I have noted that the senses can't absorb the entirety of the information inflows they confront daily, and (likely) could not have evolved to do so. Much potential sensory information is simply useless or of limited, peripheral value (quickly failing initial cost/benefit assessments), and processing every information bit would tax scarce energy and neuronal resources and carry opportunity and risk costs.[3]

If any proto-humans in human's distant linage ever were inclined to try to absorb all potential information inflows, they likely became extinct, and quickly so. As they squandered their scarce mental energy on processing information and continually sought replacement energy sources, predators would have taken advantage of their constant distraction from their immediate defense. Evolutionary forces surely have favored our archaic ancestors with brains that economized on their energy resources and who, in paying attention to information inflows, equated at the margin as efficiently as their biological constraints would allow. Therefore, those early humans who found efficient ways of balancing the cost of the added energy and other resources used to process more information against the value of the additional information in pursuit of welfare improvement must have had an advantage in the pursuit of survival and propagation.

Understandably, the brain will be very selective in the variety of the (imperfectly absorbed) information inflows it considers and then will shy from considering all details of those inflows, as noted. Much available, potential information will be ignored, just as people ignore most everything going on around them as they have a conversation in a crowded restaurant. The brain's propensity to block out "irrelevant" information and to focuses on immediate tasks at hand is obvious in how people can ignore traffic lights as they try to text while driving (or walking), sometimes with deadly consequences. People commonly don't remember many details of past events, such as whether the sky was blue or gray as they walked to work, because they were focused on getting there on time.

Indeed, again, as noted earlier, because of its limited resources, the brain compresses much sensory data observed in experiences, not recording (or committing to memory), say, the immediate fine details of the weather at the time of an event. The reason is economic, even when many details of the events, such as the color of the sky may have *some* value to reliving major events, such as when planes flew into the World Trade Center towers on September 11, 2001. The fundamental problem, given limited capacity, is economic: Neurons available for processing and storing memories are scarce, and as more and more details of events or experiences are committed to storage, the costs in terms of alternative uses of the neurons and the energy required can rise while the additional value of the details declines.[4] As a result, when recalling memories, the brain must to some degree decompress memories and then reconstruct events and experiences, filling in many details with, at times, best guesses. In the process, some details can be materially altered, even largely reconstructed (and sometimes fabricated to the point of becoming "false" memories), especially over time and with repeated recalls of given memories.[5]

However, the brain is designed with parallel processing systems—one conscious and cognitive and the other subconscious and working in the background, likely to have evolved to provide the type of redundancy in systems to increase survival chances (for reasons airline pilots and astronauts can appreciate). Sensory data that the conscious prefrontal cortex simply can't handle is not always discarded, but sometimes processed in the subconscious to support and supplement conscious thought. This subconscious processing enables people to "know more than they can tell," to use Polanyi's apt expression, and could be the foundation of intuition.

The Economics of Brain Biases and Failures

Considering the human brain's evolved propensity to economize, especially on information searches, the attention economists give in lectures and textbooks to identifying and emphasizing the role and importance of obscure or non-salient "opportunity costs" and "risk costs" in understanding decision-making is to be expected, but not from the perspective of the neoclassical economics they are teaching.

If economists take a brain-focused perspective of their discipline's foundations, they may better appreciate why many students consider such lectures as "eye-opening" and "insightful," even though the lectures may do nothing more than identify and define the concepts. If such points on non-salient costs are repeated often in, say, different contexts, their relevance can be implanted in the students' evaluative and decision algorithms, effectively making before-class non-salient economic constructs salient. Students can acquire a broader understanding of why people make many of the decisions they do, and make many wrong decisions, and student can learn how to improve their own personal and business decisions to improve their personal welfare and their firms' profitability (making the education self-fortifying).

From a brain-focused perspective on economics, neoclassical economists as educators are effectively telling their students that they will be assuming perfectly rational behavior in order to derive the rules of decision-making that such people would devise, if they could exist. They are making this kind of argument in their classes: "I understand that you face mental challenges in making decisions that improve your personal welfare and the profits of your firms. Models of perfect rationality in decision making lead to the following rules you might want to consider: Consider opportunity costs and ignore sunk costs. Equate at the margin in personal consumption decisions and in firms' production decisions, recognizing that the relevant costs and benefits change with the time period. Indeed, you might consider thinking in terms of discreet time periods, as well as in terms of simplified models (say, supply and demand curves and cost structures that can be devised for different time periods). Understand that problems of adverse selection, moral hazard, principal/agent difficulties, and tragedies of the commons can pervade business and social life." In much of the rest of their courses, economists simply dig ever deeper for progressively less prominent principles of economic behavior that most students have not considered (because, without instructions, or brain training, their value could have gone unnoticed), for example, the law of demand, comparative advantage, and diminishing marginal returns.

Once illuminated, these principles can be widely observed at work in people's behaviors and in markets, and even within the brain's own internal economy. Economists as educators, first and foremost, seek (or should seek) to adjust their students' analytical algorithms. Positive economists might be well advised to see their "professoring" role as largely didactic, if not also normative (contrary to the insistence of Milton Friedman).

Again, note that such lessons stand at sharp odds with professors' earlier lectures in which they develop the discipline's founding premise—perfectly rational behavior. If people, including students, were (or could be, given their evolutionary foundations in bygone eras, divorced from current human environments) as rational as economists assert (or just assume), lectures on rational behavior, basic cost concepts, and "laws" would contribute precious little (or nothing at the extreme) to students' education and work goals. Perfectly rational people are deemed innately capable of precisely and consistently making calculations and decisions and would already be aware of such cost concepts and laws or would be using them without awareness.[6]

Economists can largely chalk up their jobs up to the substantial breach between what they assume about human decision-making and the reality of the thinking proclivities of their students. Actually, economists as educators are, and must be, in the business of making non-salient economic constructions salient and into upgrading the rationality of their students through improvements in the efficiency of their thinking processes. In their initial lectures on rationality, neoclassical economists effectively wipe out their reason d'tre for being in front of their classes in their first lectures on rationality.

The Evolutionarily Constrained Human Brain and the Findings of Behaviorists

My brain-centered perspective can cause behaviorists to reconsider the adoption of a deductive methodology, with their experiments used to test their predictions empirically, grounded in laboratory settings, offering an extra layer of confidence in the general validity of their findings. For example, as noted in Chapter 4, behaviorists have found that students who repeated the last four digits of their Social Security numbers, and had relatively higher numbers, tended to give higher estimated prices for goods up for sale in laboratory/class settings than did students whose last four digits were lower.[7] When students recited their last four digits, they primed their brains to select the same or similar numbers for prices for goods up for sale in experiments because, I would argue, their brains could economize on energy used by defaulting to numbers just recited (less need to search the full range of numbers that could be given, especially without meaningful short-term and long-term incentives to do otherwise).

Behaviorists' concepts of "framing" and "anchoring" also can be understood as ways the brain economizes on its energy reserves. The brain could make many "mistakes," but it could still be optimizing its own efficiency and rationality and, thus, optimizing the welfare gains from human decision-making.

Marketers have reaped greater sales when they have posted sale prices in large fonts next to "original" prices in smaller fonts. Indeed, repeating firm and product names in newspaper and catalogues has the same effect—increased sales.[8] The informational content and persuasive effects (a change in preference, for example) of advertising in a variety of media have long been the explanation for increased sales derived from ad campaigns. But a brain-focused perspective offers another reason for the impact of such ads: They elevate the salience of the products' qualities, prices, and availability, and thereby induce consumers to buy because they can economize on energy that might otherwise be devoted to searching for and analyzing information on alternative goods. In "discouraging" (if that word applies) buyers to search for alternative products, readily available ads reduce the elasticity of demand over and above what would be possible if ads were only offering persuasion and product information (on, say, product attributes).

If a brain bias is involved in advertisers' use of salience in sales campaigns, it must emanate (at least in part) from the brain's evolved proclivity to economize on its internal energy in its search for relevant information for the individual's welfare improvement. If trickery is predominantly involved in the deliberate use of salience in advertising campaigns (as seems to be widely believed), resulting in energy used to lower the brain's welfare, we should expect the brain to make eventual corrections in its choice algorithms. Thus, we should expect a fading of any salience effect with time, as the brain learns (albeit imperfectly, and intentionally so) to guard against such "trickery" (if it is that) used in its accessed information sources, especially after the trick has spread among goods and sellers with its initial success. But who can say that people are worse off because of such "trickery." People can only be maximizers within their evolved decision-making constraints.

The brain's learning capacity suggests that posting clearly contrasting and more prominent sale prices with less prominent original prices will lose some effectiveness in swaying purchase decisions with consumer learning over time, which has been found to be the case.[9] Indeed, the *New York Times* reported that Amazon, the dominant online retailer in the United States, has quietly begun eliminating announcements of "sale" prices alongside "list" prices for two reasons: First, retailers have begun to face a growing number of class-action lawsuits over a form of deceptive advertising, posting "sale prices" beside "list prices" with the latter always in much smaller fonts, when in fact the list prices never applied (or applied for very short periods of time). Second, Amazon had found that the practice of sale prices no longer had a significant effect on sales, at least for many products. The data-driven company will likely eliminate the practice selectively (which has, at this writing, not been shown to be an industry trend).[10]

However, no one should expect the brain always to *eliminate* the effects of salience. With the brain's propensity to economize on all fronts, the elimination of all salience effects in buying decisions (or in any other realm) may simply be too expensive for the marginal benefits achieved. Observed effects of salience, however, are *not* necessarily evidence of the brain's inefficiency or welfare loss and *can* be evidence of the exact opposite. Purchase decisions made based on salience of key information can be made more quickly with less energy, releasing energy for other (rational) purposes, with a net improvement in decision-makers' welfare.

Behaviorists are prone to treat all of their discovered deviations from predicted behaviors based in perfect rationality not only as shortcomings of neoclassical economic models, but also as "irrationalities," or people's shortcomings in mental capacity and ability to maximize their welfare. Maybe so, from the perspective of their experiments and surveys, driven partially by a desire to demonstrate in various ways that the neoclassical economists have no clothes. But those conclusions do not exactly square with the brain-focused perspective of the discipline's core economic problem—that the human brain seeks its own maximum efficiency and welfare, via decisions that maximize the individual's welfare, given its own tight constraints on all margins. Behaviors and decisions deemed "irrationalities" from behaviorists' perspective can be seen as expected and allowed, if not sought after, collateral damage from the brain's maximizing efforts within its evolved constraints.

Observed irrationalities can often (not necessarily and not likely always) be the consequence of adopted decisions rules, based on the best available past experiences and the best-known decision algorithms, which are bound to have flaws because of the economics of developing them, and thus, will result in some faulty behavioral outcomes. But perfection in the development of the brain's algorithm is not achievable and imperfections in them are to be expected if the brain is expected to rationally allocate its own resources efficiently, with the costs and benefits of added improvements in decision-making always kept in mind. Also, the brain can adopt some algorithms as Knightian relatively absolute absolutes, with the intentions of testing their validity not so much in isolated decisions but over a portfolio of decisions and with the intent of revising them when evidence piles up that suggests some other decision-making framework is superior (not necessarily more correct or more economical).

This is to say that observed flawed decisions and behaviors, even when repeated, can be no more irrational and welfare destroying for the brain than are product failures for multiproduct firms or missed jump shots in basketball games. Flawed decisions can be seen as part and parcel of a sizable array of decisions that, on net and with time, are welfare enhancing. Indeed, any energy saved in making a flawed decision (within a portfolio of decisions) may be used to enhance the value of other decisions (not covered in behaviorists' experiments) to a degree that surpasses the value of the flawed decision, a generalization that flows readily from a brain-focused neoclassical economics, but not from either traditional neoclassical economics or behavioral economics.

Product managers for multiproduct firms can rightfully be seen as portfolio managers, with attention totally focused on the return from their *portfolios*, not from *individual* products. Similarly, as a portfolio manager of decisions, the brain probably faces more demands on a far greater portfolio than any actual product portfolio manager in the "real world." Brains should also be expected to look at their total rate of return on cross-sections of decisions.

And do note that behaviorists have been devoted to cataloging a lengthy list of "wrong" decisions people make. However, given the coverage limits of their research to date (made necessary in part by research costs), they can't jump to the conclusion that people are "predictably irrational," or even largely irrational.[11] People make daily a multitude of decisions, and behaviorists have surely studied only a minor (maybe a trivial) fraction of them, and largely under conditions far removed from being "ecologically adaptive."

Predictions from a Brain-Focused Economics

When I attempted to explain briefly to a colleague steeped in neoclassical economics my attempts in this book to shift the central "economic problem" from scarcity in the external world to scarcity in the human brain, his reaction was understandably: "Well, can you make testable predictions?"

At the most general level, my reaction is "Why not?" My brain-focused foundation for economic science has all the basic elements needed for modeling and the pursuit of science that neoclassical economics has (and certainly more than behavioral economics, which is, for the most part, devoid of a deductive theory). Robbins pitted the external world's limited resources against people's unlimited (subjective) wants. In my reconstruction, I pit the brain's limited resources against the excessive demands on their use. The human brain can reasonably be considered an evolved maximizer/optimizer—within its evolved constraints—ready-made to equate at the margin on the costs and benefits of making decisions with the goal of extending the precision, complexity, and completeness—and welfare value of decisions, both individually when economical and collectively, as decision portfolios.

Moreover, the human brain has an evolved capacity to devise algorithms for making alternative decisions and then to estimate, within evolved bounds, of the associated risks and uncertainties relative values and then to make comparative subjective valuations for the computed consequences of alternative decisions. Obviously, through learning, the brain's decision-making algorithms can be revised for improvements, when the revisions themselves pass economic (costs and benefits) assessments. Perfect (or optimum) rationality of the brain doesn't imply perfect rationality, or total correctness, in decisions, as conventionally assessed. Indeed, quite the opposite. After all, the human brain is an economy unto itself. Economists have long been comfortable with anticipated and unanticipated flaws in the operations of firms, workers, and consumers. Flaws in economies are hardly unexpected given their complexities. Indeed, they can be planned as part of cost-minimization strategies for collections of decisions through time. On balance, greater welfare gains that would not otherwise be possible. The trick for the brain is to deal with its prospective flaws from a portfolio perspective, with a net positive gain expected. I am simply suggesting that the same line of thinking can be applied to decision-making within the brain, using its own internal resources and external resources and technology (e.g., computers) economically.

There really is no basis for assuming anything other than that the brain is perfectly efficient and rational in its decision-making both for itself and for the individual human host. And there is no reason to fall back on the presumption that the brain engages in "satisficing" or works to make decisions that are "good enough." I don't understand why the brain would want to settle for less than what is doable, economically speaking, given the excessive demands made on its limited resources. Some might say the brain is "lazy" (which seems to suggest that the brain will not recklessly avoid working at maximum capacity), but such a claim seems to be tantamount to disclosing another embedded resource constraint of the brain's economy and the need for it to conserve limited energy resources as best it can to serve other physical and mental demands.

Yes, we might now *imagine* that the brain *could be* reconstituted in various ways to make even better decisions. For example, the primitive brain, limbic systems, and cerebral cortex might be better positioned and integrated for greater efficacy and with perhaps a greater capacity to store and retrieve memories through the use of more exact "addresses," much the way computers do. But of course, we don't have the option of replaying evolution for the purpose of achieving such imagined "advantages." In fact, any replay of evolution would not necessarily result in an improved brain construction compared with what we have from the evolutionary process that actually has played out over billions of years. The brain that emerges from a replay of evolution could even be worse in terms of achieving welfare improvements from its decisions. A replay of evolution would, literally, be a crap shoot on making humans smarter through more efficiently constructed brains.

On predictive power, my reconstruction of the foundation of economics has two primary effects:

- First, my reconstruction makes the basic rationality premise of the discipline more incontrovertible (or, maybe more guarded, less subject to the heavy criticisms behaviorists have leveled against perfect rationality in "human" decision-making now employed in neoclassical economics).
- Second, my reconstruction does suggest a potential for added complexity in economic modeling, since the maximizing/optimizing entity is one theoretical step removed from the usual maximizing/optimizing entity, the human being taken as a whole. Thus, modeling must include interactions between the brain's internal economy and the external economy in which humans must operate.

Also, my revision predicts that a perfectly rational brain will result in less than perfectly rational decision-making by real-world human beings, or, better yet, will result in some form of "rational rationality" that *could* rob economic modeling of the niceties of being able to theorize by seeking out first and second-order conditions for human decision-making. However, I am not willing to concede the point because "rational rationality" could be visited as "optimal rationality," which means that neoclassical analytical thinking can be applied to the brain's decision-making. But then, is the complexity of modeling under conditions of optimal rationality any greater than is required in capital theory in which there are interconnected effects of people's current purchases of capital goods (including human capital goods) and the feedback effects between capital uses and people's welfares over time? Or are the modeling problems in my revised perspective any more complex than the strings of interconnected, game-theoretic decisions business people must make in, say, oligopoly markets? Granted, such game-theoretic problems may not have easily identified predictable solutions, but is that kind of conclusion cause for pausing before transferring decision-making at the individual level to proposed "choice architects," often selected by politics, to settle decisions for a host of individuals (if not the entire population)? Surely, the supposed decision-making flaws behaviorists have uncovered in their (imperfect) experimental settings could be magnified in the macro decisions of choice architects.

Similarly, are the added complexities likely to be any more confounding than the problems in information and search theory in which people can be expected to optimize on information sought only by first considering the costs and benefits of the information itself and then the costs and benefits of seeking out the costs and benefits of the information searches? Perhaps there are added hidden complexities that I can't now imagine, because all feedback loops are not and cannot be known in advance. Theorizing must be, as in all else, a matter of assessing the problems (costs) of added complexities compared with the potential gains from theorizing, both evaluated on the same subjective scale. And modeling requires that the complexities be reduced to manageable proportions, in full recognition of the scarcity of brain resources.

Frankly, I see no reason why the various points Milton Friedman makes in his methodological essay (1953) can't be applied (with only minor adjustments) to my shift in the scarcity foundation of economic science.

I admit that I am engaging here in a form methodological entrepreneurship. Lionel Robbins did not fully understand in the early 1930s how his conceived foundations of the discipline would be received, used, extended, and crystalized considerably over the next three-quarters of a century. I am no better positioned to predict the future of my revised foundation than Robbins was—and probably less so—because I am potentially adding a layer of complexity in economic theorizing that, admittedly, I can't now fully understand and appreciate.

Most importantly, my proposed approach must pass the initial test of professional acceptance of the *prospects* (with due consideration for risk and uncertainties) of my revision having as much or more economic merit as Robbins' approach. Let the debate begin. Here, I need to offer outlines of tentative hypotheses/predictions that can be derived from my perspective of the discipline's foundation.

Prediction Prospects

I hope that at least some of the potential predictive power of my proposed shift in the discipline's foundation is now self-evident, although I have in scattered ways shown in the previous and this chapter an array of predictions, mainly relating to behaviorists' findings, that can be made from my brain-centered perspective. The most fundamental prediction is that perfect rationality in human decision-making will never be observed in people's behaviors, given the human brain evolved to be efficient and rational itself. Irrationalities (as judged by the construction of perfect rationality in neoclassical economics) in decision-making should be easily found, as they have been.

Decision Mistakes and Welfare

However, many observed irrationalities conventionally defined, need not be "mistakes," unexpected or not, with outcomes that diminish welfare. Indeed, at least a likely nontrivial share of them can be welfare enhancing to the extent that they enable the brain to be more efficient and relieve pressure on its resource and process constraints, which can make, overall, for more rational decisions regarding its internal resources and those in the external world. This means that many so-called irrationalities are part and parcel of a process of welfare enhancement, as more widely defined than in neoclassical or behavioral economics. It should follow that human welfare can be predictably undercut if all (or just many) supposed "irrationalities" are systematically eliminated through, say, nudges concocted by behaviorists or, worse yet, policymakers some distance from the varying local information that a multitude of people confront daily with their brains that have devised their own algorithms and heuristics and decision portfolios to accommodate their local conditions that don't match those of all others (especially self-appointed choice architects working with the backing of government regulations).

Propensities to Specialize and Trade

I have already noted how a brain-focused view of resource scarcity predicts an innate, evolved propensity on the part of people to search for opportunities for specializing labor and other resources and for trades. Such a propensity not only can lead to greater efficiency in the use of resources in the external world, as neoclassical (and maybe many behavioral) economists have long taught, but also trade, with specialization and growth (interconnected in Adam Smith's *Wealth of Nations*), can relieve the scarcity pressures on the brain's efforts to allocate its own resources efficiently and rationally. A major difference between Smith's approach and mine is that Smith assumed a propensity on the part of people to specialize and trade partially from his daily observations solely and from external scarcity conditions (at least as I read his treatise). I offer a brain-focused explanation for Smith's presumption and an efficiency and welfare consequence, an interaction between the mental and external spheres, that Smith and his followers do not seem to have considered or appreciated.

With specialization and trade, the brain can free some of its resources for perfecting a more limited range of skills, with the prospects of an improved welfare beyond what economists have touted for trade-inspired efficiencies in the use of external resources. In turn, making decisions about external resources can become more efficient and rational, or human rationality in decision-making (apart from the brain's efficiency and rationality) can be elevated above what it would otherwise be.

Endogenous Rationality and Welfare Improvement

Note that this brain-focused welfare gain from specialization and trade is ruled out in neoclassical economics by its founding premise, perfect rationality. Perfect decision-making can't be improved. My line of argument leaves room for improvement in rationality by making it an endogenous variable. The extent and quality of the rationality of decision-making becomes a function of external as well as internal conditions, with competitiveness of markets an important consideration. Competitive market pressures can weed out consistently irrational market participants, as Friedman posited, but it can also induce all market decision-makers—competitors—to pay closer attention to the market feedback effects and, thereby, can put pressure on their brains to devise more cost-effective (profitable and welfare enhancing) algorithms, heuristics, and decision portfolios.

After all, participants' welfares are at stake, not to mention their potential market survival. This leads to a prediction that people in pressing competitive markets will more likely be more rational than they are in some nonbusiness or nonmarket settings (including many behaviorists' laboratories) where competition is denied or made less pressing, with no offsetting experimental pressures, than in markets. Competitive market pressures can induce participants to hone their skills to equate costs and benefits at the margin, ignore sunk costs, consider opportunity costs; to more accurately discount future costs and benefits; and to make choices more consistently than, say, in social settings. Market participants, who may not be initially prone to hone their choices with economic care, can learn from others who have caved to the market pressures and have become more rational than they would otherwise be in their decision-making (by, for instance, ignoring sunk costs or considering opportunity costs). Those market participants who follow the more efficient and welfare-enhancing decisions of others can possibly lower their mental energy costs and improve their decisions, adding to the competitive pressures on other wayward decision-making holdouts. This line of argument, of course, suggests that competitors' decisions can become more rational and market outcomes can become more efficient, but only with time as feedback loops play out.

From the perspective being posited in this book, economists as educators can, again, see student value in their courses not now widely recognized. Economists can effectively tell their students that competitors in markets will enter markets, making business decisions with varying degrees of rationality (and irrationality) (as behaviorists have repeatedly found). Those who get decisions "right" will have competitive cost advantages that can increase their chances for market survival and profitability. Those who consistently make "wrong" decisions will face cost disadvantages and pressures to change their decision-making. Students have the option of learning "right" economic heuristics for business decisions through real-world market experience, which can be costly. Or the students can pay attention to the decision-making heuristics that emerge in economic courses and then apply them, when deemed appropriate, in their ongoing market decisions.

Irrationality as a Variable

Behaviorists should expect the count and pervasiveness of irrationalities in decision-making to be greater in their laboratory settings than in competitive market settings, which suggests a potential explanation for many people's hostility to reliance on markets economies (which is to say, "capitalism"): Markets can pressure participants to be more calculating and more rational than they might want to be (and incur more mental energy costs than wanted), just as competitive market pressures can force sellers (workers included) to accept lower prices than they would like to receive. That is, market participants can now have two reasons to suppress competition in their markets: Through suppression of competitive pressures, competitors can, first, hike their prices and profits. Second, they can ease energy demands on their brains. Put another way, market participants may seek market controls because the controls can allow them to relax the pressure on their brains to make more exacting decisions.

As widely recognized, the efficiency of transportation and communications can affect competitive market pressures because of increases in the scope of markets, as widely recognized, but also, as not so widely recognized, they can affect the efficiency and rationality of people's brains and their decision-making. For example, an increase in communication efficiency can lead to improvements in the mental algorithms of those who adopt the technologies, which can upgrade the rationality of their decision-making. Feedback loops improved by more efficient communications can have the same effect. Behaviorists' studies that don't allow for communications and feedback loops in laboratory settings are bound to result in more irrationalities than would be expected in real-world settings in which communications and feedback loops abound and play out over time.

Neuroscientists have found that the brain often needs repeated encounters with the same names, phone numbers, or emotional experiences (as well as economic concepts as basic as the law of demand) for the information to be etched tightly into neuro-networks that form the basis of memories, heuristics, and new or revised algorithms for decision-making. Of course, people need good reasons—namely consequential incentives—to take the time and mental energy to allow the repeated experiences to be implanted in their brain's neuro-networks. Many laboratory-based studies have provided no, or trivial incentives, for people's brains to do the work of allocating its resources among alternative uses, many of which can have consequential mental costs. This finding leads to the prediction that the pervasiveness of irrationalities should be expected to subside somewhat when subjects are offered repeated encounters with experiences and have sufficient reason to give problems in laboratory settings more than casual and momentary attention. In more concrete terms, problems associated with salience and endowment effects are likely to be less common among experienced subjects in real-world competitive settings than in laboratory settings, which are necessarily sterilized of many adaptive attributes of real-world settings.

Technology and Rationality

Computer technologies can enable people to offload many mental demands, say, from undertaking complex computations to storing facts and figures. It can, therefore, improve decision-making by freeing up some of the brain's limited neuronal resources for a variety of tasks beyond computations and data storage. Admittedly, the *net* impact of modern technologies on decision-making in the external world is not now clear. Many people may be using the time once devoted to memorizing, for example, state capitals to staring at an array of social media sites for hours each day. However, competitive market pressures may still induce more people to use the technologies to upgrade rational decision-making. For that reason, we might not be surprised if many people are hostile to the introduction of many computer technologies that make them think more competitively and rational, with cost savings and profits elevated concerns in business.

Market Power and Rationality

In conventional neoclassical economics, owners and managers of monopolies have the same drive to make "right" (rational) decisions as do competitors under any other market structures, even down to perfect competitors. Accordingly, growth in monopoly power leads only to greater curbs in production, higher prices, and greater inefficiencies. The rationality of decision-making is unchanged as the market structure is changed. The reason is simple: all decision-makers in all firms in all market structures are assumed to be perfectly rational.[12]

However, from my brain-focused perspective of markets, monopolization of markets might rightfully be expected to impair rationality in decision-making. Without monopolies' survival being threatened, as is the case for individual firms at all times under perfect competition, the brain can be expected to be less concerned about making exacting decision, simply as a matter of curbs in the various pressures to do so. Hence, we might be able to predict that as market power of firms increases, owners' and managers' brains can be expected to relax somewhat, with one consequence being less exacting (and profitable) decisions. Some of the rent effect of monopoly power can be absorbed by owners' and managers' rational brains. Irrationalities (or less exacting decisions), at least beyond some point in growing market power, are likely to rise, which suggests that the welfare loss of monopolies might be expected to be greater than the welfare, deadweight loss described in neoclassical monopoly models. Again, this is, because of the ability of firms with market power to survive even with relaxation of the rationality and efficiency of their decision-making rules, which can lessen pressure on cost containment.[13]

My line of argument leads to the conclusion that trade liberation will likely have a greater impact on economic growth than Smith and his neoclassical followers entertained. Trade liberalization can lead to people's brains being induced to work more diligently and efficiently, yielding more rational decisions in the use of their internal resources, as well as external resources.

Even pure monopolies do not escape all competitive pressures. Maybe so in their product markets, where they are protected, to one extent or another, by entry barriers. However, in conventional monopoly models, monopolies still face competitive pressures in their labor and financial markets, which can be expected to contain somewhat owners' and managers' inclinations to relax under their product-market protections.

Government monopolies, on the other hand, may face labor market pressures, but not the financial market pressures that private monopolies face daily, with their "irrationalities" showing up in downward movements in their stock prices. Government monopolies might be expected, as a consequence, to exhibit more irrationalities and greater welfare losses than private monopolies, because the latter feel more competitive pressures to adjust their mental algorithms to achieve maximum efficiency in decision-making from owners' residual claimancies. The line of argument here suggests another unheralded consequence, a potential gap in the mental acuity of workers in protected government environments and market environments, whether protected or not.

Rationality and Neuroscience

My reconstruction of the discipline allows for ties between the findings in neuroscience and economic forces and welfare. For example, street drugs have long been proven to have effects on the brain's operations, which with my approach can be tied to the efficiency and rationality of the brain's decision-making (as well as preferences for goods and services). Hence, debilitating drugs can doubly impair human welfare: first, through greater inefficiency and irrationality in the use of the users' brain's internal resources, and, second, through the impact of the impaired decision-making on the allocation of available external resources, which, through market forces, can impair the welfare of nonusers.

For example, as noted earlier, neuroeconomist Paul Zak has found that the brain chemical oxytocin affects people's trust in others and in their trustworthiness.[14] Bans on hugging children in schools, churches, and scouting organizations to protect children from overtures by pedophiles can retard children's emotional development, which can show up in lowered educational performances.[15] The hugging bans can curb the rationality and efficiency of brains' own internal decisions, which can also undercut the welfare of others through market forces.

I could go on, but won't because I intend only to be suggestive here as to how my brain-focused foundation for economics can change and improve economic thinking. In neoclassical economics, the thinking and decision-making of both economists and their subjects can't be improved. My reconstruction points to the way thinking can be improved.

Concluding Comments

Neoclassical economists have been dedicated to understanding people's interactions with each other and with the real world. In doing so, they have highlighted the importance of, say, specialization of resources (such as labor) and trade in elevating growth and human welfare through changes in the allocation of external resources. I have remained on the same methodological page in this regard.

However, I have sought to expand the "pages" (or layers) of economic analysis. With my brain-focused view of the discipline, I can't help but point to the brain's own scarcity problems that would cause it to be predisposed *naturally* to opportunities for their hosts to specialize and trade. Such a predisposition can give rise to added neoclassical economic efficiencies in resource allocation and use and to welfare gains of all involved in a market system.

I'd like economists to turn the page and come to understand that economies from specialization and trade can be more deeply seated, profound, and expansive than previously recognized and inspired by an unrecognized force, the evolved human brain's efforts to economize on its own internal resources. The turn of this page has revealed another source of economies: Institutional and policy changes can increase the efficiency and rationality of the brain's own operations, which can result in more efficient and more rational (or less irrational) human decision-making in both economists' and psychologists' realms of investigations. In turn, more rational decision-making can lead to greater human welfare that, with parallel and serial feedback information loops, can lead to even greater efficiency and rationality of the human brain.

Notes

1. As reported by a *Telegraph* Reporter (2016), citing the research of Terry Sejnowki at the Salk Institute in California.
2. As reported by Fields (2011). By age eighty the length of the brain's "wiring" is down to less than 60% of its peak at age twenty.
3. Much sensory information is buffered in the subconscious.
4. My arguments are grounded in a general proposition: The laws of diminishing marginal returns and benefits are as universal as gravity, or at least approximately close. They can't be denied in biological systems.
5. Psychologist Elizabeth Loftus asked children in her laboratory to recall their visits to Disneyland, and through her interjected suggestions caused a fourth to a third of the children over several sessions to claim with detailed descriptions that they were hugged and touched inappropriately by Pluto. Loftus' catch was that Pluto is not among the characters at Disneyland and could not have been a part of the children's visits. The literature is full of similar cases of what she describes as "implanted false memories" (Loftus 1997).
6. Neoclassical economists might explain that the time they spend on such concepts and laws is simply directed toward elevating subconscious decision-making to consciousness so that students can better understand what people are really doing (or should be doing) out of sight inside their brains. However, behaviorists' studies have shown otherwise.
7. Ariely (2008, pp. 25–29).
8. Kim (2006).
9. Akerlof (1991).
10. Streitfeld (2016).
11. See Arielle (2008).

12. In this section, I briefly cover conventional points on monopoly power, as conventionally taught in microeconomics textbooks. I may give the impression that I uncritically accept the conventional arguments, which I do not. I do not introduce my contrarian points on the conventional treatment of monopoly power because doing so would be a major digression that adds little to my goal of laying out my brain-focused view of the economics discipline. See my book with Dwight Lee, *In Defense of Monopoly*, 2008.
13. I should note, also, that because of the relaxed survival pressures monopolies face, monopolists may not work with the same diligence to restrict production all the way to the point of profit maximization, which means that monopolies' curbs in production and the deadweight loss of monopoly can be reduced somewhat from what is deduced in conventional neoclassical monopoly models.
14. Zak (2012).
15. See Shelton and McKenzie (2012–2013).

References

Akerlof, George A. 1991. Procrastination and obedience. *American Economic Review* 81 (2): 1–19.

Ariely, Dan. 2008. *Predictably Irrational: The Hidden Forces That Shape Our Decisions*. York: HarperCollins.

Fields, R. Douglas. 2011. Brain wiring: After age 20 its all downhill. *Psychology Today*, June 21.

Friedman, Milton. 1953. *The Methodology of Positive Economics*. Chicago: University of Chicago Press.

Kim, Hyeong Min. 2006. Consumers' responses to price presentation formats in rebate advertisements. *Journal of Retailing* 82 (4): 309–317

Loftus, Elizabeth F. 1997. Creating false memories. *Scientific American* 277 (September): 70–75.

Shelton, Kathryn, and Richard B. McKenzie. 2012–2013. Pedophiles and the regulation of Hugging. *Regulation* (Cato Institute), Winter.

Streitfeld, David. 2016. Amazon is quietly eliminating list prices. *New York Times*, July 3. Available online from https://www.nytimes.com/2016/07/04/business/amazon-is-quietly-eliminating-list-prices.html.

Telegraph Reporter (unnamed). 2016. Human brain can store 4.7 billion books—Ten times more than originally thought. *The Telegraph*, January 21.

Zak, Paul. 2012. *The Moral Molecule: The Source of Love and Prosperity*. Boston: Dutton.

Bibliography

Adler, Jerry. 2013. Why fire makes us human. *Smithsonian Magazine*, June.
Aiello, L., and P. Wheeler. 1995. The expensive-tissue hypothesis: The brain and the digestive system in human and primate evolution. *Current Anthropology* 36: 199–221.
Akerlof, George A. 1991. Procrastination and obedience. *American Economic Review* 81 (2): 1–19.
Allais, M. 1953. Le comportement del'homme rationnel devant le risqué, critique des postulats et axioms de l'ecole Americaine. *Econometrics* 21: 503–546.
Ariely, Dan. 2008. *Predictably Irrational: The Hidden Forces That Shape Our Decisions.* New York: HarperCollins.
Arkes, Hal R., and Catherine Blumer. 1985. The psychology of sunk cost. *Organizational Behavior and Human Decision Processes* 35 (February): 124–140.
Aronson, E., and J. Mills. 1959. The effects of the severity of the initiation on liking for a group. *Journal of Abnormal and Social Psychology* 59: 177–181.
Bear, Adam, 2016. What neuroscience says about free will. *Scientific American*, June 16.
Becker, Gary S. 1962. Irrational behavior and economic theory. *Journal of Political Economy* 70 (1, February): 1–13.
Becker, Gary S. 1963. A reply to Israel Kirzner. *Journal of Political Economy* 71 (February): 82–83.
Becker, Gary S. 1971. *The Economics of Discrimination*. Chicago: University of Chicago Press (originally published in 1957).
Becker, Gary S. 1976. *The Economic Approach to Human Behavior*. Chicago: University of Chicago Press.

R. B. McKenzie, *A Brain-Focused Foundation for Economic Science*,
https://doi.org/10.1007/978-3-319-76810-6

Becker, Gary S. 1993. *A Treatise on the Family* (expanded edition). Cambridge, MA: Harvard University Press.

Becker, Gary S. 1994. *Human Capital: A Theoretical and Empirical Approach.* Chicago: University of Chicago Press.

Becker, Gary S. 1996. *Accounting for Tastes.* Cambridge, MA: Harvard University Press.

Becker, Gary S. 1997. *The Economics of Life.* Chicago: University of Chicago Press.

Becker, Gary S., and Kevin M. Murphy. 1988. A theory of rational addiction. *Journal of Political Economy* 96 (August): 675–700.

Bonnefon, Jean-François, Azim Shariff, and Iyad Rahwan. 2016. The social dilemma of autonomous vehicles. *Science* 352 (6291): 1573–1576.

Brown, Charles, Curtis Gilroy, and Andrew Kohen. 1982. The effect of the minimum wage on employment and unemployment. *Journal of Economic Literature* 20: 487–528.

Berg, J., J. Dickhaut, and K. McCabe. 2005. Rick preference instability across institutions: A dilemma. *Proceedings National Academy of Sciences* 102: 4209–4214.

Boehm, Christopher. 1993. Egalitarian behavior and reverse dominance hierarchy. *Current Anthropology* 14: 227–254.

Buchanan, James M., and Gordon Tulloch. 1962. *The Calculus of Consent: Logical Foundations of Constitutional Democracy.* Ann Arbor, MI: University of Michigan Press.

Buchanan, James M. 1975. *The Limits of Liberty: Between Anarchy and Leviathan.* Chicago: University of Chicago Press.

Buss, David M. 1986. Human mate selection. *American Scientist* 73: 47–51.

Buss, David M. 1988. The evolution of human sexual competition: Tactics of mate attraction. *Journal of Personality and Social Psychology* 54: 616–628.

Buss, David M. 1989. Sex differences in human mate preferences: Evolutionary hypotheses tested in 37 cultures. *Behavioral and Brain Sciences* 12: 1–14.

Buss, David M. 2003. *The Evolution of Desire: Strategies of Human Mating.* New York: Basic Books.

Buss, David M., and Michael F. Barnes. 1986. Preferences in human mate selection. *Journal of Personality and Social Psychology* 50: 559–570.

Buss, David M., et al. 1990. International preferences in selecting mates: A study of 37 societies. *Journal of Cross-Cultural Psychology* 21: 5–47.

Camerer, Colin F., and George Loewenstein. 2004. Behavioral economics: Past, present, and future. In *Advances in Behavioral Economics*, ed. Colin F. Camerer, George Loewenstein, and Matthew Rabin. Princeton, NJ: Princeton University Press.

Castro, J.M. Bermudez de, M. Martinon-Tores, S. Sarmiento, M. Lozano, J.L. Arsuaga, and E. Carbonell. 2003. Rates of anterior tooth wear in middle

Pleistocene hominines from Sima de Los Huesos (Sierra de Atapuerca, Spain). *PNAS* 100 (21, October 14): 11992–11996.
Card, David, and Alan B. Krueger. 1995. *Myth and Measurement: The New Economics of the Minimum Wage*. Princeton, NJ: Princeton University Press.
Cattau, Christopher E., et al. 2017. Rapid morphological change of a top predator with the invasion of novel prey. *Nature Ecology and Evolution* 2 (1, November 27): 108–115.
Christensen, Clayton. 1997. *Innovator's Dilemma: When New Technologies Cause Great Firms to Fail*. New York: Harper Business.
Cosmides, Leda, John Tooby, and Jerome H. Barkow. 1992. Introduction: Evolutionary psychology and conceptual integration. In *The Adapted Mind: Evolutionary Psychology and the Generation of Culture*, ed. Jerome H. Barkow, Leda Cosmides, and John Tooby, 3–18. New York: Oxford University Press.
Cowles, Alfred, and H. Jones. 1937. Some posteriori probabilities in stock market action. *Econometrica* 5: 280–294.
Darwin, Charles. 1859. *Origins of the Species by Means of Natural Selection*. New York: Random House (republished 1979).
Dawkins, Richard. 1978. *The Selfish Gene*. Oxford, UK: Oxford University Press (paperback).
Dennett, Daniel C. 2003. *Freedom Evolves*. New York: Viking Adult.
Dunbar, R.I.M. 1993. Coevolution of neocortical size, group size and language in humans. *Behavioral and Brain Sciences* 16 (4): 681–735.
Editors. 1987. The right minimum wage: "$0.00." *New York Times*, January 14.
Elder, Glen H. 1969. Appearance and education in marriage mobility. *American Sociological Review* 34 (4): 519–533.
Fama, Eugene F. 1965a. The behavior of stock market prices. *Journal of Business* 38: 34–105.
Fama, Eugene F. 1965b. Random walks in stock market prices. *Financial Analysts Journal* 21 (5, September/October): 55–59.
Fedrigo, O., A. Pfefferle, et al. 2011. A potential role for glucose transporters in the evolution of human brain size. *Brain, Behavior and Evolution* 78: 315–326.
Fields, R. Douglas. 2011. Brain wiring: After age 20 its all downhill. *Psychology Today*, June 21.
Frank, Steven A. 2009. Evolutionary foundations of cooperation and group cohesion. In *Games, Groups, and the Global Good*, ed. Simon A. Levin. Heidelberg: Springer.
Freedman, David H. 2010. *Why Experts Keep Failing Us and How to Know When Not to Trust Them*. New York: Little Brown and Company.
Friedman, Milton. 1953. *The Methodology of Positive Economics*. Chicago: University of Chicago Press.
Friedman, Milton. 2007. *Price Theory: A Provisional Text*. New Brunswick, NJ: Transaction Publishers (first published in 1962).

Friedman, Milton. 1966. *Essays in Positive Economics*. New York: University of Chicago Press.

Friedman, Milton. 1976. Inflation and unemployment. *Nobel Memorial Lecture*, December 13.

Genesove, David, and Christopher Mayer. 2001. Loss aversion and seller behavior: Evidence from the housing market. *Quarterly Journal of Economics* 116 (4, November): 1233–1260.

Gerard, H.B., and G.C. Mathewson. 1966. The effects of severity of initiation on liking for a group: A replication. *Journal of Experimental Social Psychology* 2 (July): 278–287.

Gigerenzer, Gerd, Peter M. Todd, and the ABC Research Group, editors. 1999a. *Simple Heuristics That Make Us Smart*. Oxford, UK: Oxford University Press.

Gigerenzer, Gerd, and Peter M. Todd. 1999b. Fast and frugal heuristics: The adaptive toolbox. In *Simple Heuristics That Make Us Smart*, ed. Gerd Gigerenzer, Peter M. Todd, and the ABC Research Group, 1–18. Oxford, UK: Oxford University Press.

Gigerenzer, Gerd. 2008. *Rationality for Mortals: How People Cope with Uncertainty*. New York: Oxford University Press.

Gintis, Herbert. 2000a. *Game Theory Evolving*. Princeton, NJ: Princeton University Press.

Gintis, Herbert. 2000b. Strong reciprocity and human sociality. *Journal of Theoretical Biology* 211: 169–179.

Gould, Stephen Jay. 1990. *Wonderful Life: Burgess Shale and the Nature of History*. New York: W. W. Norton.

Gourville, John T., and Dilip Soman. 1998. Payment depreciation: The effects of temporally separating payments from consumption. *Journal of Consumer Research* 25 (September): 160–174.

Hamilton, W.D. 1963. The evolution of altruistic behavior. *American Naturalist* 97 (896): 354–356.

Hamilton, W.D. 1964. The genetical evolution of social behaviour. *Journal of Theoretical Biology* 7 (1): 1–16.

Hayek, F.A. 1943. Scientism and the study of society: Part II. *Economica* 10 (37): 34–63 (reprinted in Hayek, 2010).

Hayek, F.A. 1944. Scientism and the study of society: Part III. *Economica* 11 (41): 27–39 (reprinted in Hayek, 2010).

Hayek, F.A. 1945. The use of knowledge in society. *American Economic Review* 35 (4, September): 519–530.

Hayek, F.A. 2010. *Studies on the Abuse and Decline of Reason: Text and Documents*, ed. Bruce Caldwell. Chicago, IL: University of Chicago Press.

Hoffman, Elizabeth, Kevin A. McCabe, and Vernon L. Smith. 1998. Behavioral foundations of reciprocity: Experimental economics and evolutionary psychology. *Economic Inquiry* 36: 335–352.

Holmes, Bob. 2009. Did the ice age boost human brain size? *New Scientist*, July 29.

Isaac, R. Mark, James M. Walker, and Susan H. Thomas. 1984. Divergent evidence on free riding: An experimental examination and possible explanation. *Public Choice* 43: 113–149.

Isaac, R. Mark, Kenneth F. McCue, and Charles Plott. 1985. Public goods provision in an experimental environment. *Journal of Public Economics* 26: 51–74.

Isaac, R. Mark, and D. James. 2000. Just who are you calling risk averse. *Journal of Risk and Uncertainty* 20: 177–187.

Jones, Philip, and John Cullis. 2000. Individual failure: And the analytics of social policy. *Journal of Social Policy* 29 (1): 73–93.

Kahneman, Daniel. 2011. *Thinking, Fast and Slow*. New York: Farrar, Straus and Giroux.

Kahneman, Daniel, and Amos Tversky. 1979. Prospect theory: An analysis of decisions under risk. *Econometrica* 47: 313–327.

Kahneman, Daniel, and Amos Tversky. 2000a. Choices, values, and frames, as reprinted in *Choices, Values, and Frames*, ed. Daniel Kahneman and Amos Tversky, 1–16. Cambridge, UK: Cambridge University Press.

Kahneman, Daniel, and Amos Tversky. 2000b. Prospect theory: An analysis of decision under risk, as reprinted in *Choices, Values, and Frames*, ed. Daniel Kahneman and Amos Tversky, 17–43. Cambridge, UK: Cambridge University Press.

Kahneman, Daniel, J. Knetsch, and Richard H. Thaler. 1990. Experimental tests of the endowment and the Coase Theorem. *Journal of Political Economy* 98 (6): 1325–1348.

Keynes, John Neville. 1891. *The Scope and Method of Political Economy*. London: Macmillan.

Kim, Hyeong Min. 2006. Consumers' responses to price presentation formats in rebate advertisements. *Journal of Retailing* 82 (4): 309–317.

Kim, Oliver, and Mark Walker. 1984. The free rider problem: Experimental evidence. *Public Choice* 43: 3–24.

Kirzner, Israel M. 1962. Rational action and economic theory. *Journal of Political Economy* 70 (4, August): 380–385.

Kirzner, Israel M. 1963. Rejoinder. *Journal of Political Economy* 71 (August): 82–83.

Klein, Joanna. 2016. Lacking brains, plants can still make good judgements about risks. *New York Times*, June 30.

Knauft, Bruce. 1991. Violence and sociality in human evolution. *Current Anthropology* 32: 391–428.

Korkki, Phyllis. 2016. Paying with cash hurts: That's also why it feels so good. *New York Times*, July 16. Available online from https://www.nytimes.com/2016/07/17/business/paying-with-cash-hurts-thats-also-why-itfeels-so-good.html.

Kosters, Marvin, and Finis Welch. 1972. The effects of minimum wages on the distribution of changes in aggregate employment. *American Economic Review* 62: 323–331.

Lakatos, L., and Z. Janka. 2008. Evolution of human brain and intelligence. *PubMed.gov*, July 30.

Larcom, Shaun, Ferdinand Rauch, and Tim Willems. 2017. The benefits of forced experimentation: Striking evidence from the London underground network. *Quarterly Journal of Economics* 132 (4, November): 2019–2055.

Leclerc, France, Berndt Schmitt, and Laurette Dubé. 1995. Is time like money? Decision making and waiting time. *Journal of Consumer Research* 22: 110–119.

Leonard, W., M. Robertson, et al. 2003. Metabolic correlates of hominid brain evolution. *Comparative Biochemistry and Physiology: Part A, Molecular and Integrative Physiology* 136: 5–15.

Ledyard, John O. 1995. Public goods: A survey of experimental research. In *Handbook of experimental economics*, ed. John H. Kager and Alvin E. Roth. Princeton, NJ: Princeton University Press.

Lee, Dwight. 1969. Utility analysis and repetitive gambling. *American Economist* 13 (2): 87–91.

Lewis, Michael. 2016. *The Undoing Project: A Friendship That Changed Our Minds*. New York: W.W. Norton.

Loewenstein, George, and Nachum Sicherman. 1989. Do workers prefer increasing wage profiles? *Journal of Labor Economics* 9 (1, February): 67–84.

Loftus, Elizabeth F. 1997. Creating false memories. *Scientific American* 277 (September): 70–75.

McAuliffe, Kathleen. 2011. If modern humans are so smart, why are our brains shrinking? *Discover*, January 20.

McCabe, K., and V.L. Smith. 1999. A comparison of naive and sophisticated subject behavior with game theoretic predictions. *Proceedings of the National Academy of Sciences of the USA* 97: 3777–3781.

Mankiw, N. Gregory. 1998. *Principles of Economics*, 1st ed. Fort Worth: Harcourt Publishers.

McConnell, Campbell R. 1960. *Elementary Economics: Principles, Problems and Policies*. New York: McGraw-Hill.

Marcus, Gary. 2008. *Kluge: The Haphazard Evolution of the Human Mind*. Boston: Mariner Books.

Marlowe, Frank, Coren Apicella, and Dorian Reed. 2005. Men's preferences for women's profile waist-to-hip ratio in two societies. *Evolution and Human Behavior* 26: 458–468.

Marwell, Gerald, and Ruth Ames. 1981. Economists free ride: Does anyone else? *Journal of Public Economics*. 15: 295–310.

McKenzie, Richard B. 1977. The economic dimensions of ethical behavior. *Ethics* 87 (3, April): 208–221.

McKenzie, Richard B. 1994. *Times Change: The Minimum Wage and the New York Times*. San Francisco: Pacific Research Institute.

McKenzie, Richard B. 2010a. *Predictably Rational? In Search of Defenses for Rational Behavior in Economics*. Heidelberg: Springer.

McKenzie, Richard B. 2010b. Predictably irrational or predictably rational? *Library of Economics and Liberty*.

McKenzie, Richard B. 2012. *Heavy! The Surprising Reasons America Is the Land of the Free—And the Home of the Fat*. Heidelbery, German: Springer-Verlag.

McKenzie, Richard B. 2014. *Why are there so few job losses from minimum-wage hikes?* Dallas: National Center for Policy Analysis, Study 354, April 9.

McKenzie, Richard B., and Dwight R. Lee. 2008. *In Defense of Monopoly: How Market Power Fosters Creative Production*. Ann Arbor, MI: University of Michigan Press.

Mises, Ludwig von. 1962. *The Ultimate Foundation of Economics*. New York: Martino Fine Books (republished in 2012).

Mullainathan, Sendhill. 2017. Why trying new things is so hard to do. *New York Times*, December 1.

Nease, Robert. 2016. *The Power of Fifty Bits: The New Science of Turning Good Intentions into Positive Results*. New York: HarperBusiness.

Neumark, David, and William L. Wascher. 2008. *Minimum Wages*. Cambridge, MA: MIT Press.

Olson, Mancur. 1965. *The Logic of Collective Action: Public Goods and the Theory of Groups*. Cambridge, MA: Harvard University Press.

Peterson, John M., and Charles T. Stewart. 1969. *Employment Effects of Minimum Wage Rates*. Washington, DC: American Enterprise Institute for Public Policy Research.

Plott, Charles, and K. Zeiler. 2005. The willingness to pay/willingness to accept gap, the endowment effect. Subject misconceptions and experimental procedures for eliciting valuations. *American Economic Review* 95 (3): 530–545.

Polanyi, Michael. 2009. *The Tacit Dimension* (revised edition). Chicago: University of Chicago Press.

Pratt, John W., David A. Wise, and Richard Zeckhauser. 1979. Price differences in almost competitive markets. *Quarterly Journal of Economics* 93 (2): 189–211.

Ragan, James F. 1977. Minimum wages and the youth labor market. *Review of Economics and Statistics* 59: 129–136.

Robbins, Lionel. 1935. *An Essay on the Nature and Significance of Economic Science*. Auburn, AL: Ludwig von Misses Institute(first published in 1932 and revised and reissued in 2007).

Robinson, E., et al. 2014. Will smaller plates lead to smaller waists? A systematic review and meta-analysis of the effect that experimental manipulation of dishware size has on energy consumption. *Obesity Review*, July.

Rubin, Paul H. 2002. *Darwinian Politics: The Evolutionary Origin of Freedom*. New Brunswick, NJ: Rutgers University Press.

Rubin, Paul H., and Chris Paul. 1979. An evolutionary model of taste for risk. *Economic Inquiry* 17: 585–596.

Samuelson, Paul A. 1947. *Foundations of Economic Analysis*. Cambridge, MA: Harvard University Press.

Samuelson, Paul A. 1948. *Economics*. New York: McGraw-Hill.

Samuelson, Paul A., and Peter Temin. 1976. *Economics*, 10th ed. New York: McGraw Hill.

Samuelson, Paul A., and William Nordhaus. 2009. *Economics*, 19th ed. New York: McGraw Hill.

Schabas, Margaret. 2014. *A World Ruled by Number William Stanley Jevons and the Rise of Mathematical Economics*. Princeton, NJ: Princeton University Press.

Schilthuizen, Menno. 2016. Evolution is happening faster than we thought. *New York Times*, July 23.

Shepard R.N. 1981. Psychological complementarity. In *Perceptual organization*, ed. M. Kubovy and J.R. Pomerantz, 279–342. Hillsdale, NJ: Lawrence Erlbaum Associates.

Shepard, R.N. 1990. *Mind Sights: Original Visual Illusions, Ambiguities, and other Anomalies*. New York: W. H. Freeman and Company.

Segal, David. 2016. Solar snare: Spend thousands and cut power bills by $9 a month. *New York Times*, August 13.

Shelton, Kathryn, and Richard B. McKenzie. 2012–2013. Pedophiles and the regulation of Hugging. *Regulation* 35 (Winter): 14 (Cato Institute).

Shiller, Robert J. 2005. *Irrational Exuberance*, 2nd ed. Princeton, NJ: Princeton University Press.

Shiller, Robert J. 2008. *The Subprime Solution: How Today's Global Financial Crisis Happened and What to Do about It*. Princeton, NJ: Princeton University Press.

Simon, Herbert. 1957. *Models of Man*. New York: Wiley.

Singh, Devendra. 1993. Adaptive significance of waist-to-hip ratio and female physical attractiveness. *Journal of Personality and Social Psychology* 65: 293–307.

Singh, Devendra. 1994. Is thin really beautiful and good: Relationship between waist-to-hip ration (WHR) and female attractiveness. *Personality and Individual Differences* 16: 123–132.

Skouras, Thanos, George J. Avlonitis, and Kostis A. Indounas. 2005. Economics and marketing on pricing: How and why do they differ. *Journal of Product and Brand Management* 14 (6): 362–374.

Smith, Adam. 1759, vol. I of the Glasgow Edition of the Works and Correspondence of Adam Smith. *The Theory of Moral Sentiments*, ed. D.D. Raphael and A.L. Macfie. Indianapolis: Liberty Fund, 1982.

Smith, J. Maynard. 1964. Group selection and kin selection, *Nature* 201 (4924): 1145–1147.

Smith, Vernon L. 2008. *Rationality in Economics: Constructivist and Ecological Forms*. Cambridge, UK: Cambridge University Press.

Steiner, Mary C., Natalie D. Munro, Todd A. Surovell, Eitan Tchernov, and Ofer Bar-Yosef. 1999. Paleolithic population growth pulses evidenced by small animal exploitation. *Science* 283 (5399, September 25): 190–194.

Stigler, George J. 1962. The economics of information. *Journal of Political Economy* 69 (June): 213–225.

Stigler, George J. 1975. *Citizen and the State: Essays on Regulation*. Chicago: University of Chicago Press.

Stigler, George J., and Gary S. Becker. 1977. De gustibus non est disputandum. *American Economic Review* 67 (2, March): 76–90.

Streitfeld, David. 2016. Amazon is quietly eliminating list prices. *New York Times*, July 3. Available online from https://www.nytimes.com/2016/07/04/business/amazon-is-quietly-eliminating-list-prices.html.

Swartz, Barry. 2005. *The Paradox of Choice*. New York: Harper Perennial.

Telegraph Reporter (unnamed). 2016. Human brain can store 4.7 billion books—Ten times more than originally thought. *The Telegraph*, January 21.

Taylor, Patricia A., and Norval D. Glenn. 1976. The utility of education and attractiveness for female status attainment through marriage. *American Sociological Review* 41: 484–498.

Thaler, Richard H. 1990. Anomalies: Saving, fungibility, and mental accounts. *Journal of Economic Perspectives* 4 (1): 193–2005.

Thaler, Richard H. 1991. *Quasi Rational Economics*. New York: Russell Sage Foundation.

Thaler, Richard H. 1992. *The Winner's Curse: Paradoxes and Anomalies of Economic Life*. New York: Free Press.

Thaler, Richard H. (ed.). 1993. *Advances in Behavioral Finance*. New York: Russell Sage Foundation.

Thaler, Richard H. (ed.). 2005. *Advances in Behavioral Finance*. Princeton, NJ: Princeton University Press.

Thaler, Richard H., and Cass R. Sunstein. 2009. *Nudge: Improving Decisions about Health, Wealth, and Happiness*. New York: Penguin Books.

Trivers, Robert L. 1971. The evolution of reciprocal altruism. *Quarterly Review of Biology* 46: 35–57.

Trivers, Robert L. 1985. *Social Evolution*. Menlo Park, CA: Benjamin-Cummings.

Tversky, Amos, and Daniel Kahneman. 1981. The framing of decisions and the psychology of choice. *Science* 211 (4481): 453–458.

Udry, J. Richard, and Bruce K. Eckland. 1984. Benefits of being attractive: Differential payoffs for men and women. *Psychological Reports* 54: 47–56.

Veblen, Thorsten. 1898. Why is economics not an evolutionary science? *Quarterly Journal of Economics* 12 (4): 373–397, also available online with an introduction by Jean Boulton. 2010. *E:CO Issue* 12 (2): 41–69.

Wansink, Brian. 2007. *Mindless Eating: Why We Eat More Than We Think*. New York: Bantam.

Wansink, Brian, and Koert van Ittersum. 2006. The visual illusions of food: Why plates, bowls, and spoons can vias consumption volume. *FASEB Journal* 20: A618.

Weber, Martin, and Colin F. Camerer. 1998. The disposition effect in securities trading: An experimental analysis. *Journal of Economic Behavior and Organization* 33 (2): 167–184.

Wedekind, C., T. Seebeck, F. Bettens, and A.J. Paepke. 1995. MHC-dependent mate preferences in humans. *Proceedings of the Royal Society, London* 260: 245–249.

Wilson, Edward O. 2012. *The Social Conquest of Earth*. New York: Liveright.

Wilson, James Q. 1993. *The Moral Sense*. New York: Free Press.

Wootson, Cleve R., Jr. 2017. Diet drinks are associated with weight gain, new research suggests. *Washington Post*, July 18.

Zak, Paul. 2012. *The Moral Molecule: The Source of Love and Prosperity*. Boston: Dutton.

Zak, Paul, and Stephen Knack. 2001. Trust and growth. *Economic Journal* 111 (470, March): 295–321.

Index

R. B. McKenzie, *A Brain-Focused Foundation for Economic Science*,
https://doi.org/10.1007/978-3-319-76810-6

The manufacturer's authorised representative in the EU is Springer Nature Customer Service Centre GmbH, Europaplatz 3, 69115 Heidelberg, Germany. If you have any concerns regarding our products, please contact ProductSafety@springernature.com

Printed and bound by CPI Group (UK) Ltd, Croydon, CR0 4YY
22/09/2026
02220950-0005